T0246190

Praise for *From Hoodies to Suits*

From Hoodies to Suits provides a front row seat to understanding the significant changes about to happen in financial services infrastructure and the applications that will reshape how value is transferred, settled, and stored. Tokenization of financial assets will increase efficiencies and reduce costs across an asset's life cycle, improve the efficient allocation of capital, optimize global supply chains, catalyze a new generation of software-as-a-service companies, and ultimately drive mainstream adoption. Benefits will be widespread, but ultimately result in more transparency and lower costs for borrowers and investors.

—Anthony Moro, CEO Provenance Blockchain Foundation

From Hoodies to Suits takes a novel approach detailing the benefits and innovation of blockchain technology applied to the world of finance and investment.

—Mike Cagney, Co-Founder and CEO of Figure Technologies; Co-Founder and former CEO of SOFI.

In this groundbreaking book, Annelise Osborne takes us on a journey from the tech-savvy world of "Hoodies" to the boardrooms of "Suits," illuminating the remarkable transformation of the digital asset industry. As blockchain technology emerged as a disruptor, challenging traditional finance, Osborne provides a comprehensive guide to the intersection of innovation and established financial markets.

—Perianne Boring, Founder and CEO, Chamber of Digital Commerce

Now more than ever, books like *From Hoodies to Suits* are needed to educate readers on the promise of blockchain and crypto. It's an insightful, digestible, entertaining read.

—Katherine Kirkpatrick, Chief Legal Officer, CBOE Digital

From Hoodies to Suits is an indispensable guide to blockchain technology and the finance industry. Annelise Osborne offers practical insights beyond Bitcoin to the burgeoning world of tokenization and institutional DeFi. With a critical examination of high-profile failures in the crypto space, she delineates key lessons for traditional finance, discusses the regulatory landscape, and underscores the generational shifts set to transform the industry. It's an essential read for anyone seeking to understand the future of finance and the disruptive influence of digital assets and blockchain innovation.

—Richard Walker, Senior Partner, Bain & Company

A must-read for all financial market participants, ranging from the crypto skeptics to those who understand something is happening in markets related to blockchain and crypto, but don't know quite where to start. Annelise Osborne removes the jargon and provides a common sense and understandable framework of the transformation already underway in complex markets through complex technologies. With tangible examples and a clever sense of humor, she ties the past, present, and future of market functioning driven by blockchain technology.

—Charles Mount, Chief DeFi Officer, S&P Global

Annelise Osborne succeeds brilliantly at the difficult task of explaining the complex origins and use cases of crypto finance while creating a captivating, fun to read book. This book breathes life into personalities and palpable excitement of the formation of a new industry. Bravo.

—Edward A. Glickman, Executive Chairman USA, AIP Asset Management

From Hoodies to Suits skillfully bridges the gap between traditional finance and the power of blockchain technology. Annelise Osborne presents a compelling narrative, demystifying digital assets and their transformative role in the future of financial markets. An essential read for anyone in finance.

—Jennifer Warren, Former Head of Markets Digital Strategy, Barclays

The author brilliantly traces the evolution of blockchain from its origins to its pivotal role in reshaping traditional finance. What sets this book apart is its ability to connect the dots seamlessly, skillfully illuminating the digital tipping points that traditional finance is approaching, providing readers with a roadmap to navigate the changing landscape. Whether you're a finance professional or technical architect, this must-read provides a clear understanding of how digital assets are transforming the traditional financial landscape, inspiring a vision for the future where innovation drives true value creation.

—Lora Lindsey, Principal, Value Innovation and GTM Strategy, Amazon Web Services (AWS), and former Goldman Sachs investment banker (both a hoodie and a suit)

An entertaining guide through the inevitable tech upgrade advancing the world of finance.

—Gregg Bell, Head of Growth, Binance.us

From Hoodies to Suits is an important, fascinating and fun read for everyone involved with the financial markets. It is a digestible dive into how this innovative technology provides opportunities to develop new asset classes and market infrastructure. Annelise Osborne does a wonderful job of providing unique insight and helpful guidance for those interested in how blockchain tech can evolve finance and institutional investing.

—Kari Larsen, Partner and Co-Head of the Digital Works Group at Willkie Farr & Gallagher LLP

Annelise brings her years of first-hand experience to this effort and the end result is a must-read for both those not familiar with blockchain as well as those with experience and looking to dive deeper into understanding the benefits of fintech.

—Rayne Steinberg, CEO, Co-Founder Arca; former Co-Founder, WisdomTree Asset Management

Annelise Osborne is able to explain a complex topic making it understandable to all, with entertaining stories weaved in. I highly recommend this book for anyone working in traditional finance to grasp the potential of the technological upgrade taking place.

—Marcus Grubb, ex SVP State Street Digital, Banker, Fintech and Gold Entrepreneur

A must-read for every head of trading or investment in a language they will understand and written by someone they can relate to. Look for other copies on the morning train.

—James Godfrey, Managing Partner, Secure Digital Markets

From Hoodies to Suits demonstrates the exact transition the digital assets industry is seeing in near real-time. The compelling storytelling coupled with key and lesser-known events that have gotten the market to where it is today makes this a staple for financial professionals as tokenization compounds and positions itself as the next major technological overhaul to the capital markets. Annelise does a splendid job covering all angles through her unique lens as both a TradFi player and digital assets pioneer.

—Peter Gaffney, Head of Research Security Token Advisors.

On the eve of the US's financial announcement approving a spot ETF, we are on the precipice of a cultural shift that will significantly impact finance. This shift characterized by fringe technological wizards has now moved mainstream into traditional financial institutions with their risk profiles and business know-how. Annelise Osborne has captured this tectonic shift in her entertaining and impactful book *From Hoodies to Suits*. A must-read for the neophyte to the professional—you won't be disappointed. I couldn't put it down!

—Lynne Maylor, Co-Founder, Women in Digital Assets Forum (WIDAF); Ambassador, GBBC; Chair, Boston Blockchain Association

For finance and technology executives, this book is not just recommended; it is essential reading. Osborne accelerates the perspective of the landscape, empowering decision-makers to make intelligent and well-informed choices. *From Hoodies to Suits* transcends being a mere book; it becomes a strategic tool for those steering the helm of finance and technology, equipping them with the knowledge to navigate the dynamic shifts in the industry.

—Nitin Gaur, Global Head Digital Assets, State Street

FROM HOODIES TO SUITS

FROM HOODIES TO SUITS

Innovating Digital Assets for Traditional Finance

ANNELISE OSBORNE

WILEY

Published by John Wiley & Sons, Inc., Hoboken, New Jersey.
Published simultaneously in Canada.

For general information on our other products and services or for technical support, please contact our Customer Care Department within the United States at (800) 762-2974, outside the United States at (317) 572-3993 or fax (317) 572-4002.

Wiley also publishes its books in a variety of electronic formats. Some content that appears in print may not be available in electronic formats. For more information about Wiley products, visit our web site at www.wiley.com.

Library of Congress Cataloging-in-Publication Data is Available:

ISBN 9781394231829 (Cloth)
ISBN 9781394231843 (epdf)
ISBN 9781394231836 (epub)

Cover image(s): © BLACKDAY / SHUTTERSTOCK; POSTERIORI / GETTY IMAGES
Cover design: PAUL McCARTHY

SKY10073276_042024

To my amazing sons: Rory, Jamie, and Nate

May you stay curious.

Contents

Acknowledgments

I would like to acknowledge that it takes a village. First, thank you, Mom and family, for your unwavering support. Thank you to Bill Falloon for taking a chance on a first-time author and to Richard Samson for fine-tuning. Thank you, Jen Singer, for accepting the challenge and for weekly calls to turn the book into a story. Thank you, Nikesh Dalal, for your Hoodies input and to Kari Larsen, Jason Allegrante, and Tiffany Smith for your regulatory comments. Thank you, Chris Giancarlo and Jake Ryan, for steering me through the publishing process. Thank you, Leanne Mair, for the inspiration to write my book.

Thank you to the many people that helped shape my views on digital assets and crypto over the years including Bea O'Carroll, Rebecca Rettig, Cathy Yoon, Sandy Kaul, June Ou, Mike Cagney, Christine Moy, Nitin Gaur, Jerald David, Cynthia Jackson, Jennifer Warren, Blue Macellari, Adina Fischer, Nisa Amoils, Victor Jung, Hannah Baker, Carlos Domingo, Ryan Rugg, Kate Walters, Morgan McKenney, Anthony Moro, Georges Archibald, Pat O'Meara, Frank Walczak, James Godfrey, Emmanuel Aidoo, Blair Bingham, Rayne Steinberg, Hassan Bassiri, Patrick Martinez, Marcus Grubb, Ekene Uzoma, Dave Hendricks, Kim Diamond, Gabe Benincasa, Brian Berman, Ioana Niculcea, Mark Smith, Todd Lippiatt, Alina Fisch, Michael Oved, Sam Tabar, Maggie Hsu, Braeden Andreson, Tyler Hinton, Someera Khokhar, Elsie Brown, Deborah Bussiere, Yordanka Ilieva, Kelsey Weaver, Leanne Bassett, Ronit Walney, Peter Gaffney, Ginnette Harvey, Fabian Astic, Chuck Mounts, Charles Jansen, Jerry Tang, Gabriella Kusz, Amanda Wick, Elaine Asher, Angus O'Callaghan, Jeremy Fox-Green, Tim O'Regan, and Chris King.

The CT crypto crowd: Richard Walker, Jim Knox, Pat LaVecchia, Bob Yopstille, Keith Strycula, Gregg Bell, Elizabeth Menke, Wendi Carver, Emily Goodman, Rhonda Eldridge, Keith Coyne, Jarvis Cromwell, Trip Stocker, Charlie Moore, Lynne Morton, Michael Forstl, Chris Perkins,

Sebastian Bae, Jasmine Burgess, Simon Zais, Michelle Noyes, Justin Schmidt, Bruce Morris, Anthony Bassili, and Ken Chapman.

Thank you to the TradFi crowd: Chris Patterson, Swati Sharma, Billy Jacobs, Andy Feytko, Bill O'Conner, Arvind Bajaj, Jason Hull, Charlie Manna, Nelson Braff, Ed Glickman, Mark Green, Dan Olsen, Mary Rottler, Julie Agnew, Maneesh Sagar, Mark Ripka, Chris Jones, and the many, many, many others. Thank you, Columbia Business School and William & Mary.

I am lucky to live in a collaborative and cooperative environment working to build the next interaction of finance. Thank you to the ecosystem for the many dinners, conversations, and predictions about what we will achieve.

To my lifetime of mentors, mentees, and sponsors, thank you for believing in and continuing to challenge me every day.

Disclaimer

The information provided in this book is for informational purposes only and is not intended to be construed as a source of advice. The information contained in this book does not constitute professional, legal, tax, or financial advice and should never be used without first consulting with a financial or other professional to determine what may be best for your individual needs.

This book is in no way a solicitation, endorsement, recommendation, or offer of any investment. Past performance doesn't guarantee future results. Any forward-looking statements are only general in nature and the opinion of the author.

Although the author has made every effort to ensure that the information included in this book was correct at press time and while this publication is written to provide accurate information, the author assumes no responsibility for errors, inaccuracies, omissions, or any other inconsistencies herein and hereby disclaim any liability to any party for any loss, damage, or disruption caused by errors or omissions, whether such errors or omissions result from negligence, accident, or any other cause.

The author does not make any guarantee or other promise as to any results that may be obtained from using the content of this book. You should never make any investment decision without first consulting with your own financial advisor and conducting your own research and due diligence. To the maximum extent permitted by law, the author disclaims any and all liability in the event any information, commentary, analysis, opinions, or advice contained in this book prove to be inaccurate, incomplete or unreliable, or result in any investment or other losses.

Introduction

When Facebook's Mark Zuckerberg testified before Congress in 2018, he did something remarkable: He wore a suit. A navy blue suit with a matching solid blue tie and a crisp white shirt. It was a noteworthy shift for the hoodie-wearing CEO of the tech giant that would eventually rename itself Meta, as in "metaverse." As one journalist put it at the time, "When men want to look like adults, they suit up."

The *New York Times* called it his "I'm Sorry Suit," a strategically effective symbolic gesture that he was going to accept responsibility and defer to the rules set by people who wear suits to work every day.[1]

Disgraced FTX CEO Sam Bankman-Fried, too, wore a suit, at his 2023 federal trial for what's been called "one of the largest financial frauds in history," even though he'd once insisted that T-shirts were crucial to his "brand."[2] His lawyers argued that he was just a young guy who got in over his head[3] – while he allegedly misappropriated billions of dollars of his clients' money through his trading firm and cryptocurrency exchange, both of which had attracted plenty of grown-ups to the investment table.

Even Ethereum founder, wunderkind Vitalik Buterin, has occasionally ditched his T-shirts depicting unicorns and even a "bufficorn" (buffalo plus unicorn) costume he wore to a conference to throw on a collared dress shirt and appear on stage. This from a (very) young man who reportedly launched what would become the second most popular cryptocurrency[4] after a change in the video game World of Warcraft made him cry himself to sleep.[5]

Shifting from hoodies to suits is exactly where the digital assets industry is right now. While blockchain was originally created as an alternative to banking and traditional finance by tech start-ups filled with hoodie-wearing entrepreneurs, it can actually enhance the established financial industry by bringing additional efficiency, transparency, and liquidity to capital markets. To make that shift, a different skill set is required – a skill set that the innovators of blockchain and cryptocurrencies don't have. The "Suits" of Wall Street and Main Street can build on what the "Hoodies" of tech start-ups created when they come to understand how to innovate using digital assets in traditional financial markets. That's when Hoodies and Suits can combine their talents and expertise to create the next generation of finance together.

What I Found in the Boardroom

Just before Zuckerberg was knotting his tie for Congress, I left my corporate life in traditional finance at Moody's. I was invited to join the board of a regulatory task force focused on cryptocurrencies and blockchain. Only, I knew nearly nothing about crypto, blockchain, or the initial coin offerings (ICOs), when blockchain based "coins" are sold to raise funds for a cryptocurrency project. It needed regulation. I told them, "You're talking to the wrong person. This isn't my expertise." But they were young, persistent, idealistic attorneys.

So, I watched YouTube videos about bitcoin and blockchain to understand what they were about and why the lawyers were so passionate. When I understood the basics of the technology, I recognized that the potential upgrades to traditional finance were mind-blowing. But back then, the tech-savvy Hoodies were attempting to upgrade finance without finance experience, leading to false starts and bad publicity.

When you're dealing with traditional finance, you're dealing with securities, structure, and regulation – and possible jail time for any violations. After all, finance is one of the oldest professions in the world, dating back to Mesopotamian bankers offering credit contracts. And if it's not broken, why fix it? But it can run more efficiently, and blockchain and digital assets are paving the way. It's going to take recognized structures and "responsible innovation" regulation to make them mainstream.

I had made the assumption that the industry was already deep into the process of applying the Hoodies' technologies to traditional finance, but I was wrong. Hoodies couldn't do it alone, because they lacked the experience and understanding of the intricacies of the industry, and Suits didn't understand the technology.

So, I found a partner and together we worked to create digital assets – discoverable digital representations of value that establish ownership – as smart securities, eliminating frictions and developing a more automated process, while using his broker-dealer. Together with a great team, we focused on efficiencies and programmable securities and worked to create tokenized real-world assets before the term RWA was cool. We even created securities offering to pay interest in stablecoin, a cryptocurrency that provides a stable price by being pegged to a currency or commodity, which was a first. We structured non-fungible tokens (NFTs), unique tokenized assets on the blockchain that can't be replicated, for investments in land plots, before NFTs became known for art.

I understood that digital assets would become important because the next generation of investors, who grew up with supercomputers in their pockets, will demand a different way of handling their finances and identifying their investments. For them, the speed, efficiency, transparency, and potential interoperability of the systems built by Hoodies won't be a nice-to-have. They will be a must-have. But in my first venture, we were too early for real adoption. So much had yet to be built and integrated and still does.

I recognized that it would take people with finance experience to apply the technology in a practical and usable way, and I wanted to be a part of it. I had a clear vision of what could be built. I had been that kid who wondered why I had to take cash for babysitting when I wanted my clients to transfer the money right into my bank account. This was back when ATMs were finally becoming ubiquitous at bank branches nationwide, and my mother still used checks – and checks aren't real money. They're just *access*. Even as a teenager, I saw the value in a cashless economy.

Recently, at a farmer's market in rural Alaska, I noticed that the vendors all took credit cards on mobile readers attached to their iPhones. Imagine if that had been an option for my babysitting job. Technology is changing finance. We must change with it.

Today, the market is ripe for blockchain technology in traditional finance, on Wall Street, and in corporate America. There are a lot of frictions that digital assets and blockchain can solve. The market is ready for the Suits to work with the Hoodies to make it happen, but they need to first catch up on understanding the technology and its potential applications.

We also have to create the current regulatory and interoperability landscapes. Too many banks operate on old systems written in COBOL that cannot talk to one another. There's a reason for that: There are regulations that require financial institutions to keep records, and it takes a long time to upgrade systems. So, they just kept building on old technologies, and by the time they upgrade it, it becomes irrelevant.

While the Suits tried to put Band-Aids on their antiquated systems, the Hoodies continued to build new advances in technology. They began launching ICOs in 2017, introducing more crypto coins similar to bitcoin. Their investors, located across the globe, were passionate about crypto, but they weren't accredited investors. It was what US Securities and Exchange Chairman Gary Gensler would later call "the Wild West," with unregulated exchanges, possible insider trading, and companies with obvious conflicts of interest.

In the early days, one of my attorney colleagues wrote a white paper on crypto regulation and it went viral – and nothing ever goes viral in finance. Usually, if people know your name in finance, you've done something wrong to end up in headlines of the *Wall Street Journal*. That's exactly what's happened in recent years to some of the founders of crypto. Left unchecked by the regulations that govern traditional finance, some of them went rogue and defrauded investors. Unfortunately, that's typically much of what the Suits know about digital assets. But blockchain is not bitcoin, and the technology is sound.

Today there are over one thousand blockchains worldwide, and a lot of digital assets may be unregistered securities. While it took a long time for bitcoin to take off – as of this writing, it's trading at $47,000 – it laid the foundation for the changing face of finance today. Some very large players in traditional finance have launched their own blockchains and digital assets, and investors continue to demand changes that bring traditional finance closer to instant settlement, known as T+0.

Now Is the Time for Digital Assets and Web3

Now more than ever, finance professionals, traders, asset managers, investment bankers, and corporate treasurers must understand how to apply digital assets to today's financial markets. Only then will the traditional finance industry be able to innovate and adapt to the inevitable technological changes of the near future, when Web3, which is phase three of the internet marked by decentralization, provides a world of blockchain known as the "internet of value."

While the development of cryptocurrencies and decentralized finance paved the way for upgrades to traditional finance and institutional digital assets, the Hoodies have left behind integration challenges for the Suits to address. Among them are regulatory issues. While the SEC sorts out which digital assets are securities and how this innovative technology should be regulated, Suits can prepare for traditional finance's imminent upgrade to blockchain and digital assets. These advances will bring liquidity, speed, improved operations, transparency, and much more. In fact, they already are.

The Suits who will benefit are the ones who understand the technology that the Hoodies have built and apply it to traditional finance. *From Hoodies to Suits: Innovating Digital Assets for Traditional Finance* is your guide to understanding and adopting the technologies that are revolutionizing finance.

1

Blockchain Is Not Bitcoin

"Innovation distinguishes between a leader and a follower."

– Steve Jobs

In January 2023, JPMorgan Chase Chairman and CEO Jamie Dimon appeared on CNBC's Davos outdoor set of *Squawk Box* wearing a blue parka and a smirk. Host Andrew Ross Sorkin had asked him about cryptocurrency, and Dimon cut him off.

"I think all that's been a waste of time, and why you guys waste any breath on this is totally beyond me,"[1] he delivered rapid fire.

For a moment, Sorkin was speechless. Then he asked, "Because you think the whole thing is going to zero and it's fake?"

"Bitcoin itself is a hyped-up fraud," Dimon replied. "It's a pet rock." But then Sorkin began to ask about firms like BlackRock investing in infrastructure to support cryptocurrencies, and Dimon began to soften.

"No, no, that's different," he said, extending his hand. "Blockchain is a technology ledger system that we use to move information. . . . We've used it to move money."

In short, blockchain is not bitcoin, and blockchain is the future of finance.

For Dimon, his disdain for crypto buzz was nothing new. He had testified in 2022 before Congress's House Financial Services Committee that unregulated cryptocurrencies like bitcoin were nothing more than a "decentralized Ponzi scheme" that make it easier for criminals to engage in illegal activities like money laundering and sex trafficking.

For all of Dimon's disdain for cryptocurrencies, he had a vision for the system it was built on.[2] Long before Dimon appeared on CNBC that day, JPMorgan had already been investing in building a private blockchain. The firm's Onyx digital assets tokenization platform made JPMorgan the first global bank to offer blockchain-based wholesale payment transactions. They also introduced JPM Coin, an internal digital token of depository receipts representing $1 USD that uses blockchain technology, allowing bank clients to transfer payments between internal accounts seamlessly. The company asserted that blockchain technology would free up liquidity, offer better customer experiences, and reduce friction and risk.[3] Under pressure from clients, the firm even quietly opened up access to a half-dozen crypto funds. This, despite headlines identifying Dimon as a "crypto skeptic."

Then in late 2023, JPMorgan announced a collaboration with Apollo Global Management under Project Guardian with the Monetary Authority of Singapore, which was designed to "revolutionize the asset and wealth management industry" through tokenization and smart contracts.[4] Their white paper called the launch a "critical moment at the intersection between traditional finance and blockchain technology."

The Suits had pinched blockchain from the Hoodies, marking the beginning of built-out blockchain applications working to create the future of traditional finance. Crypto had served as a proof of concept for traditional finance in the decade that bitcoin took to get traction. Yet even today, many people aren't able to distinguish the difference between bitcoin and blockchain, thinking they are one in the same, and that bitcoin is a fraud. Then they make the leap that blockchain must, too, be a fraud. But blockchain is not bitcoin. It's technology with multiple applications for the financial world today and in the future.

When Bitcoin Stole Blockchain's Thunder

On Halloween 2008, an eight-page document that would begin to change the face of money described a digital currency for peer-to-peer electronic payments worldwide. It was released under a mysterious pseudonym, Satoshi Nakamoto, whose identity has never been revealed. The white paper, entitled, "Bitcoin: A Peer-to-Peer Electronic Cash System," has widely been touted as the birth of bitcoin, considered the world's first cryptocurrency. It also introduced the concept of blockchain technology, a decentralized digital ledger of transactions that would provide the foundation for the cryptocurrency market.

Its introduction coincided with a radical shakeup in traditional finance. The subprime mortgage crisis was in full swing, and people were losing their homes. Lending practices in the early 2000s had become so relaxed, it seemed that anybody without assets, income, or employment could get a mortgage, many of which had adjustable rates. So, when the Great Recession hit and interest rates began to rise, defaults ballooned.

As the housing market plummeted, Wall Street began to melt down, and banks suddenly had loan losses on their balance sheets and foreclosures they couldn't unload. The government stepped in with a bank bailout called the Troubled Asset Relief Program (TARP), but not before Lehman Brothers closed its doors after more than a century-and-a-half on Wall Street. The average citizen saw a crumbling financial system that had been ruled by Suits who profited while people lost homes, money, and hope.

In 2008, bitcoin was revolutionary and blockchain was transformational, with applications for traditional finance that had been built and refined over thousands of years, while along the way, becoming more efficient. For the Hoodies, the timing was ripe for addressing concerns about banks and bank control. Bitcoin allowed crypto enthusiasts to take their money outside of banks, keeping them in a decentralized system with no central body oversight or outside control over their funds. For the Suits, what blockchain offered traditional finance was a foundation for the first iteration of digital assets.

The white paper revealed a new global electronic cash system that didn't need a third-party intermediary, such as banks, to function. The process of transferring bitcoin from one party to another involves what's known as bitcoin mining, where a network of energy-consuming computers work to solve challenging puzzle-like computations to create new blocks in the blockchain, confirming and recording the change of ownership. The first computer or miner to solve the computation received transaction fees, plus the reward of new bitcoins.

Yet bitcoin's white paper and concept were largely met with skepticism by jaded Hoodies who had already experienced empty promises and grand schemes when it came to the concept of cryptocurrencies. A series of decentralized digital assets had been introduced in the 1980s and 1990s, but they were subject to hacking and often lacked scalability.

Yet in January 2009, the software for the blockchain described in the white paper was launched and soon, perceptions began to change. The first person to run the Bitcoin software was Nakamoto, who sent 10 bitcoins (BTC) to a computer scientist named Hal Finney.[5] With it, Bitcoin v1.0 was released for a maximum circulation of 21 million coins.

A new monetary asset without reliance on a formal bank was appealing to many. Nakamoto wrote in the white paper, "The root problem with conventional currency is all the trust that's required to make it work. The central bank must be trusted not to debase the currency, but the history of fiat currencies is full of breaches of that trust."[6]

The value of bitcoin, $0 USD at launch, slowly increased to reach $0.09 by 2010. Then in 2021, it hit a peak of nearly $70,000[7,8] after a volatile trading history marked by peaks and troughs in confidence with many users eager for a big payoff. Bitcoin's price, and therefore, its market value, is reflected by what one party is willing to pay for it. What makes bitcoin and other cryptocurrencies unique is that they aren't tied to the full faith and credit of any country, fiscal policy, or federal reserves. Though many countries are considering a digital form of central bank money called a central bank digital currency (CBDC), bitcoin's volatile nature and lack of reserve backing leads many to label the currency as a fraud. Its value lies in its functionality, digital decentralized nature, absence of third-party control, and instantaneous money transfers.

Though bitcoin, the cryptocurrency, has received much of the press over the years, it's really the Bitcoin blockchain and the introduction of its capabilities that matter most to traditional finance executives and investors, because the blockchain laid the groundwork for a more efficient system for securities, private markets, debt instruments, payments, and back-office functions using financial structures that are in place today.

For the first time, it allowed for peer-to-peer payments with international applications, before Venmo and Zelle made it easier to transfer fiat money. Venmo and Zelle are still more restrictive than bitcoin, with a wait time for settlement, often days with limits on how much can be transferred. Bitcoin offered faster transaction timelines, quicker settlement, decreased costs, increased potential liquidity, and control over accounts, called wallets. It also offered equal access to information and the ability to verify data across the chain, eliminated user error, decreased the need for intermediaries, left money in everybody's pockets, and allowed for a digital wallet instead of hiding dollars under the mattress.

The Suits can take what the Hoodies built and make it more efficient and usable in the regulated financial markets. No longer will banks be able to hold up clients' money for five days just to cash a check or transfer funds. Blockchain isn't a replacement system for today's financial markets. It's a building block for a better way of doing business.

What Is Blockchain?

Simply put, blockchain is a system of recording information that is virtually impossible to change or hack. It is a shared immutable ledger. It is technically a large, shared database, but for simplicity's sake, think of it like a large, shared Excel sheet or Google Sheets spreadsheet that records each input into a cell. When the cell is updated, the new information is recorded in that cell, or block, as verified. The blockchain records the continuing growing list of what happens in that cell or block. Everyone on the blockchain has access to the same information, and they don't have to discern which is the latest iteration.

A good example of how blockchain could work is in title insurance, a form of indemnity insurance for real property titles. New homeowners or commercial property owners are required to pay for title insurance, which ensures the property title is clean, the property belongs to the seller, and that there are no liens that could lead to a change in ownership. If the title for each property was recorded on the blockchain as a single source of truth, then the title insurance company wouldn't be needed. The blockchain would be updated with each change, and any liens could easily be tracked back from the construction of the house or the first input of data. This is a $58 million industry with a compound annual growth rate of 7.8 percent[9] that's ripe for disruption. Blockchain could put money back in the pockets of the property owners by eliminating the added expensive and slow process of title insurance.

What Are Digital Assets?

According to Investopedia, digital assets are "anything that is created and stored digitally, is identifiable and discoverable, and has or provides value." This can include:

- cryptocurrency: a digital medium of exchange, such as bitcoin, transacted with blockchain technology, including stablecoin and CBDCs.

- security token: a digital token that can prove identity or ownership.
- non-fungible tokens (NFTs): unique digital tokens of artwork, music, and other assets that are stored and verified on blockchain and are not interchangeable.
- crypto asset: a digital asset that uses cryptography and blockchain technology for creation, ownership, and exchange. Examples include NFTs, cryptocurrency, stablecoins, and security tokens.

Enter Ethereum

In the first 12 hours after Ethereum launched their native cryptocurrency in 2014 in an Initial Coin Offering (ICO), more than 7 million ether (ETH), the ICO coin, worth over $2 million were sold.[10] By the end of the sale just 42 days later, some 60 million ETH worth about $18 million had changed hands – the second largest crowdfunded project or ICO fundraised in the history of the internet at the time.[11] By November 2023, Ethereum had a market cap of more than $242 billion.[12]

Ethereum's 22-year-old whiz kid founder, Vitalik Buterin, told *Wired* in 2016 that he'd expected naysayers to find flaws when he released a white paper proposing something new and more functional for finance than the Bitcoin blockchain provided, but they didn't. His new proposed blockchain allowed for programmable smart contracts and ETH, a cryptocurrency, which was a welcomed addition to the community.

"As it turned out, the core Ethereum idea was good, fundamentally, completely, sound,"[13] he said.

Whereas the Bitcoin blockchain is a decentralized digital currency providing a medium of exchange, Buterin's Ethereum blockchain is a decentralized global software platform. Bitcoin was created to replace national currencies as a store of value during the 2008 financial crisis, while Ethereum was designed as a peer-to-peer network that allowed for the use of smart contracts that could securely verify and execute code, opening up a world of decentralized programmable digital transfers.

These were the early days of the ICO craze, which are a bit like an initial public offering (IPO), except ICOs are launched at the inception of a company as opposed to at a stage of profitability. They also don't generally give investors any ownership or voting rights in the company. ICO investors take a bet that the tokens they buy will increase in value or have some utility to the investor. They own nothing but the tokens.

Sometimes, that's a wise gamble. Launched in 2015, Ethereum was among the first ICOs, and by 2023, the value of ETH had increased nearly 600,000 percent.[14] An ICO "whale" initial investor resurfaced that year and transferred to a dormant wallet about 8,000 ETH. Originally purchased for a reported $2,500 for a profit of $14.7 million USD.[15]

Make no mistake: Investing in ICOs was very risky. One problem with ICOs was that the Hoodies in charge were generally inexperienced at building and running companies, and investors weren't protected. Plus, the system lacked transparency and a consistent structure. The combination made ICOs ripe for fraud by bad actors or Hoodies who were unable to get their companies off the ground. And, the Suits wouldn't step in, because they recognized the need to work within regulation. To be honest, during the ICO boom of 2017, very few Suits followed or understood the technology.

Half of all ICOs failed to raise funds in 2017 and 2018, when CNBC reported that more than eight hundred cryptocurrencies were "dead," worth less than a penny.[16] One study found that 80 percent of ICOs with a minimum market cap of $50 million were actually scams,[17] typically to either target an investor's authentication credentials or to transfer crypto to their possession.

Initial Coin Offering (ICO): Like an IPO for cryptocurrency, ICOs allow companies to raise money for a new application, coin or token, or software services. It's offered at an early inception of a company idea, like seed venture funding, only it has not been regulated and typically doesn't offer ownership or voting rights. Instead, investors receive crypto tokens issued by the company and hope they appreciate in value or provide a utility offered by the company.

Consensus and Technical Terms

Blockchains use different types of consensus mechanisms to synchronize a network for agreement within the digital ledger. It's a way to ensure that only valid transactions are recorded on the blockchain. Think of it as checking the work that is being added to the blockchain to make sure it is what it's supposed to be.

While Bitcoin's consensus mechanism is Proof of Work (PoW), which reportedly gobbles up as much energy as the entire country of the Philippines,[18] Ethereum, which launched as PoW in 2015, upgraded to Proof of Stake (PoS) in 2022. Not only is Proof of Stake a greener solution, dramatically reducing energy consumption, it's a more simplified process that relies on "validators," who check new blocks in exchange for rewards above their own staked coins which are pledged to help validate transactions on the blockchain.

Ethereum has its own programming language that runs on a blockchain, and its transaction time is seconds, compared to Bitcoin's minutes.

What's a Consensus Mechanism?

Blockchains operate under different protocols, called consensus mechanisms, for verification:

Proof of Work (PoW): A consensus mechanism to synchronize and validate date and process transactions. It requires participants (miners) to solve mathematical puzzles to create new blocks and earn rewards. The Bitcoin blockchain is built on PoW.

Proof of Stake (PoS): A consensus mechanism for processing transactions on the blockchain where validators must stake some of their coins for the right to create new blocks and earn rewards. Unlike PoW, it doesn't require energy-consuming computing by cryptocurrency miners. Ethereum uses PoS.

Proof of Authority (PoA): A centralized consensus mechanism that permits a limited number of vetted and approved entities to validate blockchain transactions. It is implemented largely by private and permissioned blockchains.

What Is Blockchain to Finance?

Understanding the basics of how blockchain works is the first step to recognizing its capabilities and possibilities for the traditional financial markets of today and bridging to tomorrow. Grasping the key benefits that blockchain brings to the financial system will help create an understanding of the possibilities, including key wins, trends, and opportunities in the digital asset space. The goal of this book is to highlight digital asset opportunities in traditional finance, clear up misconceptions, and work to pave the way for adoption and progress.

Since the mid-2010s, the developing crypto market has provided lessons about wins and losses that can be applied to the institutional digital asset ecosystem where institutions like JPMorgan, Citi, and Goldman Sachs and intermediaries such as the Depository and Trust Clearing Corporation (DTCC), the Society for Worldwide Interbank Financial Telecommunications (SWIFT), NASDAQ, and the New York Stock Exchange (NYSE) are building. The irony is that Bitcoin's root philosophy was to displace the banks, but its blockchain technology has provided banks with an efficient new rail for payment, trading, back office, and transactions, allowing lower costs, increased speed, and transparency. It was a framework designed to disrupt Wall Street, but it will actually become the basis of the next generation of Wall Street and capital markets.

A blockchain creates a central source of truth that offers transferability with instantaneous settlement in a 24/7/365 market with fewer intermediaries. Benefits include the transfer of digital assets quickly and securely without one governing body. Plus, its protocols can be automated, and it's decentralized with more traceability, trust, and speed and less potential for fraud. Blockchain's features include:

It's decentralized: There's no one entity with oversight of the network. This means that the owner of a crypto asset can transfer it to anyone with a wallet.

It's immutable: Posted transactions cannot be deleted or altered.

It's transparent: Every transaction is validated on each node in the system, maintaining a copy of the digital ledger that is open source and visible.

It uses cryptography to authenticate: Each user has a unique digital signature that cannot be forged.

It's a distributed ledger: The recording of ledger activity is held on multiple computers spread across geographically diverse locations.

It's faster: Blockchain can settle transfers at much faster speeds than traditional banking systems can. No more T+2. Now it's T+0.

It's a 24/7/365 market: It also offers the ability to eliminate banking hours as it is accessible 24 hours a day, every day.

It's global: The world is no longer limited by borders. Cryptocurrencies and blockchain are a truly global technology.

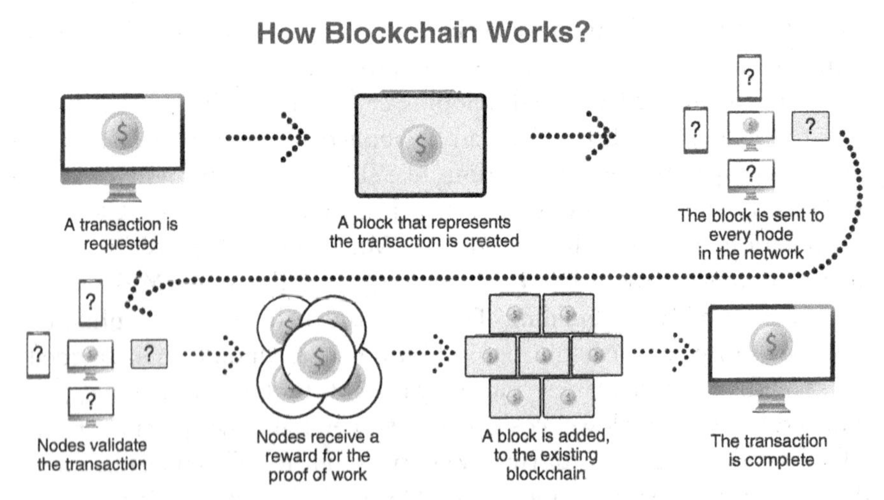

Figure 1.1 How Blockchain Works
Source: Geeks for Geeks

Figure 1.1 depicts the flow of a blockchain transaction. The entire transaction is digital from initiation to validation to adding the updating of information on a new block on the chain. The process is secure and transparent.

State Street's Global Head of Digital Asset and Technology Design, Nitin Gaur, explained, "Aggregating information within a single open

Blockchain Definitions

Block: A place where data is stored and encrypted

Hash: A string of numbers and letters that serve as a digital fingerprint for a set of data

Node: Anything with an IP address that runs a blockchain's software with the primary function to maintain the public ledger's consensus. Nodes are essentially a computer that runs a copy of the blockchain.

Nonce: A value or number that can only be used once. When blockchain miners solve for nonce, they receive a block reward.

Smart Contracts: Self-executing contracts, built into the system's code, which outline the contract between buyer and seller without oversight from a third party ledger should reduce informational asymmetry and transaction costs, a significant advantage of the transition to blockchain-based systems. For this to succeed, blockchain-based ledgers must coexist with existing ledgers . . . Financial institutions cannot create a parallel system."[19]

Public, Private, and Permissioned Blockchains

Blockchains come with varying levels of accessibility: public, private, and permissioned. This is important when considering tokenization of securities, fiduciary responsibility, regulatory compliance, and risk profiles for institutions.

Consider the introduction of the internet. Initially, companies were concerned about the risk of privacy or other potential threats posed by a public internet, so they used an intranet, a private, permissioned network used as a bulletin board to share information such as policies, procedures, and company news internally only. As user comfort grew with internet security and people began to recognize the true value of online information and communication, companies expanded access to the internet.

In 1992, there were 10 websites on the internet, and by 1996 there were two million. Today, the internet is how most companies share information and serve their clients, with some generating all of their revenue online. It allows anyone to access research, information, or shop using a desktop or a smartphone, so we no longer have to go to a library to write a research report or gather data for a quarterly report or go to physical stores and stand in the checkout line to buy things. Technology has made our lives significantly more efficient.

While financial institutions are now focused on private blockchains, traditional finance will likely eventually push toward public, permissioned blockchains as privacy technology improves and the ecosystem moves toward Web3, the internet of value. As technology improves, speed and scalability will, too. Traditional finance's shift to a public blockchain will have added privacy so that trades are not traced back to a wallet, which is a string of numbers, as currently it is possible to highlight large transactions and wallet balances.

Public Blockchains: Bitcoin and Ethereum are built as *public* blockchains that anyone can build on. This offers decentralization, as more parties are involved and ownership or control is less concentrated. These public blockchains are open source and transparent, meaning that every transaction can be viewed by anyone on the chain. The wallet addresses are pseudonymous, meaning they don't reveal the identity of the user.[20] Yet, as it stands, scalability can be limited on public blockchains because as more nodes join, the network slows down. But this is just the first inning of blockchain; faster public chains are expected to be built, as are layers that allow for enhanced privacy and added functionality.

Private Blockchain: Corda and Hyperledger are examples of private chains that are controlled by one organization, a central authority that determines who can serve as a node, a device-stakeholder that runs the software for the network. Also known as enterprise blockchain, the benefit is privacy, scalability, and control. The downside is that they aren't decentralized, they're limited in global application, but they're likely to have faster validation times than public blockchains. The blockchain's owner holds the right to override, edit, or delete entries, and with a limited number of participants, there's a risk of bad actors colluding. However, on a private chain the bad actors are easily identified because no one is anonymous.

Private blockchains can be more expensive to run, and if they are too centralized, they may be the same as a large database. In some more centralized cases, there's a question as to the benefit of a private blockchain versus a database.

Permissioned Blockchains: These have features of both private and public blockchains and they're restricted to authorized participants. While public blockchains can launch permissioned subnets for institutions, permissioned blockchains like Provenance, Canton, and Onyx allow for easier security because there are fewer people on the network to achieve consensus. Managed by a network administrator, permissioned blockchains aren't as decentralized as public blockchains. The administrator can grant access to participants and can even provide different participants access to different data offering more privacy functionality.

What Does This Have to Do with Finance?

Now that you have a basic understanding of blockchain, it's time to outline its benefits for traditional finance. Why is this important? According to a report by HSBC and Northern Trust, by 2030, 5 to 10 percent of all assets will be tokenized,[21] when the ownership is converted to digital assets. The recent generations raised with supercomputers in their pockets will demand it. (See Chapter 7.)

Transactions will be more automated, there will be less overhead and more traceability, and back-office transactions will run more smoothly. In the debt markets, we'll have instantaneous settlement and programmable securities that pay as defined in legal documents. It will no longer be a 9-to-5 business. Work will happen outside of business hours, making for a 24/7/365 market that adds to liquidity. And everything will be accessible on cell phones or whatever replaces them.

This is coming. In fact, it's already here. Soon, blockchain will be behind most every transaction because it's a more efficient system. This means that trading any sort of securities, private assets, or debt instruments will be affected. Some company systems will run on blockchain, as will collateral management, treasury management, and securities. Even new concepts like NFTs, utility benefits, and governance will be commonplace. It's a matter of embracing the future of finance.

Avoiding Kodak Moments

In 2007, Eastman Kodak (NYSE: KODK) released a cringe-worthy marketing video claiming "Kodak is back" and promising they wouldn't "play grab ass anymore."[22] Though it was meant to introduce Kodak's new digital cameras and online services, it served to highlight the denial that the company had marinated in for several decades, not to mention a lack of judgment.

Kodak continued to act as though it was in the film and chemical business, making decisions based on increasingly outdated data and philosophies. Like Blockbuster and AOL, Kodak moved too slowly and failed to innovate or adapt to changing customer preferences, thereby losing out.

Though Kodak had a market cap value of nearly $30 billion, it has fallen to about 1 percent of that today. The camera film market evaporated. Kodak squandered value by failing to recognize that the very digital cameras it had invested in were becoming commoditized, built right into smartphones with easy photo sharing available on developing social media outlets like Instagram. It was a case of too little, too late, because the company failed to leverage its new product, focusing instead on selling low-margin digital cameras and printers. Kodak had been built on old-school film that was no longer needed in the digital age. The result was a market share loss to photography competitors like Canon and Nikon and tech companies like Apple and Google.

In 2012, Kodak filed for bankruptcy. And yet, even Kodak attempted to get on the digital asset bandwagon with plans to offer KodakCoin to create permanent, immutable records of photography ownership, through an ICO in 2018. The *New York Times* called Kodak's white paper, "a 40-page mishmash of marketing buzzwords and vague diagrams,"[23] and the crypto project was never launched.

When it comes to digital assets and blockchain, traditional finance is in danger of reaching its own Kodak Moment. The institutional building continues with select Wall Street banks, asset managers, and capital market players piloting programs in the digital asset ecosystem, while many countries are researching CBDCs.

Even JPMorgan has shown signs of changing its tune on crypto, writing in a 2022 research note that bitcoin's slide in a massive one-day sell-off provided a "significant upside."[24] It's not exactly Jamie Dimon singing crypto's praises, but it is a notable shift. BlackRock CEO Larry Fink also changed his mind about bitcoin. Where he once referred to it as an "index of money laundering," he later claimed that crypto would "transcend any one currency in currency valuation,"[25] reports *The Street*. "I do think a lot of crypto is an international asset,"[26] Fink said.

While it's true that the anonymous nature of cryptocurrency has allowed a small number of bad actors to engage in criminal activities, it's important to note that only 0.15 percent of all cryptocurrency volume in 2022 was used for illegal purposes, with the overwhelming majority of crypto used for legitimate transactions.

It's clear that blockchain is here to stay, and that bitcoin is not blockchain. In fact, Nisa Amoils, venture capitalist and managing partner of A110x, said, "We have only begun to see the applications and real world use cases that will now disrupt multiple industries, not only financial services. Just as we used to say, 'online business' or 'mobile business,' 'blockchain business' will be a term of the past as it becomes ubiquitous and invisible to the end user."[27]

Once traditional finance separates out crypto from the technology it runs on, it will bring on tremendous change with great opportunities.

2

The House That Crypto Built

"They did not know it was impossible so they did it."

– Mark Twain

The most expensive pizzas ever delivered were bought with crypto. In 2010, a Florida programmer named Laszlo Hanyecz posted an offer on a bitcoin forum: 10,000 bitcoins for two pizzas. The pizzas and bitcoin were worth about 20 dollars, but that bitcoin today is now worth more than $300 million.[1] A bitcoin enthusiast from California brokered the deal, accepting the bitcoin in exchange for ordering two pizzas from Papa Johns with US cash and having them delivered to Hanyecz.[2]

What's significant is that it's the first known documented purchase of physical goods using bitcoin. To be clear, the pizza shop didn't accept bitcoin as currency, but the intermediary did. Hanyecz has since said he doesn't regret giving up bitcoin for his pizzas, and today there's a crypto project for ordering pizza that allows you to use bitcoin to buy food from Domino's Pizza. There's even an international holiday to honor Hanyecz's original purchase: May 22 is Bitcoin Pizza Day.

In the crypto community, Hanyecz is a legend because he introduced cryptocurrency to traditional markets, showing its value without a third-party authority to validate it. Thanks to his foresight, you can now use Coinstar machines in supermarkets as bitcoin ATMs. Crypto payments are stepping into the mainstream.

To many Hoodies, their fervor isn't just about the eye-opening returns that some cryptocurrency investments have created. It's about democratizing finance for everybody, removing the intermediaries, and offering access to anyone with a computer and an internet connection.

What was amazing about the launch of cryptocurrencies and the blockchains they run on was that the Hoodies had the foresight, know-how, and community-thinking to build the next iteration of finance. The Suits couldn't have pulled that off. Innovation is difficult to develop within a large institution with institutional and status quo thinking. Now, however, both mindsets are needed for the integration of this technology with traditional finance. Hoodies understand technological capabilities, and Suits understand finance. Before the market can integrate and adapt, Suits need to understand what the Hoodies have built and how we got here.

It's easy to dismiss crypto as a passing fad for young "dudes" wearing baseball caps backward and tech bros who know little about how finance works. Except for this fact: They built a global cryptocurrency industry with a market cap of $1 trillion[3] – equal to the GDP of Saudi Arabia,[4] a country that holds about 17 percent of the world's petroleum reserves.[5] Some $500 billion of the crypto market – half of the entire market cap – belongs to bitcoin. It might be the butt of jokes and ridicule in traditional finance, but crypto is here to stay. The Suits who understand, leverage, and adopt the technology will win.

What Are Cryptocurrencies (and Why Should You Care?)

The Hoodies wanted a more universal currency that's not intermediated, and they wanted people to have more freedom with and control over their money – and for banks and governments to have less. This wasn't an offshoot of Occupy Wall Street, which took over Lower Manhattan's Zuccotti Park in 2011 to protest the inequalities between the "One Percent" and everyone else. Crypto enthusiasts were more than willing to make bundles of money off their ideas and systems. Rather, they rallied for more autonomy, more transparency, fewer intermediaries, and less friction. If they could also make a revolutionary statement to the banks and a few governments along the way, that would be fine with them.

Though crypto didn't become a household word until the 21st century, its beginnings date back to 1982, when UC Berkeley's David Chaum published a paper called, "Computer Systems Established, Maintained, and Trusted by Mutually Suspicious Groups."[6] It began: "A number of organizations who do not trust one another can build and maintain a highly-secured computer system that they can all trust (if they can agree on a workable design)."

That turned out to be very prescient. Chaum had created the "blinding formula," which completes transactions without revealing the players or the contents of the deal. About a decade later, Chaum would launch what could arguably be the first cryptocurrency, a digital currency called eCash, available through his company DigiCash decades before bitcoin even existed.[7] Though his company ran out of money and filed for bankruptcy in 1998, Chaum and DigiCash were instrumental in developing the groundwork for blockchain. Most of all, he helped launch a philosophy of borderless freedom provided through technology.

Long referred to as the "Godfather of Cryptocurrency," Chaum told Coindesk in 2022, "If there's one thing that I want to communicate here, it's that forty years ago, I saw the inevitable progression of the digital world very clearly."[8]

Some crypto founders have made so much money along the way that they ended up with inflated egos and expensive lifestyles. Some outright scammed investors and a few paid the price for it. But at its core, cryptocurrencies are digital assets with value assigned by the networks they run on. It's about the technology first, collectivism, community, and then the life-changing cryptocurrency. That's the Hoodies way.

Similar to blockchains, cryptocurrencies aren't controlled by any central authority or government. They are digital currencies with no active fiscal or monetary policy or physical properties. Cryptocurrencies are fully decentralized, meaning there is no bank or central intermediary acting between one holding funds in an account or transferring the funds for payment.

Transactions are verified and recorded on a network of computers, or nodes, that follow set algorithms. The most well-known currency is bitcoin, which in 2008 was introduced with a peer-to-peer blockchain network that helps prevent double-spending and cuts down on transaction times. Today, there are approximately 23,000 different cryptocurrencies[9] and some 420 million users worldwide.[10] According to *Forbes*, the total market cap of cryptocurrencies peaked at $3 trillion in 2021 and had dropped to under $1.5 trillion by November 2023.[11]

Some cryptocurrencies don't seem to hold value while others do, despite their volatility. Some cryptocurrencies are stable in nature to mimic other currencies like the US dollar. Some are wildly volatile. Others are utility coins that provide access to specific services.

Anyone can send any amount of cryptocurrencies to anyone else, anywhere in the world, without permission from a central authority. This provides an economic freedom that traditional currencies do not offer. Some of the benefits of crypto include:

- **It's decentralized and trustless.** Holders aren't affected by a single governing entity.
- **It's fast.** Cryptos can be transferred from one account to another in minutes.
- **It's accessible.** Everyone with an internet connection can own cryptocurrencies.
- **It's secure.** Cryptography makes transactions within the system secure and cryptocurrency wallets require a private key to access.

Open-source network: A software system not owned by any one entity that's created for anyone to use it as they see fit. Bitcoin and Ethereum and other blockchains run on open-source software created by collaborative groups of developers who don't own or control the cryptocurrencies. Code and transactions are viewable for the public to see.

The open-source environment of cryptocurrencies creates a sense of "We're all in this together," a unified front. However, when you're working in finance or corporate America, privacy and asymmetry of information have created great wealth for a small subset.

Crypto's volatility, novelty, and lack of oversight have kept many investors from diving into the market. Yet even the most traditional of traditional finance players are beginning to soften. Many banking clients are requesting digital asset investment allocations, and, after a long crypto bear market that lasted nearly 500 days, many well-known investors remain in the market, including billionaires Jeff Bezos, who invested approximately $2 billion in cryptocurrencies,[12] and Bill Ackman, who declared, "Crypto is here to stay."[13]

According to a report by the CFA Institute and Financial Industry Regulatory Authority's Investor Education Foundation, crypto is the most common investment held by Generation Z investors (see Chapter 7). A whopping 32 percent of family offices currently hold digital asset investments, according to a Goldman Sachs report, and 14 percent of all US adults own bitcoin.[14] Note that crypto owners are 70 percent male and 30 percent female.

The market for crypto continues to grow. A 2023 Coinbase survey of the general population found that 20 percent own cryptocurrencies, and three-quarters of owners believe that crypto and blockchain are the future of finance.[15] Yet two-thirds of all those surveyed believe that the financial system needs major changes or a complete overhaul, and a Paxos survey found that 75 percent would buy cryptocurrencies from their banks if offered, up 12 percentage points over the previous year.[16]

Crypto isn't just bitcoin, and Suits can learn a lot about the market by examining the many types of coins and the blockchains they run on:

Bitcoin (BTC): The oldest well-known cryptocurrency, it runs on a peer-to-peer network that allows anyone to send and receive payments without intermediary involvement. It has a limited supply of 21 million coins, supporting its scarcity and value.

Wrapped bitcoin (WBTC): Created in 2019, this token was first designed to represent bitcoin on the Ethereum blockchain, giving BTC owners the option to trade outside the Bitcoin blockchain.[17] WBTC can now be used as collateral on other decentralized finance (DeFi) protocols, including MakerDAO and Compound.

Bitcoin Cash (BCH): A derivative of bitcoin designed after Bitcoin blockchain's "hard fork," when it split into two incompatible versions of the blockchain, each with its own set of rules. BCH allowed faster and less expensive transactions by increasing the block size limit.

Ethereum (ETH): Among the most popular open-source blockchain platforms, Ethereum allows holders to borrow, lend, or trade cryptocurrencies without fees or intermediaries. It relies on smart contracts, which enable programmable tokens or securities, and its holders can use its native currency to pay for some tangible goods and services.

Solana (SOL): Named after a beach near San Diego where its founders surfed, Solana blockchain and token were created to provide what Bitcoin and Ethereum lacked: effective synchronization, more attractive cost structure, and improved transaction speed. The Proof of Stake (PoS) blockchain allows for smart contract capabilities, decentralized finance (DeFi), and NFTs.

Ripple (XRP): Launched in 2012, Ripple was designed as a public, open-source, digital payment network that provides a faster and more energy-efficient option for cross-border transactions than bitcoin. Cleared of charges that it was an unregistered security, the XRP coin is now considered a commodity.

Litecoin (LTC): Created when developers were concerned that bitcoin was becoming too centrally controlled, Litecoin is a minable cryptocurrency on an open-source global payment network. Some call it "bitcoin lite" because it's a derivative or "fork" of the Bitcoin blockchain.

Stellar (XLM): Created by the founder of Mt. Gox and a co-founder of Ripple, Stellar is a public blockchain that offers developers "experiences more like cash than crypto" and that promotes itself as being "faster, cheaper, and more energy efficient" than most other blockchains.[18] Stellar's native token, Lumen (XLM), can be traded on several crypto exchanges. It has a market cap of over $3 billion.

Aave (AAVE): This Ethereum-based, permissionless lending protocol allows borrowers and lenders to interact using smart contracts instead of control by a centralized entity. In case of a market crash, Aave locks its tokens. The AAVE coin is a native governance token, which allows holders to vote on the development and direction of the protocol.[19]

MakerDAO (MKR): Launched on the Ethereum blockchain in 2017, MKR is a utility token that's used to pay fees and a governance token. It's also a recapitalization resource, created and sold to raise money in a shortfall.

Decentraland (MANA): This virtual reality platform available through Ethereum lets users create and monetize content. It's a virtual world where people purchase virtual plots of land to navigate, build, and buy and sell.[20] Think: a tokenized Sim City for Web3. Decentraland's token, MANA, and can be used to purchase investments, accessories, or in-game services.

Security token: A digital representation of ownership rights or asset value. Regulated by the US Securities and Exchange Commission (SEC), they are securities which could have similar structures to real-world asset (RWA) investments. Security tokens can be fractionalized and traded on exchanges using blockchain technology. They are also known as digital asset securities.[21]

Altcoin: Any cryptocurrency that's not bitcoin, though some include ETH in their definition as well, because many are a derivative or "fork" of either blockchain. Altcoins tend to be designed by developers who wish to provide an alternative to bitcoin, offering different consensus mechanisms or other features.

Among cryptocurrencies, there are subsets that are worth noting:

Meme Coins: A cryptocurrency that originated from an internet meme or joke. It typically holds no intrinsic value.[22] Examples include:

Dogecoin (DOGE): Created as a joke about a dog, it became popular after Elon Musk publicly sang its praises. Investors like its low price and high supply. It's inflationary, so more DOGE is printed daily, providing an infinite supply. (When Musk voiced his support of Dogecoin, it led to more demand and higher prices. Then he sold his Dogecoin after significant appreciation.)

Shiba Inu (SHIB): Created in honor of the Shiba Inu, a Japanese dog breed that serves as Dogecoin's symbol, the coin trades on Ethereum. Its white paper is referred to as a "woof paper."

Utility coins: Utility coins don't represent ownership or an investment stake but offer a utility, service, or access. They're more like poker chips: They represent value only for providing access and for exchanging one medium for another.[23] Here are some utility coins of note:

Binance Coin (BNB): Launched in 2017 as the primary token for the Binance exchange, it's one of the world's most popular utility tokens. It gives investors discounts on trading fees and other utility functions. The coin can also be traded, used to pay for goods and services using the Binance card or to pay transaction fees on the Binance blockchain.

Blackbird ($FLY): Blackbird is a blockchain-based platform for the restaurant industry. The native token, $FLY, offers incentives for both the restaurant and customer. Accessible by tapping your phone, the token connects restaurants with customers, improving guest engagement, loyalty, and payment. Diners get rewards, invitations to exclusive events, and on-platform spending power. Blackbird launched in summer 2023 and is initially focused on New York City restaurants.

Smooth Love Potion (SLP): Launched in 2017, SLP is the game digital currency of Axie Infinity, an NFT-based virtual world filled with digital collectable pets, called Axies. SLP can be utilized to breed new Axies, and players can mine SLP while playing, earn it in tournaments, or purchase it on exchanges.

Stablecoins: These currencies with a trading volume of $30 billion per day are designed to provide a stable value to protect investors from the volatility of other cryptocurrencies and mitigate price risk acting as a medium of exchange. In the DeFi world, they allow borrowing against crypto assets, hedging, or shorting. They are often pegged to fiat currencies, such as the US dollar, but they can also be collateralized by another crypto, an algorithm, or some combination thereof. Though stable in comparison to other crypto coins, they are still technically vulnerable to runs if too many investors try to cash out at once and the issuer doesn't have the reserves to back up the withdrawals. Some examples include:

Tether (USDT): The largest stablecoin with more than half the market, it's pegged to the US dollar to mitigate volatility risk. Tether is also available in other currencies with the value of all currency reserves backing the token published daily, though the company has not produced an audit of their balance sheet. That said, they are the largest player in the stablecoin market. During the TerraLuna debacle that depegged stablecoins, Tether's value dropped to $0.95 around midday but quickly bounced back to $0.998 by afternoon.[24] As of this writing, USDT is trading above $1.

USD Coin (USDC): This tokenized US dollar equivalent is pegged 1:1 to the US dollar, making it a stable cryptocurrency. It's compatible with several blockchains, including Ethereum and Solana. Reserves are liquid in nature, including short-term treasuries and US cash deposits, and they're audited.

DAI: This algorithmic decentralized stablecoin, which runs on Ethereum, is backed by collateral on the MakerDAO platform. It employs game theory to balance economic incentives for price stabilization. It's over-collateralized by other cryptocurrencies and real-world assets, including US treasuries, to keep its value at $1 USD.

Binance (BUSD): A US dollar–denominated stablecoin issued by the largest exchange, BUSD is backed by cash reserves and equivalents and minted in partnership with Paxos Trust.

TrueUSD (TUSD): A fully collateralized and legally protected token pegged to the US dollar, TUSD maintains a 1:1 ratio. It's designed to be transparent, so it doesn't use a special algorithm. Instead, it uses several escrow accounts to lower risk, increase transparency, and prevent theft. TUSD offers real-time attestations for its reserves.

Paxos Standard (USDP): Formerly known as Paxos Standard (PAX), USDP is a stablecoin with a $1 USD value on the Ethereum blockchain and regulated by the New York State Department of Financial Services. Other stablecoins launched by Paxos include Pax Gold (PXG), which is backed by gold, and PayPal USD (PYUSD), created in collaboration with PayPal.

The stablecoins listed above are an important part of the ecosystem as they are similar to $1 USD though they run on digital rails. Banks and other traditional finance companies are looking to create stablecoins for their clients and the institutional digital asset ecosystem.

A Stable Crypto

In 2022, transactions of USD stablecoins accounted for about 40 percent of all value transacted on blockchain and totaled approximately $6.87 trillion, surpassing Mastercard and PayPal volumes. One of the greatest benefits of stablecoin is that it makes it possible for traditional finance products to be a part of the crypto marketplace. Margin calls can be automated using stablecoins, which is important in the 24/7/365 digital world with prices constantly moving. If a natively digital bond is issued as a smart security using stablecoin, and that stablecoin can be programmed to pay when it's supposed to, right into the wallet of its owner, it keeps the process decentralized and automated. It also provides a stable reference for trade or transaction – the US dollar. That's why stablecoins are the backbone of trading on the blockchain.

In 2023, Moody's began working on a scoring system for stablecoins based on "the quality of attestations on the reserves backing them," reports *Bloomberg*.[25] The scoring system highlights the institutional recognition of stablecoin benefits.

ERC-20 tokens: By far the most popular token standard, the ERC-20 token is created on the Ethereum blockchain and allows for smart contract-enabled tokens that are fungible in nature, meaning it can be swapped interchangeably, like $20 bills. ERC-20 and smart contract logic opened the door for digital assets and DeFi. Other token standards include ERC-721, the Ethereum token standard for NFTs, and ERC-1155, a multi-token standard.

Commodity-backed stablecoins: Collateralized by silver, gold, oil, real estate, and other commodities, these stablecoins offer stability by their link to the underlying asset. Tether Gold (XAUt) and Paxos Gold (PAXG) are examples of gold-backed stablecoins. AgroToken has three stablecoins collateralized by soybean, corn, or wheat.

Cryptocurrency Exchange: An online marketplace where investors can buy, sell, and trade cryptocurrencies and digital assets.

Crypto Exchanges: From a Single Peer-to-Peer Trade to the NYSE

On January 12, 2009, Satoshi Nakamoto, the pseudonym for the never-identified creator of Bitcoin, sent 10 bitcoins to Hal Finney, the software developer and cryptographer. It was a test transaction, transmitted before bitcoin even had a quotable price. Some people have since speculated that Finney *is* Nakamoto, or was; Finney died of ALS, Lou Gehrig's disease, in 2014. Either way, it was a pioneering moment, effectively launching the first cryptocurrency transaction.

But what were they exchanging if there was no physical representation of bitcoin? There weren't dollar bills or gold bars to trade, and yet the transaction was the transfer of value between two parties, plain and simple. Today, crypto transactions are records stored on blockchain and validated and verified by a network. But back then, the only way to get bitcoin was by mining it or arranging a trade, peer to peer, and that was risky because it required trust. Then again, bitcoin was worth nearly nothing, so how risky was it?

> **Crypto mining:** Mining is using a computer to solve complex mathematical problems – like a puzzle – to produce a block of validated transactions on a digital ledger in exchange for coins. Bitcoin mining is one example, and it uses extensive computing power, and therefore, energy, to complete. According to the *New York Times*, China was the leading bitcoin mining industry until 2021, when the country effectively kicked them out, citing its high energy use.[26] The practice then grew rapidly in the United States, where each mining operation reportedly uses on average about 30,000 times as much power as the average household. In fact, it's so electricity intensive that Greenpeace said bitcoin mining "devours energy at an alarming scale, rivaling nations like Chile and Denmark."

Bitcoin Market: Created to allow investors to buy and sell bitcoin peer to peer using PayPal as a fiat exchange, it was later shut down by PayPal, who cited fraudulent trades by some users. But by then, the value of bitcoin had increased to nearly $24. Over the years, several exchanges emerged to provide a mechanism for trade. Some of them, like Mt. Gox, which handled the lion's share of bitcoin trades for a few years, were later shut down after hackers stole cryptocurrency from them (see Chapter 4).

Silk Road: Launched on the dark web, it helped users buy and sell illegal drugs and other illicit items using bitcoin. Its founder, Ross Ulbricht, was later arrested by the FBI, and then convicted and imprisoned for life on charges that included money laundering, hacking, and conspiracy to traffic narcotics. Silk Road was also shut down.[27,28]

Coinbase: In 2012, an Airbnb programmer and a former Goldman Sachs trader launched Coinbase, now one of the largest crypto exchanges with some 108 million users who hold more than $128 billion in assets worldwide. It was one of the first major crypto businesses to go public in the United States, on the NASDAQ exchange, beginning in 2021. *Barron's* reported that the Coinbase IPO "lived up to the hype," and *Fortune* shared that it ranked the seventh largest new listing of all time.[29,30,31]

Binance: Launched in 2017 by a former developer for high-frequency trading, Binance grew to be the largest global crypto exchange. At the last funding round, the value was reported to be over $4.5 billion, and it supports more than one hundred types of coins. After China banned crypto trading, the company relocated to Singapore. Binance and its founder Changpeng Zhao, known as CZ, have since faced regulatory scrutiny in the United States.[32]

In June 2023, the SEC filed charges against Binance and CZ for operating unregistered exchanges and misleading customers, ultimately classifying Binance's stablecoin BUSD as a security.[33] The *New York Times* reported, "Regulators have long seen the exchange, which has said it does $65 billion in average daily trading volume, as a major target in their quest to bring to heel a crypto industry that has been built around an explicitly anti-government ethos."[34] Then in November 2023, CZ stepped down from his role at Binance with plans to plead guilty to violating US anti-money-laundering requirements.[35]

NPR called Binance a "crypto Amazon,"[36] a one-stop shop for lending, research, and trading that's unlike anything available in traditional finance, which is bound by rules that protect investors from risk and conflicts of interest.

Alternative Trading System (ATS): An SEC-regulated electronic trading system that matches buyers and sellers for securities typically managed by broker-dealers. Regulations are not as stringent for an ATS as for an exchange, and it can add liquidity to a digital asset post-launch. Trading on an ATS is not publicly available and can be helpful for trading large transactions to mitigate price fluctuations.

Transfer agent: An intermediary who facilitates trades by maintaining a record of ownership of securities, canceling and issuing certificates, and managing distributions. As the digital asset ecosystem develops, many of these functions can be done on chain and through smart contracts.

Tokenization platform: A tech-enabled platform that creates and manages the actual tokens or digital asset securities.

While networks and exchanges continued to launch and grow, regulators began to take note. Some founders made preemptive choices designed to follow SEC guidelines.

tZero: Launched by online retailer Overstock, this blockchain-based exchange was designed to provide oversight to security token offerings. It's a designated alternative trading system (ATS), so it's regulated by the SEC and the Financial Industry Regulatory Authority (FINRA), though not all of its tokens are registered under the US Securities Act of 1933.[37] TZero provides trading of both private securities and digital assets and boasts over 44 million shares traded on the platform.[38] Recognizing the growing world of alternative investments, private markets, and digital assets, ICE, the parent company to the NYSE, made a strategic investment in tZero in 2022.

Securitize: Spun out of SPiCE VC, Securitize was co-founded by Carlos Domingo and Jamie Finn with a mission to decrease friction and create liquidity in the private sector. They are an SEC registered transfer agent, an ATS, and a broker dealer for digital assets. Issuances include common stock of Exodus, a credit-rated tokenized fund in Japan, and a debt security token issues by NBA player Spencer Dinwiddie. Securitize have also worked with KKR and Hamilton Lane to distribute tokenized shares of specific private funds.

Gemini: Launched in 2015 and regulated by the New York Department of Financial Services, the Gemini exchange allows users to buy, sell, trade, and store more than 120 cryptocurrencies.[39] Founded by Cameron and Tyler Winklevoss, the twins made famous by suing Mark Zuckerberg over the origins of Facebook, Gemini is well regarded by both inexperienced and experienced traders.[40] Selling "innovative security solutions" and ease of use, Gemini offers a mobile app for trading, plus a credit card that earns crypto on purchases.[41]

Kraken: Yes, this exchange is named after the mythical Norwegian sea monster. Built as a digital currency marketplace for gamers, it's now the world's third largest crypto exchange for more than two hundred currencies, reaching a daily trading volume of $333 million. But Kraken, too, fell into trouble with regulators when it was ordered to turn over its users' information to the Internal Revenue Service in the summer of 2023.[42] The SEC sued Kraken in late 2023 for illegally operating as a securities exchange without first registering with the agency.[43]

What's in Your Wallet?

A cryptocurrency wallet stores public and private keys, which are passwords for accessing your crypto or digital assets. Wallets can come as hardware, like a thumb drive, or a mobile app or other software. Users can even get a paper wallet. That is, the keys are written on paper and stored in a safe place, which is great for thwarting hacking, but makes it harder to use crypto, which is, of course, digital.

Satoshi Nakamoto and Hal Finney had the first wallets, which they used to trade the first bitcoin. Here's how you send crypto to a wallet:

1. Enter the recipient's wallet address, which is a string of 26 to 35 alphanumeric characters.
2. Choose the amount of cryptocurrency to send.
3. Use your private key to sign the transaction.
4. Pay the transaction fee.
5. Send the crypto.

To receive crypto, you simply accept the payment.

Types of Crypto Wallets

Custodial: Hosted by a third party, such as a traditional custodian, bank, or a crypto exchange, that stores the user's keys for them.

Non-custodial: The user is responsible for securing their own keys. Most crypto wallets are non-custodial. No other party holds keys to your wallet.

Hot wallets: Software that stores private keys. They are easily accessible and always connected to the internet. Think of the wallet apps on your phone or a plug in browser. This makes them more vulnerable to potential hacks and theft.

Cold wallets: An offline wallet for storing crypto. Think: thumb drive. It's stored on a platform that's not connected to the internet, better protecting it from hacking and theft than hot wallets can. However, they can be physically lost or stolen.

Isn't Crypto Really Just for Embezzling?

It's easy to think that crypto is just a bunch of toys for Hoodies, an overhyped flash-in-the pan, mired in scams and volatility. Like in any financial system, there are bad actors, and crypto has had its fair share. But the checks and balances of the blockchain create a public record of ownership that can thwart would-be criminals. In short, blockchain creates witnesses.

When Sarah Meiklejohn was studying for her PhD at the University of California at San Diego in 2011, she began researching blockchain, and she was interested in the payments tagged by keys with some two- or three-dozen characters. The *Washington Post*[44] reported that she discovered a way to collapse bitcoin's addresses into single identities along a traceable chain. She could follow the money.

The *Post*'s Dina Temple-Raston writes, "If you understand this much about the mechanics of bitcoin and the blockchain, then the whole smokey world of crypto starts to open up."[45] You can trace the money chain, making blockchain a forensic accountant's dream. That's because crypto is a fingerprint and blockchain is often open source. Every coin and every transaction has a number attached to it, and its movements are trackable along the chain. That makes money laundering for drugs or other illicit activities difficult, and forensic accounting, easier.

In the early days of crypto, the Suits wouldn't get involved because there wasn't any regulation. Yet they could have helped structure deals and scale companies, skills that many Hoodies, who are experts in tech, not finance, lacked. But the system simply didn't operate like traditional finance does, and the news headlines continually tied crypto to fraud. And yet, the Chainalysis annual Crypto Crime Report found that illicit schemes in 2022 accounted for less than 1 percent of total volume.[46] Meanwhile, the United Nations Office on Drugs and Crime estimates that between 2 and 5 percent of global GDP each year is connected with money laundering and illicit activity.[47] Fiat currencies are still more likely to attract criminal activity than crypto is.

Crypto's reputation wasn't legitimate, and that turned off the Suits. It also lacked a user-friendly interface, like a banking app that presents all your cash or investments in one place. Crypto was a bit rough around the edges.

But Hoodies are not reckless. They're inexperienced in finance, yes, but they still saw the value of a decentralized system built on blockchain, and as demonstrated in Chapter 1, blockchain is not crypto. Jamie Dimon recognized that early, and so, JPMorgan was among the first banks to introduce its own internal coin. To Dimon, crypto might be a useless toy, but the very system it's built on and the digital assets it can provide proved valuable even to staunch traditional finance institutions like JPMorgan.

The Birth and Growth of Decentralized Finance

The advent of crypto ushered in the new age of decentralized finance or a finance ecosystem that is not controlled by a centralized entity. The technology that runs its blockchain networks is the basis for DeFi, which *Forbes* calls "the antithesis to the way in which the world's financial system currently operates."[48] It has and will continue to influence what investors expect from their financial experience, and it will have effects on traditional finance in the short and long term. There's no turning back now.

The Hoodies created a crypto economy with billions of dollars a day of money transacting. Though crypto has experienced sometimes drastic fluctuations in value, it's here to stay. The number of cryptocurrencies globally grew steadily through the 2010s, with a dip in 2022 and 2023. By February 2023, more than 8,000 cryptocurrencies were in circulation, and it's estimated that the top 20 make up about 90 percent of the market.

BlackRock CEO Larry Fink, one of the most influential finance titans, said, "We do believe that if we can create more tokenization of assets and securities – that's what bitcoin is – it could revolutionize finance."[49] In his annual letter to investors, Fink warned that the United States was lagging behind countries like India, Brazil, and parts of Africa when it comes to digital payments. "The tokenization of asset classes offers the prospect of driving efficiencies in capital markets, shortening value chains, and improving cost and access for investors,"[50] he said.

This new technology attached to crypto allows more flexibility and the ability to create new structures, much like the way the derivatives market arose. But first, we need to create our traditional structures on top of it. Once systems are in place, we can create new structures that will make it through a risk committee at a bank and even be recognized as less risky.

DeFi Is the Future of Finance

As discussed, DeFi doesn't rely on a centralized institution, such as a bank, instead allowing for peer-to-peer exchange, lending, or borrowing using blockchain technology and smart contracts. Those smart contracts set Ethereum and other decentralized applications apart from bitcoin by ensuring that transactions on the blockchain are legitimate, according to the provisions of the agreement.[51] It's a contract between parties based on predetermined parameters that must be met, no intermediary required.

Decentralized Apps (dApps): These are digital applications that run on blockchain or a peer-to-peer network outside the control of a centralized authority. These dApps are software programs that safeguard user privacy by not requiring users to submit personal information to use the app. Instead, smart contracts help facilitate transactions between anonymous parties. But their end-user experience can leave a lot to be desired.

Examples of dApps include Aave, an open-sourced liquidity protocol that runs on Ethereum and lets users lend, borrow, and stake crypto with anonymity. With the Auger dApp, users can create predictions and bet on sports, economic, or world events. Other popular dApps include UniSwap, a decentral exchange, and OpenSea, an NFT marketplace.

DeFi solves some problems inherent in the traditional finance system.

The investor holds the money and retains control instead of an intermediary financial institution.

1. Transactions are peer to peer or eliminate a majority of intermediaries or counterparties.
2. Fund transfers occur in minutes or seconds, not days.
3. Anyone, including the unbanked, can participate.
4. It's available 24/7/365, not just when the market is open.
5. It's transparent and trusted.

Hoodies represented a philosophy that decentralization evened the playing field for all, opening up access and opportunity. But as soon as they started trading cryptocurrencies and "investing" in ICOs, that is finance. They're banking.

Suits represent companies, revenue, earnings, and wealth, and they're seeing the value represented by the technology behind cryptos. A Suit doesn't have to worry that money's sitting in escrow or if there's another Lehman Brothers event on the horizon. To sell stock, there are seven intermediaries that take a cut, and the trader has to wait for T+2, two days to clear. On the blockchain, intermediaries are eliminated, and that trader gets the money today, pushing the trade to immediate settlement.

When the Suits start to see the value of DeFi, it's only a matter of time until these principles seep into traditional finance. If the 2008 financial crisis served as fuel for the rise of bitcoin as the leading cryptocurrency, events in traditional banking in the subsequent years set the stage for the rise of DeFi. While 2008 saw the largest bank collapse – Washington Mutual's demise after a run on the bank drained it of some $16 billion in 10 days – 2023 experienced the second and third largest to date, when First Republic Bank and Silicon Valley Bank failed within six weeks of each other.

Ninety percent of Silicon Valley Bank's deposits, made largely by tech start-ups, exceeded the FDIC's $250,000 insurable maximum, putting depositors at risk.[52] Traditional finance can experience mismanagement or face regulatory pressures not inherent in DeFi, and involves layers of intermediaries, adding costs, delays, and risks that don't constrain DeFi. While intermediaries can deliver checks and balances, centralized authorities can subject investors to fees, restrictions, and delays.

So, no wonder the circumstances were ripe for the introduction of blockchains.

Programmable tasks: Automatic, self-executing actions, such as borrowing, investing, or lending, executed by smart contracts on a blockchain without an intermediary.

While bitcoin introduced a peer-to-peer electronic cash system rooted in software code without oversight from a centralized entity, such as a bank or government treasury, Ethereum set the stage for DeFi, which gives investors four key benefits: **autonomy**, **decentralization**, **transparency**, and **trust**.

With DeFi, you can hold and control your own money, work directly with peers without interference, count on an accurate record of all transactions, and trust the records and smart contracts' immutability, or the inability to be changed. What's more, DeFi tends to offer attractive yields and new forms of collateral.

Plenty of Interest: CeFi/DeFi Lending and Staking

By the end of 2020, the top three bitcoin lending services had grown their holdings by a record 734 percent.[53] It was all about the yields, which were paid in crypto. By December, reports Decrypt, BlockFi's APY for bitcoin lending was 6 percent, Nexo's was also 6 percent but rose to 8 percent when paid out in Nexo tokens, and Celsius Network hit 4.51 percent.[54] As Decrypt reported, "The three firms are all planning on expanding [in 2021], anticipating further growth in the Bitcoin lending industry."[55]

CeFi (Centralized Finance): A system similar to traditional finance where intermediaries have centralized control over the flow of money and transactions. CeFi platforms include BlockFi, Nexos, and Celsius Network, which all serve as intermediaries.

DeFi (Decentralized Finance): A system that doesn't have a central authority or intermediary and uses blockchain technology and smart contracts for peer-to-peer execution. The transaction is recorded on a public blockchain. DeFi lenders include Aave, MakerDAO, and Compound.

In 2023, Celsius, which had more than a half-million customers with a total of $4.4 billion in interest-bearing accounts, filed for Chapter 11 protection,[56] just one of several crypto lenders to go bankrupt. Celsius claimed "poor asset deployment decisions" and repercussions from the aftermath of the TerraLuna collapse. BlockFi, too, went bankrupt, citing its exposure to Sam Bankman-Fried's FTX (see Chapter 4), which caused a liquidity crisis.[57] The company was the first to be charged for failing to register its crypto lending product with the SEC, and agreed to pay a $50 million penalty. Nexo survived but was fined $45 million by the SEC for violating federal securities law and wound up settling without admitting wrongdoing.

Though lending on crypto, BlockFi, Celsius, and Nexos are CeFi companies because loan participants rely on a centralized intermediary. True DeFi lending is peer to peer and uses smart contracts for execution on a decentralized application. For example, the Aave protocol supports users to borrow and lend multiple crypto coins. Smart contracts control the preset agreements for funds disbursed, fees, and collateral ratios. MakerDAO is also a DeFi protocol, focused on their stablecoin DAI, which is borrowed when ETH is deposited into smart contract Maker Vaults. The value of posted ETH is always higher than the DAI borrowed for overcollateralization and risk protections.

It was the end of the 2020-to-2022 crypto lending boom, but not the end of lending crypto. During the rush, the Crypto Fear and Greed Index,[58] which assesses the overall state of the market and assigns a number from zero to 100, consistently hit highs in the seventies and eighties after an initial dip due to the COVID-19 pandemic. Fear was low and greed was high, and lots of people wanted in on it (see Figure 2.1).

Crypto lending allows investors to lend coins to borrowers who pay them back with interest, which in 2020 ranged from 1 to 8 percent.[59] Typically, borrowers must stake their own cryptocurrencies as collateral, more than it's worth, so it's overcollateralized, making it easier for loan platforms to cover losses. It's a personal loan secured by crypto.

It's been popular for several reasons, including relatively fast loan approval speed and flexible payment schedules. Most crypto loans don't

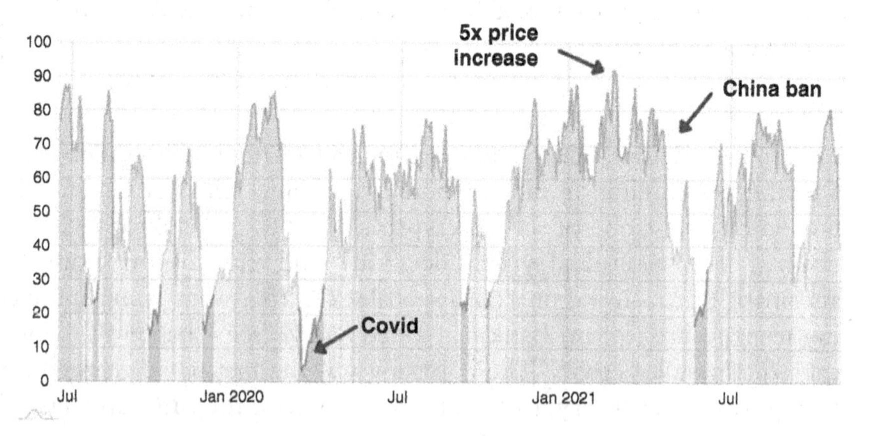

Figure 2.1 Crypto Fear and Greed Index
Source: Alternative.me

require a credit check because the loans are overcollateralized by generally liquid assets. But it's crypto, and crypto can be volatile. It's also unregulated. No wonder a favorite crypto term is HODL, or "Hold On for Dear Life," which, rumor has it, originated as a typo for "holding" by a supposedly drunk crypto enthusiast on a bitcoin online forum. It allows regular investors to never sell crypto but borrow against it and maybe even double down.

Crypto's propensity for volatility increases the likelihood of crypto lending and borrowing margin calls, which, along with liquidations, can be automated. Despite the sizable bumps crypto lending went through in 2022, it continued to grow. In 2023, Coinbase launched a digital asset lending platform for large institutional investors, raising $57 million for the launch.[60]

Campbell Harvey, co-author of *DeFi and the Future of Finance*, told *Cointelegraph*[61] that the crypto lending market was ripe in 2022 for risk management practices common in traditional finance. He didn't think crypto lending was dead, but the SEC was getting nervous about it, issuing an investor alert in 2023[62] about crypto platforms because, unlike traditional finance firms, they aren't required to register with the agency. The SEC sought to register crypto lending companies, with Chair Gary Gensler saying that the practice of crypto lending "sounds a little like an investment company, or a bank, you might say," reports *Reuters*.[63]

At the same time that crypto lending saw a boost in popularity, staking emerged. *Cointelegraph* explains: "Defi staking works through smart contracts, pieces of code representing automated financial agreements between two or more parties that offer excellent incentives for crypto enthusiasts willing to stake (lock up) their assets and engage in a more active presence in the network."[64] In other words, you lock your crypto into a smart contract and in return, you get rewarded at rates higher than typical savings accounts typically provide. It's directly related to Proof of Stake (PoS) networks like Ethereum and Binance, and not Proof of Work (PoW) blockchains like Bitcoin (see Chapter 1). It's a way to generate income by becoming a validator for payments. If you don't do your job right, you risk losing parts or all of the crypto you staked.

Moneywise summed it up this way: "Staking is leasing your crypto to the blockchain, and lending is leasing your crypto to a borrower."[65] Staking is not mining, which requires hardware and lots of computing power. It's relatively low risk, but stakers can lose if the price tanks.

Crypto Incentives

The story in 2021 was the incentives programs that crypto networks launched, offering rewards, such as NFTs and free coins, for lenders and buyers. Rewards are thought to have value but, like cryptocurrencies, not all actually do. One of the most well-known incentives programs was Polygon's $40 million reward, or 1 percent of their MATIC tokens, funded by its nonprofit Polygon Foundation to entice users to deposit and borrow assets on Aave's Polygon marketplace.[66] The liquidity mining program was designed to attract more liquidity to the network. Other platforms followed suit: Avalanche's $180 million program, Fantom's $370 million program, and Binance's $100 million liquidity incentive program.[67]

But the United Kingdom's Financial Conduct Authority (FCA) set its sights on crypto incentives, such as airdrops of free tokens to encourage investments, proposing a ban in 2023 to "strike the right balance between protecting people and enabling sustainable innovation in the sector," said the FCA to CoinDesk.[68]

DeFi Derivatives

In DeFi, derivatives are supported by smart contracts hosted on a blockchain, offering investors an opportunity to bet on tokenized versions of real-world assets (RWAs), such as stocks, bonds, commodities, or crypto, without holding the underlying asset. It's a hedge, but in DeFi, the derivatives are automated through smart contracts with no need for intermediaries and turned into synthetic tokens that aren't owned by the user.

One example is wrapped bitcoin (WBTC), which is tied to bitcoin. It can be minted only when the original token is deposited, thereby allowing redemption without risk. There are many more out there and many that are being developed. DeFi opens the doors for new types of derivatives.

Now more than ever, crypto and digital assets need the Suits, and now more than ever, the Suits can use their skills and knowledge to transform a revolutionary industry that started as a good idea by the Hoodies into something that can benefit millions of investors.

Major institutions are beginning to see the value of digital assets. Citi, Deutsche Bank, and JPMorgan introduced deposit tokens for clients, allowing faster and more efficient payments including cross border initiatives.[69] Apollo, KKR, and Hamilton Lane have tokenized private funds. HSBC used FX Everywhere to process trades using blockchain technology. Tassat used blockchain for real-time, business-to-business payments, and in 2023, the US Federal Reserve launched FedNow,[70] an instant payment infrastructure to send and receive money 24/7/365. FedNow is not a blockchain-based program, but it does highlight the demand for instant payments. Nearly three dozen banks and credit unions participated, and the Fed promised that the service isn't a form of currency or a step toward eliminating cash.[71]

The House That Crypto Built is still standing, and the Suits can give it the upgrade investors deserve.

3

Crypto as a Proof of Concept for Traditional Finance's Capital Markets

"The Stone Age didn't end because they ran out of stones."

– Unknown

When PayPal announced in August 2023 that it was launching its own stablecoin for its 435 million users – a first for a global payments company – Ron Lieber, the *New York Times*' "Your Money" columnist, admitted in an open letter to young crypto enthusiasts, "You were right. It's not a passing fad."[1] Coindesk meanwhile called the new stablecoin, available to PayPal's U.S. customers, "training wheels" for decentralized finance (DeFi),[2] and *Forbes* said it's "likely to be a trendsetter" that could set off a stampede.[3]

Whatever people labeled it, PayPal's entry into the digital assets market signaled a shift in the industry. It was the farthest that digital assets and blockchain had made it toward mainstream adoption. Naturally, there was a lot of buzz. Columbia Business School adjunct professor

Omid Malekan offered both a statement and a warning on *Medium*: "PayPal issuing its own stablecoin is big, marking a major milestone in the continuing evolution of crypto." He added that "legacy banks and payment providers who do nothing will fade away."[4] When it comes to digital assets, now more than ever, if you snooze, you lose.

PayPal had announced that its US customers could transfer its new stablecoin, PYUSD, to compatible external wallets, send payments to other PayPal customers, use the stablecoin for other types of payments, and convert other cryptocurrencies to and from PYUSD. The coin could also be exchanged for US dollars at any time.[5]

Years earlier, Facebook had tried and failed to launch its own stablecoin project, Libra, later renamed Diem, but it couldn't survive Congressional scrutiny, and parent company Meta shut down its cryptocurrency endeavor in 2022 (see Chapter 4).

But PayPal had several things going for it that Facebook did not. Issued by Paxos Trust Co., its PYUSD was pegged to the US dollar and US Treasuries. Unlike Meta, which was facing scrutiny for the Cambridge Analytica privacy scandal, PayPal didn't have their CEO hauled in front of a congressional subcommittee. PayPal instead chose to work with regulators, and by the time the company announced its own digital coin in 2023, lawmakers had spent several years catching up-to-speed on the pluses and minuses of digital assets. In short, the timing was right and so was the player.[6]

Even so, Bank of America issued a statement declaring that the new PayPal stablecoin wouldn't "lead to accelerated regulatory clarity."[7] In fact, Congresswoman Maxine Waters (D-CA), the top Democrat on the House Financial Services Committee and a crypto skeptic, was "deeply concerned" that the PayPal stablecoin, which she labeled "a new form of money," lacked federal oversight, and called for "prudential authority" to address runs, risks, and the "concentration of economic power."[8]

The hammer came down in late 2023 when the US Securities and Exchange Commission (SEC) issued a subpoena requesting documentation related to PYUSD. Former Paxos executive Austin Campbell told CoinDesk the move was "intimidation" and a "power grab," and accused the SEC of targeting PayPal based on "headline value" because of its name recognition, or else, he said, they would have gone after other more established coins.

CoinDesk had once described PayPal's entry into stablecoins as "crypto, sans crypto – or fintech with the benefit of blockchain."[9] It had elements of the so-called "two wolves" of crypto: the money side and the tech side. This was a vote of confidence for the tech side by the money people. In other words, the Suits were giving blockchain a thumbs-up, or as Coindesk editor Zack Seward put it, "This is a giant fintech firm saying that transmitting value dollars is better on blockchains."[10]

Indeed PayPal had a stronger relationship with Congress than Facebook, which prided itself on asking for forgiveness, not permission. Along the way, the political tides had changed on stablecoin. As *Bankless* podcaster Ryan Sean Adams tweeted, "I think people are massively underestimating the chances the US Gov may flip bullish on stablecoins and choose to pursue a policy of exporting them to the world."[11]

In 2023, that idea was in jeopardy.

Much had changed since Mark Zuckerberg put on a blue suit and appeared before Congresswoman Waters's committee for a public dressing down. She had told him, "Given the company size and reach, it should be clear why we have serious concerns about your plans to establish a global digital currency that would challenge the US dollar. In fact, you have opened up a serious discussion about whether Facebook should be broken up."

One thing is certain: There is much to learn from crypto's test runs, false starts, and victories.

What Traditional Finance Can Learn from Crypto

This chapter is about the technology, structures, and usability created by Hoodies, not whether a token is a security or if bitcoin has value. Sometimes, the benefits of blockchain get lost in the "crypto is a scam" weeds, missing some of the industry's early wins: more efficient systems for payments, trading, lending, investing, and supply chains. For 15 years, the Hoodies have been working out the kinks in crypto, blockchain, and decentralized finance, paving the way to adoption in the institutional capital markets.

Goldman Sachs's head of digital assets, Mathew McDermott, told CNBC in 2023, "We're at such an early stage in terms of its adoption, but as you look across the marketplace and you see the breadth of financial institutions building out their digital asset teams, their digital asset strategies, be that the sell side or the buy side, it's just super exciting and I think there's a real recognition there."[12]

Though crypto was not built by Hoodies for an institutional audience, the thought process behind its foundation lays the groundwork on which institutional players – Suits – can build out payments, securities, and business systems. We'll look at payments, funding, lending, blockchain functionality, non-fungible tokens, registration, governance rights, royalty payments programs, and owner utility benefits.

Changing How Payments Are Made

Bitcoin is becoming an acceptable form of payment at a growing number of retailers, with bitcoin ATMs popping up in cities around the United States. Retailers such as Microsoft, Starbucks, Overstock, AT&T, Dell, Pavilion Hotel and Resorts, and AMC Theaters accept bitcoin, partnering with companies like BitPay, Bakkt, or Flexa's software. At Walmart, shoppers can use bitcoin to purchase gift cards usable at the store. Payment applications like PayPal, Robinhood, Venmo, and Zelle also recognize bitcoin, and some universities accept crypto payments.

While credit card transaction fees typically cost merchants 1 to 3 percent, the processing, or "gas," fees associated with crypto payments are typically less, especially when fewer people are using the network. Though a credit card transaction takes just seconds, the funds can take up to three days to transfer, which is why an account statement may list transactions as "pending." Personal checks can take two days to clear while the bank "floats" the money in the meantime, earning interest on their balance sheets. Allowing consumers to reinvest those funds to put to work sooner could assist in more working capital and higher liquidity.

Today, a bitcoin transaction can take minutes to an hour to complete, but once the transfer is made, the money has changed hands. Still, that's a long time to wait for your Starbucks order.

Yet digital assets offer instantaneous settlement, which means having immediate access to your funds when a transaction closes. This gives control over cash flow back to the bank clients and offers users the opportunity to access the funds right away. It also lowers the risk of counterparty risk and fraud.

Pat LaVecchia, Founder and CEO of Oasis Pro Markets, called digital assets a "part of an evolution of the financial system," adding that "infrastructure developed with blockchain technology is driving the industry forward, enabling lower costs, faster settlement times, and transparency that benefit both institutional markets and investors."[13] He sees it as a critical part of moving traditional finance from Web2 to Web3.

Bank of America's "Beyond Crypto: Tokenization" report explains that cross-border payments and transfers now can take seven days to settle, involve five or more intermediaries, and cost ten times more than domestic payments. "Cross-border payments cost corporations $120 billion in transaction fees in 2020 and are heavily reliant on manual processes," the report said.[14] Blockchain can change this.

In 2022, the Federal Reserve Bank of New York issued a paper about atomic settlement, an exchange of two linked assets that combines instant and simultaneous settlement. In traditional finance, on the other hand, the trade and the settlement are separate processes that can take several days, the traditional T+2 settlement. So, the authors asked, "How can each party ensure that, when the time comes to settle the trade, the other will keep their side of the bargain?" citing settlement failures in Treasury markets reaching as high as 400 billion a day in 2008.[15] The Fed recognizes that new distributed ledger technologies can change traditional finance for the better by changing settlements.

Counterparties to transactions are paying attention to blockchain and digital assets. A paper published by the Depository Trust and Clearing Corporation (DTCC) announced support for T+0 settlement times allowed by the distributed ledger technologies (DLT), claiming that their client response had been overwhelmingly positive.[16]

Moving to T+0, or same-day settlement, would have a significant positive effect in the cash and securities financing markets. The key benefits would be liquidity flows, a reduction in overnight funding costs, and optimal uses for assets for collateral and capital purposes. Similarly, counterparty risk, credit risk, collateral liquidity, and margin and capital requirements also benefit.

Many countries are looking into creating central bank digital currencies (CBDC) backed by reserves in part because fiat or paper dollars

Central bank digital currency (CBDC): The Federal Reserve defines the CBDC as "a digital form of central bank money that is widely available to the general public."[17] It's a digital dollar and programmable money.

aren't as important as they were before credit cards and apps allowed for money transfers. Similarly, a digital dollar would aid in optimizing monetary and fiscal policy. That said, a CBDC is a sovereign currency and can't afford to fail.

The infrastructure to host both CBDC and institutional digital assets is the same, so when CBDCs are streamlined, it will open the doors for other digital assets and tokenized products.

One big difference is that CBDCs would be a liability of the central bank, not commercial banks.[18] But commercial banks may push back, because they earn money by lending out money they hold in deposits to earn the spread between the savings account interest paid and the interest received from borrowers. This will affect how the future of banking will shake out.

US Secretary of Treasury Janet Yellen highlighted the benefits of a CBDC when she said that a digital dollar could help lower transaction costs and support a faster payment infrastructure in the US.[19] Currently, China is piloting a digital yuan project, and Reuters reported that 130 countries are looking into CBDCs.[20]

Shifts in Funding

Initial Coin Offerings (ICOs) (see Chapter 2) began as an innovative form of funding that may have skirted regulatory oversight but filled a demand for both the companies in funding and the investors looking for alternative opportunities. Admittedly, there was fraud in ICOs, but not all participants were bad actors. Had Hoodies and Suits worked together at that time, perhaps fewer investors would have lost money.

In 2018, the largest ICO to date raised $4.2 billion for the Block.one's blockchain EOS. It was larger than the top three venture-funded projects of that year combined: Epic Games, Uber, and Juul. Block.one was focused on developing a smart contract platform competitor to Ethereum to transact faster. Yet nothing much has happened since.

A year earlier, AirSwap's ICO, which represented the Hoodie mentality of collectivism, community, and open source, raised $36 million in just 24 hours. Launched by a Brooklyn team of programmers and traders who reportedly met at either business school or Burning Man, AirSwap is a peer-to-peer trading bulletin board that doesn't charge fees for trades. By removing the intermediaries, AirSwap provides off-chain negotiation with on-chain settlement. Counterparty risk is eliminated.

AirSwap built a global community with strong marketing, representing about 23 million followers at the time of the ICO, which provided the funders with AirSwap's utility and governance token, AST. A Bloomberg video available on YouTube called, "What Happens at a Crypto ICO,"[21] highlights the successful ICO and shows the well-intentioned Hoodies at work. Not all ICOs were fraudulent.

Funding rails through digital assets open up new opportunities. Take private investments, for example. Today, it's difficult to trade out of a private investment. Financial circumstances can change in five years for individual investors or investment funds. Many require a hold until maturity, which could be from 5 to 10 years. Generally, if a private asset is sold prior to redemption, it's at a steep discount. The discount or bid-ask spread is primarily because it's deemed that the seller had more information than the buyer.

With digital assets, value information could be included on the token for full transparency, which could decrease the bid-ask spread. Also, it's difficult to find an active secondary market for a fund interest or private security. Digital assets open up potential liquidity, offering trading on an alternative trading system (ATS) or exchange.

For asset managers who raise money through the retail channel for projects, offering investors the option to sell or trade prior to the completion of the project is a benefit to their investor base. Tokenization can provide this option. A retail investor can be affected financially by tuition and other college costs, a sick family member, or a change in work situation. For the manager, the change in ownership will not affect the end project or add additional risk.

Asset managers and private equity firms are looking for more opportunities to expand their investor base and grow assets under management. The ideal investors are small in number and large in check size, which keeps the administrative and marketing burden to a minimum. However, most asset managers are seeking funding from a relatively select group of funders, which includes pension, endowment, sovereign wealth, insurance, or ultra-high-net-worth family offices. How do you grow when relying on the same pool of investors?

"If I'm an asset manager, it means I can no longer afford to ignore the retail or the individual investor," Daniel Celeghin, managing partner at Indefi, said. "If I want to stick to serving these large institutions, I'm going to be [serving] a smaller and smaller pool of business, which will be increasingly more competitive."

The wealth dynamic is changing. The retail family wealth is slightly higher than institutional wealth, and currently institutional wealth has access to the alternative investment market with very limited access to such opportunities for retail family wealth (see Figure 3.1).

One benefit of blockchain technology is that it decreases the administrative burden, opening up the potential for more investors without the additional heavy lift. Currently, the investor relation team has a long list of tasks to perform for subscriptions making small checks not worth the effort. Automated systems will decrease the labor hours required to onboard additional investors, which could also open the door for a lower allowed minimum investment. The changing demand of the next generation of investors (see Chapter 7) will greatly expand the investor pool for the asset manager.

A number of institutional asset managers have launched digital funds or are looking to do so, including, but not limited to Apollo Global

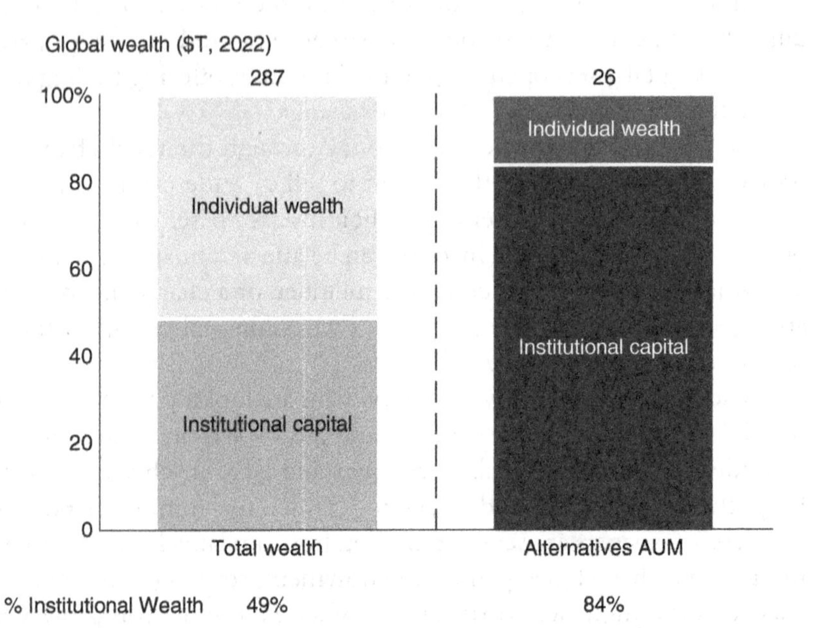

Figure 3.1 Private Asset AUM Is Currently Highly Concentrated in Institutional Capital

Source: Used with permission from Bain & Company

Management, Franklin Templeton, Hamilton Lane, KKR, and WisdomTree (see Chapter 6).

All of these funds have offered lower minimum investments for digital assets, opening up a wider pool of investors. Apollo Global Management has plans to offer a natively digital fund on the blockchain as well. The move is a bridge from traditional paper-based deals to digital transactions.

Expanding the World of Lending

Hoodies used cryptocurrencies and stablecoins to create a decentralized, global technology-based banking system that's open to everyone without the need for traditional intermediaries. There is no centralized authority in DeFi. It consists of decentralized exchanges, synthetic derivatives, and lending protocols. One thing Suits can take from DeFi is the lending opportunities created as the new technology opens up new avenues.

In traditional finance, lending is generally performed by banks, insurance companies, or alternative lenders. For example, a bank client deposits funds and, in return, receives a low interest rate on the deposited principal. The bank then lends out the deposited money to a borrower as a loan for a higher interest rate with the understanding that the money will be paid back within a specific period of time. The bank makes money on the interest rate spread between the rate paid to the depositor and the rate received from the borrower. In this transaction, the bank is the intermediary between the depositors and the lenders.

With DeFi, depositors still earn interest on their deposits, but they don't have to entrust their money to a bank or counterparty, instead holding their funds in a digital wallet that represents an account on the blockchain.

Let's look at Compound Finance, "an algorithmic, autonomous interest rate protocol built for developers, to unlock a universe of open financial applications" that's rated B– by Standard & Poor's. In other words, they employ technology to allow users to lend and borrow cryptocurrency or crypto assets without an intermediary. And the company itself underwent a traditional risk assessment by obtaining a traditional credit rating.

A borrower from the Compound protocol needs to supply some sort of cryptocurrency as collateral. Let's say it's 100 USDC; each USDC is a stablecoin equivalent to $1 USD. Depending on the currency, the borrower can then borrow up to a certain percent of the collateral. Let's say 75 percent, so $75 worth of ETH. It doesn't have to be the token supplied, but the collateralization ratio depends on the specific currency. No credit score is required as the loan is overcollateralized by the initial amount supplied. If the 75 percent collateral requirement is not met because the collateral loses relative value, the account is automatically liquidated – like an automated margin call – which could be from accrued interest or from the decreasing value of the supplied coin. There is a cost to liquidation which can range but is approximately 8 percent.

To supply collateral to the Compound protocol, it's similar to depositing funds in your bank account. It earns interest, which is tied to the interest rate determined on liquidity or the size of the pool for the cryptocurrency, even if the user borrows against it. The cryptocurrency supplied is added to a large pool of that same cryptocurrency that others have supplied as well. Small pools equate to higher rates, and large pools to lower rates. Interest is accrued approximately every 15 seconds.[22]

For example, Bob supplied $1,000 worth of ETH and received a 1.2 percent interest rate for the deposit. Then he borrowed $750 worth of USDC at a rate of 2.5 percent. Bob believes in the future value of ETH (HODL), and doesn't want to sell his initial ETH holding, but at the same time, he wants to free up some funds. If Bob uses the borrowed $750 to buy Apple stock (NASDAQ: APPL) at a return of 20 percent for the year, he would have made $150 while still holding on to his ETH, which could have also appreciated.

Obviously, this could go in the other direction as well. It is a gamble. But he has a stop at the initial $1,000 collateral because of the immediate liquidation if it hits the top collateralization limit. Bob still has his initial ETH investment value, minus the liquidation penalty.

Now assume that Alice supplied $1,000 worth of USDC in the Compound Protocol and received a 4 percent interest rate, and she borrowed $750 worth of ETH for a 5 percent interest rate. Here, Alice still has her $1,000 of USDC on which she earned $40 for the year and was able to borrow $750 for a cost of $37.50 plus a few transaction fees. If Alice holds on to the $750 worth of ETH and the price of the ETH doubles, she will have made a 75 percent return while still holding on to her USDC.

Tokenized products with an accurate price feed will be able to be pledged as collateral for loans in a more efficient manner than is possible today. When the world of tokenized assets expands, this will be a huge growth area. Counterparty risk shifts in the lending example. This can be done without a bank. In the Compound example, Alice and Bob are pledging to a Compound pool, so technically there is an intermediary, but the lending is automated and it is considered DeFi.

Non-Fungible Tokens

Non-fungible tokens (NFTs) are a digital representation of a single unique product that can be traded on certain exchanges. Think of snowflakes, houses, trees, or people. All are unique, or non-fungible, and could each be represented by an NFT. No two are exactly the same. US dollar bills, on the other hand, may have different serial numbers but they are technically interchangeable and, therefore, fungible.

Digital art represents the largest use case of NFTs to date. The NFT boom started in 2017 with the launch of Dapper Labs' CryptoKitties and Larva Labs' CryptoPunks. The first NFT game to receive widespread attention, CryptoKitties allowed players to purchase, breed, and trade virtual NFT cats. CryptoPunks dealt in unique digital artworks, all unique as one of the first art collections generated by an algorithm. These two projects were very popular among the crypto, gaming, and tech crowds.

NFTs reached the mainstream in 2021 when the prestigious auction house Christie's sold a digital art NFT collection by Beeple. Its top piece, called *Everydays: The First 5000 Days*, sold for $69.3 million.[23] The top NFT sale to date, *The Merge* by Pak, sold for $91.8 million at auction to a consortium of 28,000 collectors.

It's hard to not mention the coveted Bored Ape Yacht Club in NFTs as they pushed digital art to pop culture. These sought-after collectibles feature ten thousand unique ape works of art. Owning a Bored Ape NFT also allows access into an exclusive community of live events, merchandise, and voting rights.[24]

Other opportunities for NFTs are within the metaverse, which McKinsey & Company describes as "emerging 3D-enabled digital space that uses virtual reality, augmented reality, and other advanced internet and semiconductor technology to allow people to have lifelike personal and business experiences online."[25] In the metaverse, NFTs represent land plots, property, or wearables, all of which can be traded or sold online. The best-known metaverse, Decentraland, reportedly has eight thousand daily active users.[26] In 2021, a plot of virtual land in Decentraland sold for $2.4 million.[27]

Well-known retailers are using NFT collectibles as brand marketing. Adidas has designed NFT clothes for the metaverse as a virtual wearable fashion line, which sold out almost immediately after the launch, generating $23 million.[28,29]

With 1.5 million users, NBA Top Shot allows sports fans to create NFTs of their favorite basketball players' game footage.[30] Gucci and Christie's are collaborating on an NFT collection that will use generative AI, shedding light on how the technology may shape the art and fashion of tomorrow.[31]

Starbucks Odyssey is an NFT loyalty program that sold out their 2,000 unique NFTs in just 20 minutes and still delivers new perks, including exclusive experiences.[32] Even Walmart announced plans to offer NFTs,[33] while Amazon is giving out NFTs as an in-game currency to its Prime subscribers in its game Mojo Melee, built on the Polygon blockchain.[34] Amazon Prime Gaming has also partnered with Mythical Games and Blankos Block Party.

In an effort to stay relevant with the next generations, brands such as Nike and Uniqlo are creating NFTs, while many video games have created in-game assets.[35]

The potential for NFT applications in finance is exciting. Anything that is unique could be digitally represented as a non-fungible token. Consider loans and structured finance. While certain structural features are standardized, such as interest rates, terms, and collateral, every loan is tied to unique pledged assets and unique terms. Each loan could be similar, but not the same. If the loan was created as an NFT, it would be digital and could use smart contracts, and the loan could be structured to pay out interest to a specific account (or wallet). The loan NFTs could be grouped into a portfolio and structured as digital securities for an asset-backed securitization, collateralized loan obligation, or mortgage-backed securitization.

For land, home builders could sell individual plots as NFTs. The data, value information, and chain of ownership would be stored on the NFT, making it easier to transfer, buy, and sell. In addition, all liens would be recorded against the on-chain asset to be valid, making title insurance redundant. Similarly, NFTs could change the car title industry. Currently, when a car is purchased, the owner receives a paper title, but it would be more efficient and traceable if the title were an NFT. It would also be less likely to be lost when it's accessible on the blockchain, where it lives.

Then, there is digital identity. We need identities and records for employment, travel, driving, proof of birth, health records, and investor accreditation. All of these identifications are paper-based, but the same entities dispensing identifications could move identity into a digital form. For finance, NFTs could represent an investor's accreditation and a financial institution's Know Your Customer (KYC)/Anti-Money Laundering (AML) compliance requirements, which are designed to establish a customer's identity, monitor financial activity, and prevent and detect fraud.

Security and Bond Registration

During Hurricane Katrina, a safety deposit box submerged at a bank nearly floated away with some $250,000 of bearer bonds inside.[36] Unlike most other bonds, bearer bonds are not registered, so they can be redeemed by whoever possesses them. So, it's no wonder that the US government, fearing their use for illicit activities, prohibited the issuance of bearer bonds beginning in 1982. In an effort to protect investors and the IRS, all bonds and securities today are registered to an individual or company.

In bond transactions, proxy votes, or any situations that require a majority or a two-thirds' shareholder vote for approval, tracking bondholder ownership can prove time consuming and difficult to identify. Bond ownership is typically held in book entry form where paper certificates aren't issued but the issuer keeps a record of buyers' names. When bonds are traded, the registry is not always updated.

Blockchain can solve sole registration issues as an immutable ledger for financial transactions, offering increased trust, transparency, and traceability. It also eliminates the possibility of user error and centralized control.

Blockchain offers:

- **trust** as an immutable record of ownership that cannot be tampered with or deleted.
- **transparency** of recording, providing access to the same information for all permissioned members.
- **traceability**, providing an audit trail of ownership detailing any and all changes.

Blockchain can provide a more efficient method of registration for both the transfer agent and the company stock ledger, which is an internal ledger that includes redemptions, splits, issuances, transfers, and different classes of stock issuances. Traditional registration is similar to a database. The registry can be very complicated, with the possibility of user error or omission. Mergers and acquisitions have fallen apart due to lack of clarity on the capitalization table. Blockchain can provide transparency.

Public companies are required to use transfer agents, an important fiduciary business that maintains a registry of ownership, record changes, disperse dividends, and issue and cancel certificates. It is the responsibility of the transfer agent to maintain accurate records, but transfer agents are people, not systems, that use archaic technology that's slow to be innovated. It's a commoditized service that has yet to become truly digital. What's more, charges have been filed against transfer agents for failure to perform duties, committing fraud, or other violations. There is also the potential for user error in recording information. Blockchain solves these problems.

Improved Governance Rights

The Hoodies created a new organizational and community governance structure, the system by which entities are directed and controlled, called the Decentralized Autonomous Organization (DAO). Similar to a cooperative where everyone has ownership and a vote that's binding, it's an entity with no management, CEO, board of directors, or centralized decision makers.[37] The organization is totally flat.

Benefits of DAOs include a community of like-minded people with one common goal or strategy. It is seen as a more democratic way to run an organization. Smart contracts have internal conflict resolution of prewritten rules included in the code for the organization's digital shares. DAOs can be more adaptable to market conditions assuming everyone has the same vision and vote.

Drawbacks of DAOs include potential loss of corporate efficiency, or time to resolution for decision-making if there are bottlenecks in proposals and voting on company action. If there is a disagreement or apathy, governance is difficult and leadership tends to emerge. That said, as all levels of members are technically flat in a DAO, any member could be liable for action taken by the organization. There are regulatory concerns as DAOs are not legal in all states, and for those that are, they are registered as limited liability corporations (LLCs).

The largest DAO, MakerDAO, is responsible for the Maker Protocol, which includes "adjusting policy for the DAI stablecoin, choosing new collateral types, and improving governance itself."

There are still questions about regulatory clarity and concerns for security, which is dependent on the code used to create the DAO. How will issues be handled when the DAO has financial problems or the community breaks from the initial underlying thesis? The jury is still out on the effectiveness of these organizations; however, the acceptance of the structure by many highlights the call for collectivism, individualism, control, and new ideas.

While it's unlikely that DAO's governance rights will become mainstream or adopted by traditional finance, digital assets offer "responsibility, accountability, awareness, impartiality, and transparency," which is the definition of good governance.

Blockchain does provide increased transparency and efficiency in shareholder voting, which would result in fewer errors, enhanced legitimacy, and increased quality of the voting process. It could also improve fairness among stakeholders. Sharing data between stakeholders can improve trust and provide an immutable audit trail.

Accessible Royalty Payments

Royalty payments are a prime use case of digital collectibles, and music is one of the first industries to dive in. Royalty payments are made to the owner of an asset for the use of intellectual property, a product, or a patent. Musicians receive royalties when their original songs are played on the radio, on streaming apps, or in a movie or a video game. The ability for artists to sell their royalties helps to connect them with fans and to get deeper with their fan base. It also allows fans to profit alongside their favorite songs or artists.

For instance, three hundred NFT shares in megastar Rihanna's hit song, "Bitch Better Have My Money," sold out in minutes, coinciding with her 2023 Super Bowl performance. The NFT purchasers would own 0.00333 percent of future royalties for the lifetime ownership of the copyright of the song, which has streamed more than 760 million times, paid not less than twice per year. The NFTs are tradeable, with returns in the first year expected at 6 percent. It was the song's producer who sold his interest, allowing him to create liquidity for his own private asset.[38]

Prior to the Rihanna song sale, the band, the Chainsmokers, gave five thousand fans NFTs representing 1 percent of ownership of their 2022 album, *So Far So Good*. The fans received album royalties with the option to sell the NFTs, providing an incentive to get ownership in the album for no upfront cost.

"A number of artists have done this in the past, but not for free," the Chainsmokers told their fans. "It was important for us to do it this way because this isn't about profiting off some new tech for us. It's about connecting more deeply with you and harnessing a new disruptive technology in an effective way that truly shows what is possible as we head towards a Web3 world."[39]

This was the first time that the royalties were distributed via NFT for an album. Nas and Diplo had previously released NFTs linked to royalties for certain songs, but not full albums.

This trend is expected to continue in other industries, including gaming, oil and gas, fashion, book publishing, and entertainment. The royalty structure of the gaming industry is complicated.[40] Revenue is earned not just through game sales but advertising, in game purchases, or subscriptions. The more complicated the structure, the more technology can help to streamline the process for transparent calculations and tracing of information. The gaming industry is relatively new and heavy in technology, so it makes sense that the integration with tokenization has a lighter lift. Tokenizing the royalty of games allows for potential investors not associated with the industry to diversify their portfolio in an emerging high-growth industry. It would also allow heavy users of the games to participate in the upside for all of the hours they invest in the game itself.

Royalties in oil and gas are interesting, in part because royalties can be tied with land and passed down from generation to generation. Using tokenization to fractionalize royalties would allow for a more streamlined process with less room for error in calculations. It could also allow for trust and estate benefits and would supply potential liquidity for owners of rights if they choose to sell down a portion of their royalties.

Tokenizing royalties allows for ownership to be transparent with fewer intermediaries, ideally lowering costs and allowing potential liquidity with the tokens tradable on a marketplace. The digital data trail shows that royalties were earned, and the funds were distributed to the holders without intermediaries extracting value. It also decreases the possibility of fraud, miscalculations, or misuse.

Novel Utility Benefits

According to Jeff Dorman, CIO of Arca, "Tokenization can distribute investment gains more fairly. Just think if Amazon had been tokenized by its users rather than run for shareholders."[41] Assets can be both an investment and a utility. The investment benefits are from the profitability and company performance of Amazon while the utility benefits are from a useful and potentially valuable perk from Amazon, such as free shipping, streaming, and discounts.

Currently, investors who want to benefit from the profitability in Amazon purchase its stock (NASDAQ: AMZN) out of their brokerage accounts. Amazon shoppers, the profit generators, who seek to benefit from free shipping, streaming, and food discounts, purchase Amazon Prime from the Amazon store. AMZN is the investment and Amazon Prime is the utility. Imagine the benefits of combining them and the interest aligning. Subscribers of Amazon Prime would be incentivized to bring business to Amazon and then benefit from the appreciation of the stock. This could be facilitated through tokenization or digital assets.

Currently, there are 153 million Amazon Prime members in the United States alone, comprising approximately 65 percent of Amazon shoppers, each paying $139 per year. Around the world, there are 200 million Prime Members[42] – significantly more than the number of AMZN stockholders, who are not currently receiving a dividend, yet benefit from stock appreciation. The interest is highlighted in the numbers. Structuring the ownership interest through tokenization would allow for a merger which could benefit the AMZN bottom line.

A real life example of utility benefits was launched in 2018 with AspenCoin, the first large-scale tokenization of real-world assets in the United States[43] (see Chapter 5). Ownership of the token offered the holders entry into an exclusive community and specialized benefits. While many hotels have rewards programs, they aren't typically tied with ownership.

The takeaway here is the opportunity to align financial incentives and utility benefits to create a more efficient structure. Putting the focus on ways to entice investors outside of just the straight investment criteria could help both build the brand and increase the value. Similarly, enticing the end user or consumer and allowing them to participate in the upside of the company they are contributing to building could add tremendous value.

It could be argued that institutional investors are not looking for upgraded rooms or discounts on Whole Food sales. However, those perks could save the company money on travel or be used as perks to top employees or clients. There is the possibility that the perks or unity offered could be monetized and traded depending on the structure.

Considering that 51 percent of the wealth in the United States is in family or retail wealth, all investments don't need to be structured for and targeted to institutions. Generational changes of the investor base (see Chapter 7) will require more investing options than accepting the same structures that have been tried over time. Millennials and Generation Z are more individual-focused, yet community-minded than past generations. Combining utility within investment opportunities could be very attractive to the growing investor base.

Imagine an owner of General Motors stock (NYSE: GM) is offered the benefit of an early sale of a limited series Corvette. Or, what if Madison Square Garden Sports Corp. (NYSE: MSGS) offered stock owners access to events with New York Knicks players? What if Microsoft (NASDAQ: MSFT) offered the utility to a tech help desk for stock owners? These utility benefits could add value to the stock and potentially help boost revenue.

Tokenization isn't the only way to make this happen, but it is the only way to make it happen efficiently and optimally. Digital assets are programmable, scalable, and tradable. As former Barclays CEO Bob Diamond told the *Financial Times*, digital currencies have a "very important place" in finance.[44] They are the future.

4

What FTX, Hubris, and Crypto's Other Mistakes Can Teach Traditional Finance

"It's fine to celebrate success, but it is more important to heed the lessons of failure."

– Bill Gates

Sam Bankman-Fried spent the winter after his extradition from the Bahamas under house arrest at his parents' Palo Alto home on a $250 million bond.[1] He had become notorious for the collapse of the cryptocurrency exchange FTX, a major blow to the already shaky reputation of the crypto market.

If there's one person who best represents all that's gone wrong in the crypto craze, it's Bankman-Fried, once the richest person under 30 in the world. At just 25 years old, the MIT graduate and former Jane Street Capital trader known as SBF co-founded Alameda Research, a quantitative trading firm that specialized in crypto, and later built the FTX exchange with the promise of higher yields than traditional banks could offer.

For a few years, Alameda bought and sold bitcoin and other cryptocurrencies, keeping the difference in spread and appreciation. As the price of crypto continued to soar, hedge funds began to participate, and Alameda now had competition. So, SBF decided to build his own crypto exchange, FTX, with its own utility coin, FTT, to help fund and facilitate Alameda's business. It worked – until it didn't.

Owning both a trading firm and an exchange represented a fundamental conflict of interest. As a trading firm, Alameda made money by buying and selling crypto at different rates on various exchanges worldwide. The classic buy low and sell high. They could also use leverage to inflate trading profits. As an exchange, FTX was one of the largest in cryptocurrency, making money off of trades, loans, and derivatives. But this arrangement lacked oversight and separation. In fact, the US Securities and Exchange Commission (SEC) clearly defines conflicts between market intermediaries of the principal and agent,[2] which can lead to market manipulation or misappropriation of funds.

All the while, Alameda and FTX made lots of money. The *New York Times* reported that Alameda claimed in 2021 to take in $1 billion in annual revenue through crypto trading fees. That same year, FTX, then the world's third largest cryptocurrency exchange, made over $1 billion in annual revenue.[3] In a two-year period, 80 investors poured almost $2 billion in funding into FTX.[4] Money was flowing.

It seemed like FTX and SBF were everywhere. The exchange secured naming rights for the Miami Heat basketball team's home arena for $135 million and signed a deal to place its logo on Major League Baseball umpire uniforms.[5] SBF donated millions to congressional representatives through political action committees[6] and reportedly helped to craft crypto-related policy.[7] He was even spotted with his arm around House Financial Services Committee Chair Maxine Waters (D-CA), the very congresswoman who would later haul him before her committee to account for "actions that've harmed over one million people and wiped out the hard-earned life savings of so many."[8]

During FTX's heyday, numerous celebrities endorsed Bankman-Fried and promoted his exchange. *Shark Tank*'s Kevin O'Leary became both an investor and a spokesperson, and basketball superstar Steph Curry promised that, though he wasn't a crypto expert, "with FTX, I have everything I need to buy, sell, and trade crypto safely."[9] It seemed as though you didn't have to understand crypto trading or the blockchain technology it ran on to make money off it.

But it wouldn't last. At a dinner in Manhattan celebrating the industry, Kristin Smith, executive director of the Blockchain Association, reportedly addressed the elephant in the room before FTX's fall: "Sam is selling out the industry to get a monopoly for FTX."[10]

Seven-time Super Bowl winning quarterback Tom Brady filmed a commercial that asked, "Crypto. FTX. You in?" But by the end of 2022, he was out, and so was everyone else. Brady and his then-wife, supermodel Gisele Bündchen, had received a combined $48 million in stock in exchange for their "ambassador" roles at FTX,[11] but in just a few days, its value vanished.

SBF had become a crypto hero, but few understood the problems inherent with his business model. Money was being funneled from FTX to Alameda Research with a large commingling and siphoning of billions of dollars of customer funds. In the down market, FTX funds propped up Alameda in billions of dollars or risky trades. FTX management, lacking business experience and an understanding of corporate controls, also funded their own lavish lifestyles.

CNBC reported in 2022, "The quant trading firm Sam Bankman-Fried founded was able to quietly use customer funds from his exchange FTX in a way that flew under the radar of investors, employees and auditors in the process, according to a source."[12] Alameda had borrowed billions from FTX and allegedly spent, traded, or donated it. An asset manager shouldn't have unfettered access to an exchange. It's a conflict of interest, and in this case, a set-up for fraud.

Without a board of directors or regulations, FTX lacked oversight, and they didn't turn to any Suits for guidance. While FTX and Alameda clients and investors in the FTT token lost money, the biggest losers are the investors who funded the almost $2 billion into FTX over multiple inflated financial statements and valuations.

The trouble started when Binance chief executive Changpeng Zhao, known as CZ, sounded the alarms about FTX's financial stability, driving down the price of FTT and frightening investors. After a three-day run on deposits, FTX suffered an $8 billion shortfall, further instilling distrust in crypto and the technology it runs on. As the curtain was pulled back and the market reacted, SBF quickly lost most of his FTX fortune as his $32 billion company descended into bankruptcy and endured investigations by the SEC and the Justice Department.[13]

On Twitter, Circle co-founder and CEO Jeremy Allaire called it crypto's "Lehman Bros. moment," adding how disappointed he was that the very financial technology that had arisen out of the 2008 banking crisis had collapsed into its own version of the same thing.[14] But FTX was built on risky trading, including selling futures to amateur investors that isn't legal in the United States. It's why SBF had moved his base to Hong Kong.

CZ originally offered to bail out FTX, but later killed the deal because of issues with "corporate due diligence." The value of both bitcoin and ETH also dropped, and the *New York Times* reported that "FTX's rapid fall suggests that no company in this freewheeling, loosely regulated industry is safe from extreme volatility."[15] Repercussions continue through the institutional digital asset industry as people question blockchain's risk and compliance and put projects on hold.

How did this happen? Alameda took a margin position on FTX, borrowing funds from the exchange to the tune of billions of dollars. Bankman-Fried later admitted to missing signs of trouble and inaccurately assessing risk. The SEC and the Justice Department investigated whether FTX improperly used investor's funds to prop up Alameda, arresting SBF in December 2022 on charges that he defrauded customers and lenders, among others.[16]

In the bankruptcy filing, John J. Ray III, the CEO who took over FTX after Bankman-Fried resigned, wrote: "Never in my career have I seen such a complete failure of corporate controls and such a complete absence of trustworthy financial information as occurred here." He added that the situation was unprecedented, involving control in "the hands of a very small group of inexperienced, unsophisticated, and potentially compromised individuals."[17]

Kevin O'Leary later told Hasan Minhaj on *The Daily Show* that FTX was "nothing but a start-up" – a $23 billion one – and that historically, 80 percent of investments in start-ups lose money. Yet in 2021, FTX "was the hottest deal on the street," O'Leary said, and investors were "a who's who of venture capital."[18] As with most financial meltdowns, the blame was put on "bad actors."

Minhaj, who called FTX a "Bahamian orgy," said, "Someone burned down the house while Mom and Dad left." FTX had raised a stunning amount of money – nearly $2 billion with a valuation of $32 billion – and then lost it all. It was a notable example of a Hoodie lacking the experience to understand the responsibilities of being a fiduciary. If he did understand what he was doing, then his actions were criminal, as a court would later find.

The *Washington Post* likened crypto investing to a ritzy casino where "the sights and sounds of winning don't mean the vast majority of people are richer than when they started playing."[19] The new technology – blockchain – wasn't the problem. People were. It's bad actors, not bad tech. It takes seasoned experts to apply the Hoodies' new technology to a centuries-old, highly regulated institution like finance. That's where the Suits will be able to build on and improve upon the lessons from mistakes that have been made so far.

In an online interview with SBF at the DealBook Summit[20] shortly after the FTX collapse, the *New York Times*'s Andrew Ross-Sorkin said that some believed SBF was a young man who had made a series of "terrible, terrible, very bad decisions," while others were sure he'd committed a massive fraud – a Ponzi scheme. Ross-Sorkin asked him about his tweet that said FTX was an $8 billion accounting mistake. SBF claimed he didn't run Alameda and, therefore, had no conflict of interest, even though he owned it, claiming, "I didn't knowingly commingle funds." He did, however, admit that the companies were intertwined, "tied together substantially more than I ever wanted it to be."[21]

"I substantially underestimated what the scale of a market crash could look like and what the speed of it could look like and how correlated it would be,"[22] he claimed. Bankman-Fried continued to paint a picture of himself in the media as a hapless victim, but a debtor's report by FTX reveals something else entirely. Not only were there accounting mistakes, but threats to employees who spoke up, and a complete lack of financial and accounting controls through a system where business expenses were reportedly approved via emoji and some 80,000 transactions tracked on QuickBooks were left unprocessed and labeled, "Ask My Accountant." Even SBF's Stanford professor parents benefited with gifted houses worth $26 million and Dad on the payroll.[23]

The US attorney's office for the Southern District of New York later alleged that SBF knowingly defrauded customers of upwards of $10 billion in what US Attorney Damian Williams called, "one of the biggest financial frauds in American history."[24] In November 2023, SBF was found guilty on all seven charges of fraud and conspiracy, with prosecutors claiming he'd used FTX as his own "personal piggy bank."[25]

The *New York Times*'s Ginia Bellafante called SBF "crypto's Icarus,"[26] describing the fraud he orchestrated in a complicated new industry as simple as "shifting around and repurposing other people's assets for his own use."

FTX's Lesson: The bottom line is that young Hoodies shouldn't run companies dealing with regulated securities worth so much money without oversight from Suits, who understand the ins and outs of finance.

LUNA/Terra: "LUNAtic" Millionaires Lose It All

FTX may have been the biggest fraud in crypto, but LUNA proved to be its own kind of epic mistake. Created in 2018 by Stanford graduate and South Korean entrepreneur Do Kwon, who called his investors "LUNAtics," LUNA quickly began creating millionaires, turning Kwon into a bit of a cult hero and the leader of a multi-billion-dollar empire. The Terra stablecoin offered a 20 percent annual yield[27] on the Anchor protocol in what some have called "Ponzinomics," a multi-level marketing scheme for tech bros looking for a quick and enormous payout.

Yet LUNA was beloved by its community, largely because of its sizable returns. At its peak, the market value for stablecoin Terra Classic UST was more than $40 billion.[28] LUNAtics were enthralled, almost cult-like in their enthusiasm for the cryptocurrency and the blockchain it ran on. They used yellow moon emojis in their Twitter handles to identify one another, and crypto asset management firm Galaxy Digital's successful billionaire founder Mike Novogratz even showed off his LUNA-themed tattoo to his nearly half-a-million Twitter followers. Renowned crypto podcaster Anthony "Pomp" Pompliano shared a video about how LUNA could transform the entire finance system, saying, "If the team successfully does this, they will show the playbook for central banks and stablecoins on how to back other assets with Bitcoin." LUNA was supposed to be an algorithmic solution to crypto's volatility.

The two stablecoins were supposed to balance each other out – Terra (earth) and LUNA (moon) – so that when the value of Terra UST dropped, LUNA holders automatically traded their coins, which propped up the price of UST. It wasn't fiat-backed like other stablecoins. It was backed by its sister token, LUNA. This was supposed to keep the supply and demand of both Terra and LUNA in balance so that they would continue to trade at their target value.

Excitement about LUNA was high in early 2022 as Terra became one of the hottest crypto projects in history. At one point, Terra had the fourth largest market cap in crypto. Kwon announced the launch of Luna Foundation Guard, an organization that raised $1 billion through the sale of LUNA tokens to buy bitcoin, with Jump Crypto and Three Arrows Capital as lead investors. Three Arrows co-founder Kyle Davies tweeted that spring, "Grandpa, what was the world like when $LUNA was less than three digits?"[29]

Kwon's outsized personality fueled the mania. He named his newborn daughter Luna, tweeting, "My dearest creation named after my greatest invention," adding that if he'd had a son, he'd have named him, "Stable Kwon."[30] Shortly before his company imploded, he predicted in a podcast that 95 percent of crypto coins would die in a few years, "but there's also entertainment in watching companies die, too."

Kwon was allowing depositors to withdraw at any time, and when one owner dumped billions of UST into the market in the spring 2022, it lost its peg to the US dollar, and LUNA's value plummeted 99 percent to a fraction of a fraction of a cent, losing billions of dollars in value in just a few days after a major sell-off began. It was a crypto run on the bank.[31]

This caused a massive number of LUNA to be minted, saturating the market. The algorithms couldn't keep up with the demand for cash, and Terra lacked cash or assets in reserve. Binance stopped trading, and the Luna Foundation Guard tried to offset the bleeding by selling off bitcoin, which drove down the value of the entire crypto market. *Forbes* estimated that some $60 billion of digital currency was wiped out because of the LUNA crash.[32] On Twitter and Google Search, "cryptocrash" trended.

Paolo Ardoino CTO of Tether tweeted, "Reminder that Tether is honouring USDT redemptions at $1 via tether.to. >300M redeemed in last 24h without a sweat drop." But Tether, the largest stablecoin, lost $20 billion in market value after the Terra collapse, and fell off its peg to the US dollar, but was still redeemable for one dollar.

Terra blockchain validators stopped activity and its Discord network shut down discussion to thwart widespread panic. Subreddit followers on the TerraLuna thread were apoplectic, with some reporting losing their life savings in the LUNA crash. Links to a suicide hotline were reportedly pinned to the thread. One Redditor wrote, "Why would anyone intelligent want to own Luna when it can be devalued on a whim, and why would you trust UST when it's essentially backed by nothing?" Another answered, "I think the answer is that 99.9 percent of everyone playing these coins had no idea what they're doing or how any of it (supposedly) works."[33] Hindsight is 20/20.

When the algorithm worked, it worked very well. But Kwon had publicly announced how Luna could fall apart, and someone took him up on it. The *New York Times* reported instances of Kwon's trash-talking as the key to Luna's downfall.[34] The Hoodies were playing a dangerous game of roulette. Kwon claimed Luna was never a scam, but instead, a market experiment gone wrong. He was even contrite, tweeting in May 2022, "I am heartbroken about the pain my invention has brought on all of you."[35]

When US Secretary of the Treasury Janet Yellen testified before the House Financial Services Committee days later, she associated stablecoins with "the same kind of risks that we have known for centuries in connection with bank runs." She called for regulation as the use of digital assets increases.

Kwon, a former "Forbes 30 Under 30," launched a new blockchain to offer a LUNA coin without a Terra stablecoin. Though he had been heralded as a pioneer in DeFi, in actuality, he was running the network in a very centralized way. He was later sentenced to four months in a Montenegro jail after he was found guilty of forgery and faces prison time in South Korea and the United States, where he's been charged with eight counts, including wire, commodities, and securities fraud. If Suits were at the table, could this disaster have been averted?

On the first anniversary of the crash, crypto enthusiasts called for risk management structures and due diligence.[36] Simply put, when the price of a stablecoin substantially deviates from the peg, investors panic, and UST, which was tied to its sister cryptocurrency, LUNA, relied on an algorithm to maintain its price. That can work only in a bull market when confidence is high. Once a stablecoin loses its peg and traders redeem their stablecoin, the price plummets, as it did with UST. The International Monetary Fund labeled it the "superficial allure of crypto," and called for strong regulations over the "negative consequences of crypto experimentation."[37]

"Any crypto-based financial system would likely be subject to regular destabilizing booms and busts," wrote the IMF, claiming that attempts to decentralize finance were an illusion. "Policymakers should not be swayed by the dubious promises of decentralization and democratization." Selling crypto, says the IMF, has been easy because it's a "compelling indictment of our current financial system," which had its own epic failure in 2008. But those problems were political, not technological, and technology is the main selling point for crypto and blockchain.

LUNA's Lessons: Algorithmic trading doesn't always win, Nobel Prize or not.

Crypto Wasn't the Start of Algorithmic Disaster

The much-loved LUNA wasn't the first time that an algorithm led to a financial collapse. In the nineties, Long-Term Capital Management (LTCM), a hedge fund in its heyday, had to be bailed out by the US government.[38] Founded by a Salomon Brothers bond trader named John Meriwether, with shareholders that included Nobel Prize–winning economists, LTCM used a systematic plan based on the Black Scholes formula, a multivariate mathematical equation that provides the fair price of a European stock option based on six variables. It offered a mathematical way to value a stock option. In short, it used an algorithm.

Investors put in $10 million each to have access to the fund, and they weren't allowed to withdraw money for three years. In the mid-nineties, LTCM gave average annual returns of a staggering 40 percent. At its peak, LTCM held more than $1 billion of investor capital, buoyed by a promise: an arbitrage strategy that could take advantage of temporary changes in market behavior, thereby reducing risk to zero.

But when the markets started to behave irrationally, a crisis began to spread across Asian markets, and yet LTCM stuck to the model, seeing it as an opportunity. The firm borrowed $200 billion from several prominent Wall Street banks and made highly leveraged bets. When Russia defaulted on debts, LTCM's billions in equity were wiped out, and the Fed bailed them out to save the industry. It was another example of algorithms working in an up market, but not a down one.

Decades later, LUNA's downfall, which CNET called "one of the most stunning crypto crashes ever recorded,"[39] set off a ripple effect in the cryptocurrency market. Voyager and Celsius, whose founder Alex Mashinsky was charged by the Justice Department with securities fraud, filed for bankruptcy.[40] Three Arrows, meanwhile, was forced into liquidation, and some investors lost their life savings.

In finance, where there are losers, there are winners, too. Hedge fund Pantera Capital had a 100x return on its $1.7 million investment by liquidating most of its LUNA holdings before the collapse.[41]

But make no mistake: LUNA's crash was a major strike against stablecoins that aren't pegged to a fiat currency and a blow for crypto.

Forbes estimated that the "crypto winter" it triggered would last until 2026, and by 2023, *Business Insider* would proclaim that "nobody really cares about crypto anymore."[42] Warren Buffet declared, "cryptocurrencies will come to bad endings."[43]

Yet the beginnings keep on coming as Hoodies continue to find ways to make crypto work.

LTCM's Lesson: Any time there's a high return, however short-lived, someone will figure out how to replicate its process.

Libra/Diem: Facebook's Stablecoin Fail Sheds Light on Regulation

You know something has potential for big returns when the tech behemoths show interest. Enter Facebook, which released a white paper in 2019 for its cryptocurrency and blockchain-based financial project, then called Libra and later Diem. It would be backed by bank deposits and short-term government securities and governed by a not-for-profit consortium called the "Libra Association," which boasted among its founding members several big names in finance and tech, including Andreessen Horowitz, Coinbase, Mastercard, Stripe, and Uber. Libra wasn't pegged to any fiat currencies, but it was backed by a basket of multiple currencies, and so, investors wouldn't always be able to redeem the Libra token for a fixed amount.[44]

Congress was unimpressed. Two years later, Senate Democrats sent a letter to Facebook chief executive Mark Zuckerberg, claiming that the company "cannot be trusted to manage cryptocurrency." Zuckerberg had already appeared – in a business suit – before the House Financial Service Committee, where Chair Maxine Waters (D-CA) voiced concerns about a global digital currency that would "challenge the US dollar." Even at Libra/Diem's inception, Congresswoman Waters had expressed doubt, asking Zuckerberg to hold the project until Congress and regulators could investigate.

This didn't square with Facebook's mantra: "Move fast and break things." They saw Libra/Diem as a bitcoin competitor, a currency with decentralized ownership built on open-source blockchain technology. The difference was that Libra/Diem, a stablecoin, would be backed by low-risk assets. Facebook would build its own digital wallet, take a piece of the transaction fees, and capture user transaction data – the privacy part that rankled some in Congress.

But Facebook's reputation, thanks to the high-profile Cambridge Analytica privacy scandal, set obstacles for the media giant. The *Financial Times* quoted an unnamed US government official who said, "Diem spent years trying to reverse-engineer their project to fix all of its faults. But they could never fix being linked to Facebook. It was their original sin."[45]

Meanwhile some of the project's backers, including Visa and Mastercard, began to reconsider their involvement, distancing themselves from Facebook. The tech behemoth had created Diem with grand plans to revolutionize global financial services, making it easier to move money across borders, but regulatory scrutiny intervened. Zuckerberg wanted Diem to rival WeChat Pay, a mobile digital wallet system and app built on China's Tencent, their version of Facebook, with more than a billion active monthly users. Like Apple Pay, WeChat Pay lets consumers use their smartphones for payments, linking their bank accounts or credit cards to their digital wallets. Users can also send money to friends and family, like a Venmo or Zelle.

WeChat Pay charges a transaction fee to transfer funds from the wallet, and it's that fee that Facebook wanted to get a piece of through its own version of the WeChat Pay project. But by 2022, its vision of a billion-plus user digital payment system had died. In late January, Meta announced it was canceling Libra/Diem.

It had faced heavy scrutiny from the start, not just from Congress, but worldwide. Five European countries created a task force to stop Libra in Europe in 2019, and one Australian professor said the access to billions of Facebook users at the project's outset meant this "alternative money" could move from "too small to care" to "too big to fail" very quickly.[46] Then the likes of PayPal and Mastercard began jumping ship. Its name change did nothing to shake its association with its early failures and from Facebook, which was soon criticized for seeking forgiveness instead of permission.

Political economist David Atlee summed it up: "Hopefully, Diem's example will serve as a reminder that the importance of regulatory negotiations should not be underestimated."

Libra/Diem's Lessons: It's a prime example of the Hoodies' growing pains. They'd developed technology that could revolutionize finance but concerns about regulations and security slowed it down considerably. Yet it's these regulations that will smooth out volatility and create safety.

Dogecoin: A Billionaire's Hubris Draws Hot Water

By the summer of 2023, Elon Musk was in trouble over Dogecoin. He was accused of insider trading in a class action lawsuit by investors, who claim the Tesla CEO and owner of X, the social media site formerly known as Twitter, had manipulated DOGE prices. It was alleged that he did so through social media posts and his 2021 *Saturday Night Live* appearance, in which he said the cryptocurrency, which he asserted was "as real" as a dollar bill, would "take over the world."

After he changed Twitter's app logo from its blue bird to Dogecoin's Shiba Inu dog, prices for Dogecoin spiked about 30 percent in a single day.[47] He's been accused of driving up Dogecoin's price more than 36,000 percent which then, no surprise, crashed.[48] Had he done that with a stock price, he'd be in hot water with the SEC.

Dogecoin's Lesson: Social media can move markets. The lawsuit, which Musk called a "fanciful work of fiction," could spur interest in more regulation and compliance, imposing stricter standards that Hoodies may find constricting, but Suits may find appealing.

Hacking Shouldn't Be the Headline (Yet It Is)

The headlines of the past decade about crypto network hacking[49] miss an important point: The hacks have never occurred within a blockchain. Rather, they've been on centralized exchanges, on bridges between blockchains, or because of smart contracts with security holes or owners not protecting their keys. Yet we continue to see headlines such as "The Largest Cryptocurrency Hacks So Far" and the biggest "Crypto Heists."

Seven in 10 of the top hacks have occurred on blockchain bridges, reports *Forbes*,[50] where transactions are temporarily held by a centralized body between blockchains, tempting hackers. That has to do with the "interoperability problem," because separate blockchains can't

Trusted bridges: Also called custodial bridges, they require users to temporarily forfeit their digital assets to a third party, a custodian.

Trustless bridges: Instead of centralized third parties, smart contracts are used to fulfill transfer requests. Considered experimental, the algorithms have been targets of hackers.

communicate with each other. So users put them on bridges, which are essentially an escrow system bridging between blockchains that aren't as secure as the blockchains themselves.

One of the most notorious crypto hacks happened on the Japanese bitcoin exchange, Mt. Gox. It started in 2011 and lasted for a few years before it was discovered. At the time, Mt. Gox reportedly handled 7 in 10 bitcoin transactions worldwide. Some 740,000 bitcoins worth €460 million at the time were stolen in what headlines called "Bitcoin's Biggest Heist."

It's believed that the hacker accessed the Mt. Gox system through a compromised computer that belonged to an auditor of the company and altered the value of bitcoin (BTC) to one cent, transferring and selling 2,000 BTC. It went undetected because the Mt. Gox system recorded the thefts as transfers. Most Mt. Gox victims never had their crypto returned, and the network filed for bankruptcy in 2014. Two Russian nationals were later indicted by the US federal government for conspiracy to commit money laundering in the attack.

This happened because, in the early days of crypto, some developers failed to add testing and security protocols that could prevent such an attack, allowing sensitive information, including key pairs for data encryption and decryption, to be exploited. The attack didn't occur on the blockchain, but on the exchange. While the blockchain is resistant to hacking, the exchange is not, and once the hackers got a hold of individual keys, which are long passwords to their digital wallets, they managed to get access to their currencies, too, over a period of three years.

Also in 2014, the biggest hack in DeFi history to date drained some $600 million from the Poly Network when a hacker or hackers using the pseudonym "Mr. White Hat" stole thousands of digital tokens by exploiting a vulnerability in the network. They later returned most of the stolen funds after the platform offered a half-million-dollar bounty and a job as "chief security advisor." CNBC reported that the hacker may have realized it would be too difficult to launder the money considering the transactions are recorded on the blockchain, making DeFi's very transparency the network's savior. Later, someone claiming to be the hacker promised a "happy ending" and apologized: "Sorry for the inconvenience!"

One day after its 2021 launch, Meerkat Finance claimed it was hacked on the Binance Smart Chain, losing more than $30 million worth of BUSD and BNB tokens. But some crypto experts suspected it was actually an "exit scam" perpetuated by the Meerkat team itself, though Binance could not prove it.

But few crypto companies are performing full audits, for code or reserves, even though code audits are required for cybersecurity for all projects. Even proof-of-reserves reports for stablecoins are limited in assurances because they're limited to a snapshot in time, a single day within a year. One accounting professor described to the *Wall Street Journal*, "The verifications are useless unless auditors constantly provide them due to the high trading volatility of crypto values."[51] Bring on the Suits.

Wormhole's Security Flaw Highlights Problems with Bridges

But it was 2022's Wormhole hack, the second largest crypto theft from a DeFi protocol to date, that exemplifies the security problem with bridges. The hack centered on a cross-chain bridge, Wormhole, which lets users move cryptocurrencies between the Solana blockchain and others, including Ethereum. The total take was nearly $325 million. The hacker found an in through a bug in the smart contract code that allowed them to mint "wrapped Ethereum" (wETH), which is ETH wrapped in a smart contract that allows it to function as an ERC20 standard, making it compatible to dApps and other chains. All that newly minted wETH was not actually backed by ETH, but created by a hack in the code, which could have led to a crash of the entire system.

After attempts to negotiate with the hacker failed, Wormhole's parent company, Jump Trading, replaced the stolen crypto, thwarting a DeFi "bank run." Chainalysis called for rigorous code audits to avoid future hacks, saying, "If users can bridge funds across chains, it means each chain's assets are only as secure as the other chains they connect to."[52]

Wormhole's Lessons: Interoperability between blockchains needs to be developed more securely, and regular security code audits should be required to find and fix bugs.

Of the largest crypto hacks, with more than $20 billion of cryptocurrency stolen in 2022, the most lucrative occurred on bridges or other transfer locations.

Ronin Network – $625 million: The hacker forged fake withdrawals using private keys on the bridge between transactions.

(*Continued*)

Poly Network – $611 million: Hackers exploited a vulnerability in the smart contract, allowing them to override the instructions for swapping tokens among the three blockchains it bridges: Binance, Ethereum, and Polygon.

Binance – $570 million: Hackers created extra Binance Coins (BNB) by exploiting a cross-chain bridge through a bug in a smart contract. Transactions were paused after hackers got away with some 2 million BNB tokens.

Three Arrows Capital: Setting off a Contagion

The crypto crash of 2022, which *New York Magazine* called "a classic dash for the exits,"[53] signaled the end of an era. Investors were able to make huge profits with limited regulation, but without full regulation, the bottom fell out of the startup sector in an old-school financial panic.

Three Arrows Capital is believed by some crypto investors to be at the center of this failure. Run by two Andover graduates, Su Zhu and Kyle Davies, the Singapore-based Three Arrows purportedly had no outside investors, and yet many crypto lenders had deposited funds in exchange for interest. As the *Intelligencer* reported, "Three Arrows continued to be a giant funnel for borrowed capital" during a crypto lending boom.[54] At its peak, the fund oversaw more than $4 billion.[55]

The duo used leverage trading on crypto exchanges under the premise of the "supercycle," a theory created by Zhu in which an extended bull run would see bitcoin hitting $2.5 million per BTC. He later admitted that his thesis was "regrettably wrong."

When the crypto market crashed in 2022, Three Arrows Capital failed to meet its margin calls and was forced to liquidate some $10 billion in assets, triggering a domino effect that took down other crypto companies and investors. Among the losers, Blockchain.com lost some $270 million in loans, and Voyager Digital filed for Chapter 11 bankruptcy when Three Arrows couldn't pay back its $670 million in loans. Three Arrows was even involved in the Terra/LUNA stablecoin crash, which its founders claimed was the cause of its demise. According to the *Wall Street Journal,* Three Arrows had invested $200 million in Luna, which was rendered useless in the crash.[56]

Nik Bhatia, professor of finance and business economics at the University of Southern California, told CNBC that the company was "supposed to be the adult in the room."[57]

Those adults, now in their mid-thirties, were reportedly hiding in Bali, taking mushrooms and painting in cafés, the *New York Times* said in 2023. They faced death threats but no arrests and, apparently, felt no remorse.

"Remorse for what?" Davies reportedly asked, even after a creditor likened them to Bernie Madoff.[58] The pair has since started a new company, Open Exchange, promising to donate revenue to Three Arrows' creditors in the name of "good karma."[59]

Three Arrows' Lessons: Bull markets don't last forever, and if it seems too good to be true, it probably is.

What to Learn from Crypto's Initial Blunders

The Suits could have mitigated so many of crypto's early mistakes. Going forward, there are opportunities to be positioned at the forefront of an evolving industry that will change finance. To do that, Hoodies and Suits need to work together, and several factors must be addressed:

Appropriate Governance: Suits at the table would ensure that controls, risk, compliance, and regulatory considerations are enacted and followed.

Cybersecurity and Audits: With the most egregious hacks occurring on bridges and exchanges, an investment in cybersecurity and code audits for all crypto and DeFi platforms could mitigate future damage. This includes enhancing security on digital wallets, shoring up smart contracts, and using data providers to verify and cross-check market information.

Adding risk management: Employing checks and balances and risk management protocols would help reduce volatility and increase safety for investors. In fact, Duke University finance professor and co-author of *DeFi and the Future of Finance* Campbell Harvey told Coin Telegraph that there is a safe middle ground between undercollateralized crypto lending and overcollateralized traditional loans, if risk management practices were put in place.[60]

Smart regulation: One thing that the Suits can get behind is smart regulation of the digital asset industry, opening the door for institutional digital assets. After all, finance, money, and investments are among the most regulated industries with a focus on protecting investors' pockets. The next few years will likely see more congressional bills designed to regulate the industry out of its Wild West mentality and into the 21st century. That said, innovation is difficult to regulate as technological advances will continue and are hard to predict.

The *New York Times* reported that 2022's arrests, bankruptcies, and losses in crypto made room for the underlying technology to shine. "It was like a four-keg frat party that the cops busted. Those still standing are proud to say that they weren't distracted by the revelry," business reporter David Segal wrote.[61]

It's time for the Suits to run the party.

5

Institutional Digital Assets: Securities, Only Better

"If I had asked the public what they wanted, they would have said a faster horse."

– Henry Ford

In 2018, Figure Technologies co-founders June Ou and former SoFi (NASDAQ: SOFI) CEO Mike Cagney launched Provenance Blockchain, now the second largest open-source, public, and decentralized blockchain for financial services, based on the idea that blockchain would make lending more efficient. Provenance was created for the financial services industry with financial assets in mind, not cryptocurrencies. Its website promotes it as "blockchain for institutions"[1] designed for financial services.

To push adoption, the co-founders created institutional use cases through their company, Figure Technologies, to prove out the benefits. They recognized the value of blockchain for online lending, harnessing the technology for digital home equity lines of credit (HELOCs) and digital mortgages that bring speed, efficiency, and reduced costs to home lending. They have even securitized their loans. Transactions have expanded to include HELOCs, home equity loans, mortgages, personal loans, piggyback loans, student loans, crypto loans, warehoused loans, whole loan sales, and securitized loans. They have transacted almost $30 billion on the Provenance blockchain.

Figure proved out approximately 150 basis points of cost savings for deals. It was so attractive that alternative asset manager Apollo Global Management, among others, entered into an agreement to collaborate on blockchain initiatives.

The institutional buyer base for the loans appreciate the detailed transparent nature of the data on the blockchain loans.

"So if you're looking at a loan, you can see all the data, you can see all the documents, you can see the validation we put in place," Ou explained. "That made [the buyers] very excited because that's normally not what you would see when you buy a pool of loans."[2]

As a few companies have developed programs, most have yet to recognize the full cost savings blockchain affords. Yet the cost-saving formula, initial savings estimate, and use cases proved so attractive that alternative asset manager Apollo Global Management, Hamilton Lane, and others entered into agreements to collaborate on blockchain initiatives.

Figure started with home loans and has since expanded to securitizations, all as natively digital assets. The brilliance and beauty of what Ou and Cagney created was the true use case program built out that can point to the benefits of blockchain. Plus, the product was attractive to institutional buyers. It wasn't a proof of concept but a more efficient lending company. This is only the beginning.

Institutional Digital Assets Matter Now More Than Ever

While cryptocurrencies have use cases, the focus of this book is institutional digital asset securities, tokenized traditional securities in digital form that are represented and recorded on a blockchain. This can include bonds, alternative investments, or private funds that are tokenized and represented on the blockchain. They're not a new asset class, but an upgrade to traditional finance. Digital assets can also be cryptocurrencies, stablecoins, non-fungible tokens (NFTs), central bank digital currency (CBDCs), and tokenized assets. In fact, some institutions are offering their clients access to digital asset departments that focus on research, trading, and investments in bitcoin, ether, and other cryptocurrencies as a new asset class.

Why do institutional digital assets matter in traditional finance? Finance has multiple layers of intermediaries that look at data but in separate silos. Newly available technology has offered a better way to do things with an opportunity to create more efficient securities. The adoption of blockchain technology will drastically change structures, distribution, and efficiencies of securities and investments over the coming years.

In a 2023 NASDAQ article called, "Will the Digital Asset Boom Be Bigger Than the Internet?" Merlin Rothfeld predicted innovative leaps that would change lives: "The present-day innovation that may one day rival the gains and importance of the Dot-Com era is the upgrading of the global financial system with digital assets and cryptocurrencies. At present, there are over 24,000 different crypto projects attempting to capitalize on the prospects of a much more digitally connected and decentralized financial world."[3] We are early in the adoption but laying the foundation to build. In fact, Citi estimates tokenization of $4 to $5 trillion of digital securities by 2030 (see Figure 5.1).

Key Benefits to Institutional Digital Assets

Digital assets require financial benefits for any sort of adoption. These benefits can be hard to quantify until programs like Figure Technologies' blockchain roll out. JPMorgan, ahead of the game in building and using blockchain for their repo business, believed their blockchain-based cost savings by the end of 2024 would be $20 million.[4] Many estimated 35 percent to 65 percent lower deal costs; however, it hasn't been proven out consistently.

But without cost savings or increased revenue, why change? Big picture, institutional digital assets offer an increase in revenues and decreased costs while saving time, eliminating errors, and offering operational efficiencies. The decrease in issuance costs and timing will open the markets to a broader array of transactions including smaller deals.

Tokenization is "securitization done on steroids," Franklin Templeton's CEO Jenny Johnson, a leading innovator in the space, said. Benefits are plentiful. She explains, "One is it allows a payment mechanism. Number two, it allows smart contracts to be programmed into the token.

Note: We assume 6.5% nominal GDP growth rate for all asset classes. We estimate 1% of NFC & Quasi Sovereign Debt, 7.5% of Real Estate funds, 10% of PE/VC, and 2% of Securities Lending & Borrowing to be tokenized by 2030.

Figure 5.1 Tokenization Total Addressable Market in Trillions of Dollars
Source: citi 2023/Citigroup.

And three, because it's a general ledger, it has a source of truth. So, whoever has that token, all rights in that token are granted to that person."

Generally, primary benefits of blockchain technology for digital assets include:

- peer-to-peer transferability
- immutability
- traceability
- near real-time settlement
- transaction transparency
- fractional ownership
- potential for greater liquidity

- lower counterparty risk
- decreased reliance on intermediaries
- automation

Blockchain technology will enable use cases and structures that are not possible given the current legacy system.

Smart Securities: Programmable and Self-Executing

In 1994, computer scientist and cryptographer Nick Szabo introduced the term "smart contract," defined by Crypto.com as "a set of promises, specified in digital form, including protocols within which the parties perform on these promises."[5] Thanks to the Ethereum blockchain, smart securities can be programmed using smart contracts, computer programs that are self-executing when certain conditions are met.

Smart contracts are not controlled by a central administrator, and they can be used to automate business processes including payment, escrows, lending, margin calls, distributions, compliance, and sourcing external data.[6] Smart contracts are also binding and immutable and can transact between Party A and Party B (see Figure 5.2).

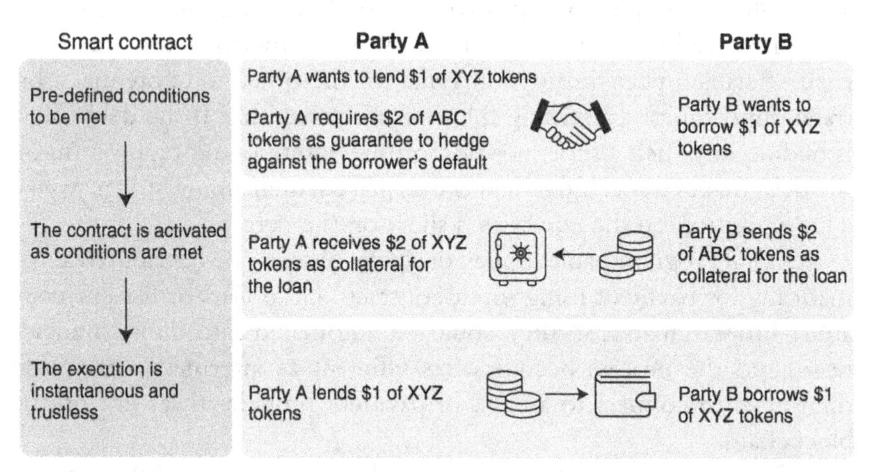

Figure 5.2 The Functioning of a Smart Contract in a Transaction between Two Parties

Source: Moody's Investor Service

Smart contracts are not yet *legally* binding, but the expectation is that, in time, they will be both legally self-executing and self-enforcing. Regulatory authorities are examining smart contracts and similarities to contracts which require an offer, consideration, and acceptance to be valid.

Justin Chapman, Northern Trust's head of digital assets and financial markets, told *American Banker* that blockchain-based smart contracts partly cut out third parties for the enforcement of legal contracts, "boosting productivity by around 20 percent on simple deals and up to 70 percent on more complex ones."[7]

Imagine a bond that automatically distributes interest into the buyer's account, calculates principal and interest accrued, and manages escrow payments. Think of the bond's legal documents and commercial terms mapped out on an Excel spreadsheet that holds many programmable mathematical or conditional equations. Equations can be programmed and, therefore, the commercial terms of the legal document can be programmed onto the security, which would be auditable and executable. The payment data could be included and updated instantaneously, so no one would have to wait 45 days to check the remittance report. Even voting and governance events could be automated.

Imagine a digital representation of a private investment that offers transparency on value, collateral information, distributions, voting rights, and automated compliance features. Imagine a digital mezzanine loan that includes the updated data on the senior loan, the collateral value, and up-to-the-minute payment data. It's tradeable and can be fractionalized. Imagine both the debt and equity of a transaction are tokenized, each offering a peer through on value for the other and potential arbitrage opportunities, assuming they are both tradeable. If the debt token is trading low, then a short position on the equity or a long position on the debt makes sense. If the debt is overpriced, then an investor may take a long position on the equity or a short on the debt.

Digital programmable money or stablecoins can be distributed automatically for payment using smart contracts. US dollars or fiat currency aren't programmable, so they could be automated into digital transactions, and the process becomes less efficient as intermediaries would then need to connect to a bank or payment provider that's not on the blockchain.

These automated securities reduce the requirements of the servicer or transfer agent and decrease the risk for personal error, and as well as labor hours required.

Built-In Security

Digital asset securities offer different types of protection. First is the programmable nature that allows compliance to be included and coded into the securities. For regulatory purposes, buyers of all securities must go through Know Your Customer (KYC)/Anti-Money Laundering (AML) screenings which help prevent financing for terrorism or other illegal activities. KYC is about ensuring that a customer or buyer's identity is verified. AML is focused on where the money is coming from and going to, which requires due diligence, policies and procedures, and risk assessments.

Once a buyer has been reviewed and cleared for KYC/AML and approved access to buy a digital security, they are whitelisted. The digital asset security can be sold or transferred only to a party on the whitelist, allowing built-in compliance features for these securities. Similarly, restrictions could be put in place. If the United States introduces sanctions against a certain country and limits their investors, digital securities allow for a more efficient management, which could prohibit trading to anyone within that country.

Blockchain records ownership, so if a security is lost or stolen, that digital asset can be burned or retired, and a new digital asset security can be minted or created. On the whitelist, trades can only happen with approved wallets. Therefore, for digital asset securities, theft is not a significant concern.

Despite the public nature of blockchain, privacy can be protected. Institutions are using permissioned or private chains to limit access. The development of zero knowledge proofs will increase privacy features and allow for further innovation.

Digital assets are also immutable, which means that information cannot be altered. When new information is added to the digital asset, the previous information will still be there. The chain builds onto itself and cannot be reverse-engineered.

The security risk in all technology is cyberattacks, which have targeted some smart contracts, typically because of poor coding or logical flaws. Smart contracts should be audited and tested.

Faster, Less Expensive Settlements

Today, settling a trade can take one day or one week. The traditional process includes trade, clearing, and then settlement. Any settlement delays tend to involve processing, which also allows for collateral transfer, gathering funds, and payment transfer.

For blockchain payment transactions, the payment's instantaneous nature, where once the deal is matched it is settled, depends on the speed of the blockchain, as some may take seconds and others, minutes. The benefits of real-time settlement in trades include potential increased liquidity in the marketplace, decreased counterparty risk, and reduced trading costs.

Not only is the increase in timing beneficial, but the decrease in costs is, too. In June 2023, Bank of America reported, "We also note that settlement costs are rising ~14 percent each year and 5 to 10 percent of trades fail each day, driven largely by human error and the seven non-interoperable systems for which the average trade is routed, indicating the significant implications that a distributed (shared) ledger enabling real-time, or customizable, settlement provides."

The automated nature of blockchain and digital assets will decrease human error, settlement times, and settlement costs.

The challenges of real-time settlement include possibility for error and the inability to recall a trade. That would prevent traders from trading on a secured basis, because they would have to use securities as collateral at the time of the trade.

Lower Counterparty Risk

Counterparties in financial transactions include banks, transfer agents, clearinghouses, broker dealers, custodians, exchanges, the buyer, and the seller. Counterparty risk is associated with the risk of one party failing to fulfill its duty in a transaction.

In 2008, counterparty risk was highlighted after 25 banks, including giants Lehman Brothers and Bear Stearns, failed.[8] These banks were counterparties to multitudes of transactions, and Lehman's bankruptcy triggered a wave of defaults and margin calls on derivatives contracts. The Bear Stearns collapse left other counterparties with losses as well.

Some counterparties can also be fraudulent. By 2022, overall fraud had reached $8.8 billion in losses, with investment scams the most common type, costing investors upwards of $3.8 billion – double the amount in 2021.[9]

Automated transactions using smart contracts cut out the need for trusting counterparties, because execution is based on predefined terms, reducing the risk of default or fraud. Many digital transactions are peer-to-peer, eliminating counterparties or middlemen.

Quicker settlement lowers counterparty risk. Decreasing settlement times from T+2 or two days to T+0, or real-time settlement, decreases the time the trade could fail or one party could fail to fulfill the trade agreement. In transparency, the digital asset and crypto ecosystem have had their share of bad actors. There have been fraudulent counterparties, and the financial press headlines have made that clear (see Chapter 4).

Tokenization: the process of converting asset ownership rights into shares that are digitally represented on the blockchain. It will help make financial markets more efficient with transparency, data, and trading, opening up potential liquidity, allowing easier transfer of digital ownership tokens, offering a secondary marketplace of buyers, and including access to value information. Tokenized digital assets are securities or commodities and can be fractionalized and traded on exchanges or ATSs.

As James Angel, associate professor at Georgetown University, told CNBC, "A traditional stock certificate is nothing more than a token that represents ownership of the keys of a company."

Potential Liquidity and Transferability

Digital assets could help create greater liquidity in non-liquid markets, those without multiple parties making trades daily. To make a market liquid, there must be willing buyers, sellers, and a market price, where selling the asset does not materially affect the price. For example, the stock market is a liquid market, and Alphabet Stock (NASDAQ: GOOGL) is a liquid stock. It is possible that some very large trades could change the market price even in public markets; however, liquid markets transactions generally don't move the price.

Illiquid assets are harder to sell, with fewer potential buyers and softer pricing. Plus, they're not quickly converted to cash or cash equivalents. Examples include real-world assets (RWAs) such as private company equity, real estate assets, art works, and debt instruments, and they can be tokenized and represented by a digital asset. These assets are more unique in nature than a fungible share of company stock and can be smaller in size.

Many exchanges and ATSs provide digital assets with a marketplace for bringing together buyers and sellers who can transact digitally and instantaneously, offering a secondary marketplace for what were traditionally illiquid investments. The digital nature makes the transaction's transfer frictionless. Due diligence can still be performed but the transfer does not require the lengthy legal work that most of these investments required for a trade.

Generally, illiquid assets require extensive due diligence to transact. That's because a lack of available information makes them opaque, and difficulties in finding buyers and their high fixed transaction costs cause inefficiencies. Digital assets have the potential to hold information which can aid sharing data for value and credit calculations. Everyone can have access to the same information.

In private securities, there is a lack of trust, with one party assuming the seller has more information than the buyer. This leads to a premium on top of the bid-ask spread as a discount is applied to the price. Digital assets can include real-time data and asset information to assess the value, execute the transaction, and transfer ownership when conditions are met so it is trustless and counterparty risk is taken out of the equation. This in turn can decrease the additional risk premium spread.

Demand for the world of private and alternative assets is growing. Retail investors are looking to increase exposure to the asset class typically open only to institutions. The next generations are looking for alternatives and digital investment opportunities outside of the stock market. Tokenization will help open these markets, as most of the assets in demand are currently deemed illiquid. As liquidity grows, markets become more efficient, spreads decrease, and confidence grows.

Standards in Digital Assets

As the digital asset ecosystem grows, institutional proof of concepts will become pilot programs, which will become actual programs. These programs will create the standards for the industry, which will define rules and structures that help compatibility, interoperability, and ease of transactions. They also help with the ease of data exchange, security, and performance when the data is accessible in a machine-readable format.

In 2023, there were more than 1,000 blockchains.[10] That is a lot of noise. For the industry to transact and embrace the technology, there must be consistency in digital asset securities and a set of recognized standards.

Use Cases

Digital assets will provide more efficient and effective banking, capital markets, and payments, aiding corporate finance, public finance, and personal finance. Digital assets can provide access to new market participants, including the option to trade out of an investment, as opposed to holding it to maturity.

Diving into use cases, we examine tokenization, collateral and treasury management, CBDCs, insurance, and intellectual property.

Tokenization

Experts estimate that the tokenized assets market will reach $16 trillion of global illiquid assets by 2030.[11] Institutions are taking note. *Forbes* summed it up in "Asset Tokenization: A Trillion Dollar Market Opportunity: JPMorgan, BlackRock, and Goldman Sachs Think So."[12] Various financial instruments can be tokenized, including RWAs, funds, and debt. The process benefits owners, investors, and service providers through capital efficiency, democratization, and cost savings.

McKinsey broke down some benefits of tokenization (see Figure 5.3).

Cost efficiency is the real winner, but increases in potential revenue should not be overlooked, as digital assets will deliver both benefits.

Tokenizing Real-World Assets: Many institutions are looking into creating tokenized RWAs, which exist off-chain but are tokenized with asset and ownership rights moved on-chain. The first institutional tokenized RWA was the Aspen St. Regis Hotel, which launched as the Aspen Coin in 2018. The owners, Elevated Returns, sold 18.9 percent of the asset ownership through an $18 million Reg D fundraise to accredited investors.[13] The Aspen Coin or digital asset token represents an ownership interest in the Aspen, Colorado, hotel, offering utility benefits, including room upgrades and a tier-based program with cash back on hotel stays. Secondary trading, which began in 2020, has reportedly

Potential benefits from tokenization, by stakeholder type, nonexhaustive

	Asset owners		Service providers		Investors	
	Revenue opportunity	Cost efficiency	Revenue opportunity	Cost efficiency	Revenue opportunity	Cost efficiency
Improved capital efficiency Lower cost of capital and free up capital in transit					✓	✓
Democratization of access Access to new secondary markets; greater liquidity					✓	
Access to new pools of capital with lower minimum investment required	✓					
Operational cost savings Opportunities to embed manual and error-prone product-structuring and asset-servicing tasks into the token smart contract and eventually across a portfolio		✓		✓		✓
Enhanced compliance, auditability, and transparency Embedding of rules and credentials into the token smart contract (eg, investor qualification, carbon credit verification)		✓		✓		✓
Cheaper and more nimble infrastructure Open-source technology driven by thousands of Web3 developers and billions of investment dollars		✓		✓		✓

McKinsey & Company

Figure 5.3 Potential Benefits from Tokenization
Source: McKinsey & Company

done well. However, no similar RWA institutional grade digital asset project has been launched since.

Another use case of RWA tokenization is Pablo Picasso's 1964 work, *Fillette au Béret.* Its ownership rights were tokenized into four thousand tokens in a fundraise of over $4 million USD.

"We really tokenized the painting itself, and we issued securities that represent direct ownership in the painting," Thomas Eichenberger, head

Source: Elevated Returns

Source: Picasso Foundation

of business units at Sygnum, the world's first regulated digital asset bank, based in Switzerland and Singapore, told *Forbes*. "So, we basically completely eliminated that layer of the Special Purpose Vehicle, which makes it much more powerful. Not only in terms of reducing costs – because you don't need to pay for an SPV – but also in terms of emotional connection. [When you invest] you really own a piece of the painting. You don't own some part of a shell."[14] Trading on Sygnum's platform provides trading opportunities, and their value is expected to appreciate with the value of the art.

Much institutional focus is on RWAs for businesses looking to capture new business lines, expand current business, or not be left behind. Almost any traditional asset investment can be tokenized.

Outside of blockchain benefits already mentioned, there will be additional advantages. Binance's 2023 report on Real World Assets says, "The main driving force behind bringing real world assets onto the blockchain is the belief that, in the long-term, DeFi will offer unique opportunities and market efficiencies to asset holders, which cannot be found in traditional financial systems."

Tokenizing Real Estate: Real estate is often the first thought in tokenized real-world assets because it's illiquid and requires a large minimum investment. Tokenizing real estate can add transparency by providing information on the property and collateral. It can add accessibility by allowing for lower minimum investment, opening the opportunity to a wider base of investors. It also adds potential liquidity because digital assets can be traded on an ATS to a possible broad base of buyers.

Residential real estate could be represented by an NFT and not fractionalized. Or, a single-family house could be tokenized and owned by multiple parties, which opens up different structures and future investment opportunities.

Commercial real estate equity can similarly be tokenized. It can bear resemblance to a tenant in common (TIC) structure with voting and control rights described in the deal contracts. The general partner and limited partner investments could be tokenized. It would open up the opportunity to trade out of potential investments and could include stipulations of buyer's approval. The investment could be similar in legal structure as it is today but offer optionality and opportunity.

Investing in a real estate investment trust (REIT) allows exposure to real estate but generally to a specific sector. What if an investor doesn't want exposure to national retail or office properties but instead, actually wants exposure to the city of Denver? Or Miami? Or Austin? Investors would be able to invest in multiple tokenized investments in a geographic region. There are many new opportunities digital assets could allow for diversification and portfolio optimization.

How does this differentiate from crowdfunding? Some tokenization projects will be crowdfunding in nature and others will be institutional. The Jumpstart Our Business Start-ups (JOBS) Act, signed into law in 2012, opened up investment opportunities to non-accredited investors by allowing small business funding without SEC registration referred to as crowdfunding. Raising small amounts of money for projects or ventures from many people, typically online, became popular. Designed to protect less savvy investors, the SEC typically limits investments to accredited investors, defined by income or net worth. But crowdfunding, estimated to reach $1.14 billion in 2023, opened investing to a larger pool of people, without requiring accreditation status and allowing for smaller investments on an average deal size of about $28,000.

Most crowdfunding platforms, which typically have non-institutional level sponsors, have yet to prove to be successful, and the process has a negative connotation for some because it hasn't been the success story that many had hoped for. Yet, crowdfunding could use tokenization for operational efficiencies, and potentially generating additional revenue, and decreasing costs for traditional structures.

Tokenizing Funds: Blockchain adoption will change fund efficiencies, distribution methods, and investor types over the coming years. A tokenized fund issues digital tokens or shares on a blockchain that represents direct interests in the fund. The tokenized interests can be traded and recorded on the blockchain.

The advantage of tokenization for funds is faster settlement, lower cost, built-in compliance, larger potential investor base, and increased liquidity. Funds are looking for ways to decrease expenses and increase assets under management (AUM), and tokenization can help with both.

There are many counterparties in funds including fund administrator, transfer agent, distributor, and servicers. With the added efficiency of blockchain, will they be required for transactions? Many of the services can be provided by blockchain technology.

Many funds have a cumbersome subscription process that can be automated and streamlined without adding additional risk. Smart contracts can build in compliance issues which are more efficient. Automation leads to fewer manual errors, a single source of truth equating to fewer reconciliations required, and speed. The automation enables an easier process that could open up the funds to a greater number of investors at potentially a lower minimum investment.

Tokenizing Private Equity Funds: Apollo, Franklin Templeton, Hamilton Lane, and KKR have already tokenized private funds. Apollo is aiming to raise $50 billion from retail investors by 2026,[15] and KKR announced that they expect private wealth to account for 30 to 50 percent of their fundraising in the next few years.[16] In a search for growing AUM within private equity, giants like Blackstone are looking to expand their investor base in the retail segment. Their goal is to reach $250 billion from the eligible retail investor segment by 2027.

The strategy makes sense, because retail investors hold 51 percent of the wealth and, thus far, only 49 percent of corporate wealth that has been the investing target[17] (see Chapter 3). Bain estimates that the number of investors in alternatives will increase 130 percent, which includes an expectation of retail investors to more than triple their investments (see Figure 5.4).

For a long time, business schools touted a balanced portfolio, investing 60 percent in stocks and 40 percent in bonds to reduce volatility. Anyone close to retirement would take on less risk with investments more weighted toward fixed income, while younger investors would have more stock-heavy portfolios.

But that's changing. BlackRock's 2023 survey of family offices revealed a different asset allocation model. The ultra-high net worth are

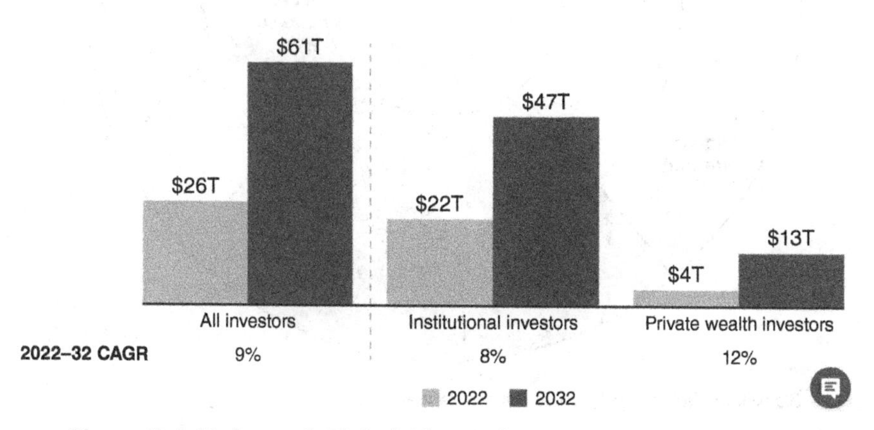

Figure 5.4 Estimated Global Alternatives AUM by Investor Type
Source: Used with permission from Bain & Company

invested 60 percent in traditional asset classes and 40 percent in alternative asset classes (see Figure 5.5).

What do the family offices who have amassed billions of dollars know that old school business professors don't? Or, has the investment appetite and world changed to accommodate the shifting demands of investors?

Similarly, Citi published a report showing the different income levels and investment portfolios (see Figure 5.6). The mass affluent are significantly underweight alternative investments by comparison. Offering retail investors allocations in funds has been difficult due to high minimum investment amounts and the manual subscription process. For investors, there is limited liquidity, if at all, and long investment holds.

In addition, the institutional invested share of global AUM is expected to decrease from 31 percent in 2021 to 26 percent in 2030, whereas the share of retail investors will increase from 52 percent to 61 percent of

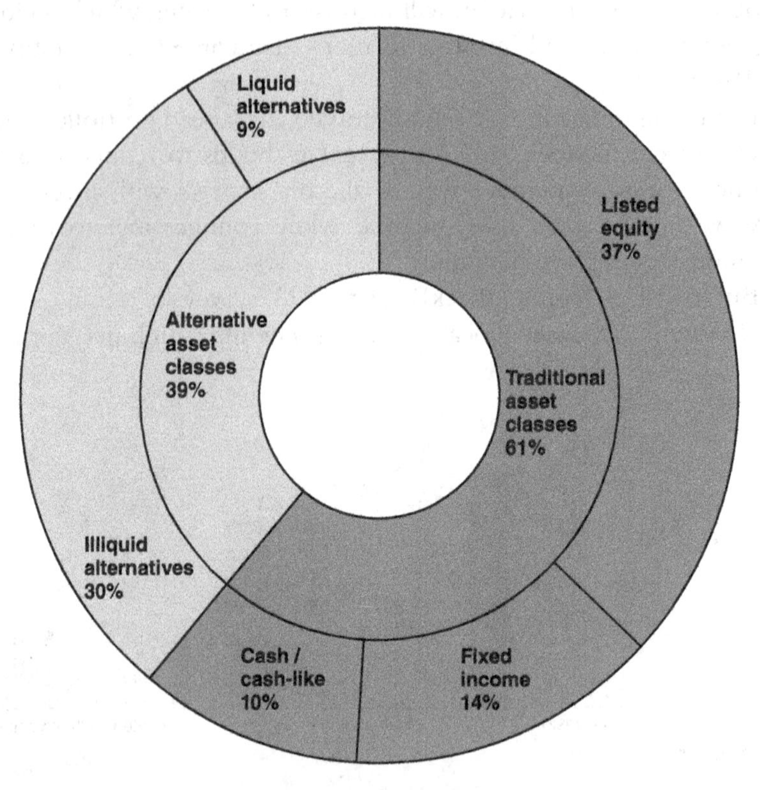

Figure 5.5 Investor Portfolio Allocations across Asset Classes
Source: BlackRock

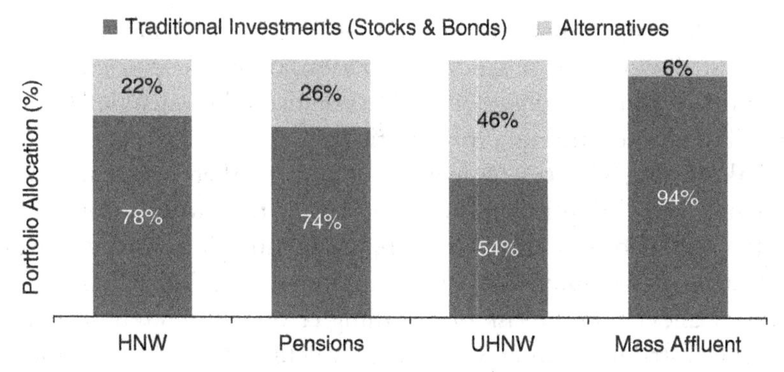

Figure 5.6 Investor Portfolio Allocations
Source: Adapted from citi

global AUM for the same time period.[18] Even more, the fees generated from institutions have decreased significantly. Therefore, to grow AUM, the retail or individual wealth is a very important segment.

Tokenized funds offer retail investors access or optionality to liquidity, which traditional fund formats do not. Digital assets with automated workflows also make the process of increased numbers of investors more streamlined while maintaining the required compliance. As institutional digital asset adoption increases, tokenized funds are expected to be normalized.

Tokenizing Mutual and Money Market Funds: The SEC defines a mutual fund as "a company that pools money from many investors and invests the money in securities such as stocks, bonds, and short-term debt"[19] and money market funds as a type of mutual fund that "invests in high quality, short-term debt securities and pays dividends that generally reflect short-term interest rates."

In future iterations of mutual funds, tokenization will add cost reductions, more efficiencies, and expanded distribution. Arca Labs, Franklin Templeton, Ondo Finance, and Wisdom Tree have all tokenized money market funds, which generally have a net asset value of $1 USD. Outside of the general benefit from investing in stable liquid products, these investments can be used in ways similar to a stablecoin, but with yield generated and KYC/AML built in.

Tokenizing ETFs: First launched in 1993, an exchange traded fund (ETF) is similar to a mutual fund as a pooled money investing in a basket of stocks, bonds, or financial instruments, but ETFs can be traded during the day on exchanges. The ETF's claim to fame is its low cost basis and diverse nature of the investment. Tokenizing ETFs brings more efficiency, allowing for broader distribution, transparency of assets, and performance and cost reductions. ETFs could also be expanded to previously illiquid assets through tokenization.

Tokenizing Debt: The loan and bonds markets are prime targets for digital asset adoption gained efficiencies that would immediately benefit fixed income. Digital assets are programmable, so many processes for debt could be automated and streamlined, offering a single source of record, alleviating the risk of recording errors on different ledgers for the same instrument. Interest could be calculated on days or hours as opposed to monthly.

A standard digital format could save hours, errors, and fees. A digital small business loan program could speed up lending for approximately nine thousand borrowers a year or the 43 million Americans who borrow money for student loans.

"Digitalization could not only generate savings but also expand and diversify debt markets," reports Moody's. "Lower issuance costs and automated processes can enable new actors, such as small and medium-sized enterprises, to issue bonds." Currently, the fixed costs associated with issuances require a higher issuance size to spread out the costs. If costs can be lower, smaller deals can be done more economically.

Moody's graphic details the streamlined process of a digital bond highlighting fewer intermediaries to potentially include only the issuer, custodian, and noteholder (see Figure 5.7).

As firms create digital bond programs, many use the same traditional counterparties in an effort to step up the transition to the digital world. In time, the number of counterparties relied upon in a digital bond transaction is anticipated to shrink.

Tokenizing Bonds: Corporate and municipal bonds could both benefit from tokenization. Most bonds follow a standard structure that can be codified and programmed with smart contracts onto smart securities. Automation and decreasing counterparties could aid in cost reduction. The digital nature could increase trading liquidity and transparency of collateral and data, which could lead to tighter pricing. As the market matures for digital bonds, smaller deals with lower fixed costs will transact. Marketplaces would help smaller companies or municipalities issue debt with lower upfront and placement costs. Payment data and credit data could be updated in real time. Ownership would also be kept in real time with automated transfer reporting.

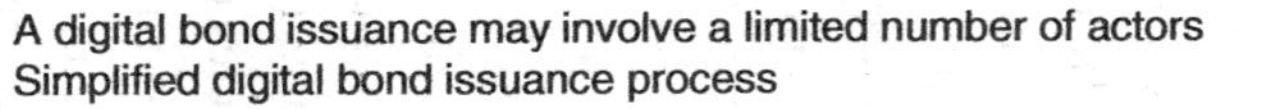

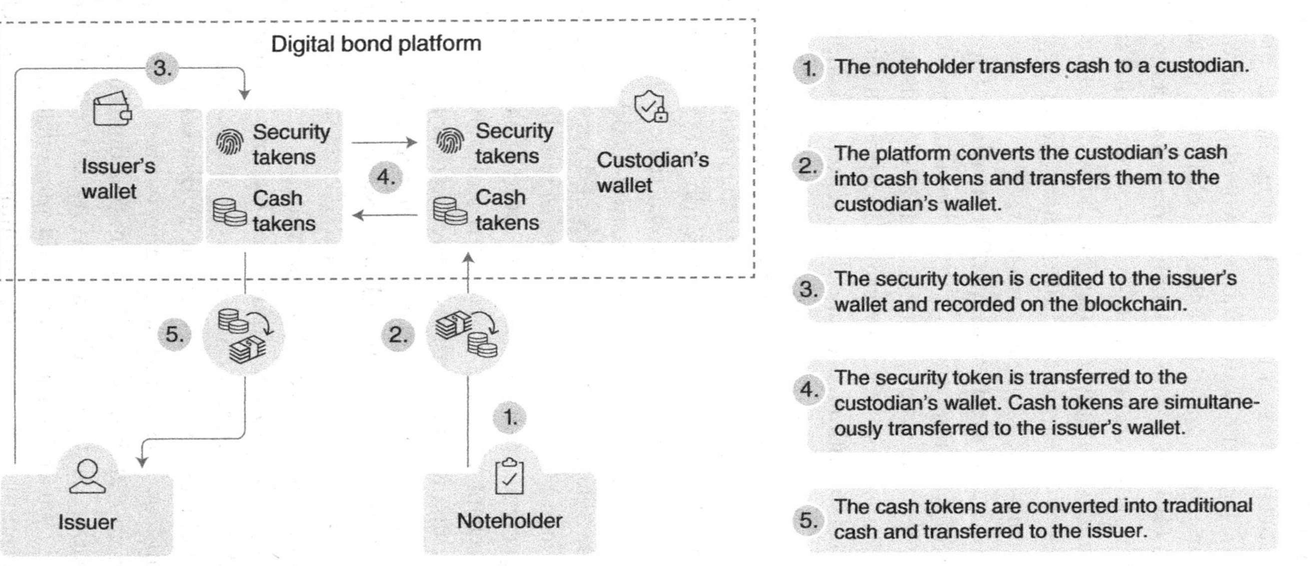

Figure 5.7 Simplified Digital Bond Issuance Process

Source: Moody's Investor Service

Tokenizing Mortgages: Mortgage payments and structure are based mathematical equations that can be programmed or conditionally programmed for payment, distributions, ownership, and transfer data, as well as real-time credit and payment data. Commercial and residential mortgages and HELOCs would benefit from blockchain tokenization. The transparent nature and current data points of digital mortgages can help primary and secondary trading. Similarly, digital assets will offer lower deal costs as the market matures. Figure Technologies is already writing blockchain-based digital mortgages.

Tokenizing Structured Products/Derivatives: The more complicated the product, the more efficiency that digital assets can add for structured products, derivatives, or synthetics, with blockchain streamlining the process, leaving much less room for error. Benefits will include real-time data, automated distributions, account management, multiple calculations of interest, and collateral management. Currently, servicers are required to sort through for errors and ensure payments to proper accounts. Digitization and automation can decrease errors and streamline servicing.

Tokenizing Trade Finance: The World Trade Organization estimates that 80 to 90 percent of international trade is financed by trade finance,[20] the process of financing international and domestic trade or commerce to facilitate the flow of goods and services. Trade finance could benefit from blockchain-based systems which could lower counterparty risk, decrease errors, and increase speed of payments. The industry is heavily reliant on paper documents and transacting in different jurisdictions, which is laden with risks, such as delayed payments, duplicate financings, manual errors, and invoice factoring. Though the system is antiquated, many countries, the United Nations, and large corporations are working to digitize trade finance.[21] Given the complexities and number of borders, it is expected to take time.

Tokenizing Insurance: Insurance requires coordination and cooperation of many different counterparties and making the rails more automated and efficient would be beneficial. Blockchain can help automate claims and payments and share information between reinsurers and companies in real time, saving time, improving transparency, incorporating regulation, and protecting against fraud. Certain policies could be triggered via smart contracts and paid immediately, which in time would lower premiums. Allianz is streamlining cross-border claims with blockchain, which has decreased processing from months to minutes and lowered costs by 10 percent.

Like commercial banks, however, insurance companies have been around a long time and typically have old technology stacks, making the ability to create interoperability a heavy initial lift to upgrade systems. That said, the insurance industry had embraced innovation from the policy side. "The insurance industry has been quick to adapt to the ever-evolving technology of blockchain and digital assets," James Knox, Managing Director, Regional Technology and Blockchain Practice Leader, Aon, said. "Insurers started offering slashing insurance for parties involved in staking. Insurers are also offering insurance for smart contract failures and exposures. As the blockchain and digital asset industry continues to scale, insurers will find ways to address related exposures with insurance remedies."[22]

Tokenizing Intellectual Property: Tokenizing intellectual property (IP) allows investors and innovators to monetize patents to be more easily sold, traded, or commercialized. In 2020, IPwe launched an NFT marketplace for patents which helped make IP a more liquid asset class. According to Brian Berman, a co-founder of IPwe, "Today, global intangibles are valued at $74 trillion. Our goal? Unlock this immense corporate potential with Smart Intangible Asset Management."[23]

Tokenizing Music and Royalties: Music artists can monetize past hits, albums, or catalogs to receive money today by selling royalties and music rights. Using blockchain, artists can tokenize royalty streams, which would allow for a more diverse investor base and the opportunity for fans to invest in their favorite songs, which can be represented by NFTs that pay out shares of revenue and royalties. Royalty streams or songs can be fractionalized through tokenization, with shares earning a portion of the revenues. Artists could tokenize concert tickets as NFTs to prevent scalping, not only financially benefiting artists but also helping them connect with fans or investors.

Tokenization of income streams isn't limited to musical artists. It is applicable in athletic contracts, sports teams, movies, video games, oil and gas, and more.

Tokenizing Commodities: Commodities can be represented as digital assets, and tokenization allows for fractionalization, ease of transfer, lower counterparty risk, and peer-to-peer transfer. Tokenized assets can also be pledged as collateral.

One example is gold, long considered a low-risk hedge against inflation and economic uncertainty. The $1 billion tokenized gold market allows for portfolio diversification, providing exposure to gold without physically holding the bars or the expense of an ETF. Other commodities that have been tokenized include art, diamonds, petroleum, natural gas, silver, and other precious metals.

Even uranium has been tokenized. Sanmiguel Capital Investment based in the Bahamas announced in 2023 the launch of Uranium3o8 ($U), the first token to be backed by uranium. At launch, $U wasn't available to US investors because it wasn't registered with the SEC.

Tokenizing Front Office Benefits: The front office, or the customer-facing division of the firm, can benefit from digital assets, which decrease time per transaction, thereby increasing the possible number of deals. In addition, smaller deals may take less time and money, opening up the industry to more liquidity.

More than just a faster transfer of payment, digital assets can create more streamlined underwriting, automated data, and less room for error or questions about versions of documents or spreadsheets. Blockchain can increase trust by providing more transparency in transactions. Fewer intermediaries should decrease the transaction closing time as well.

Blockchain can help create standardization and potentially decrease legal fees, which are typically the highest deal costs. There is a question about code being law, which will be debated over the coming years. However, with some other technologies, there are ways to decrease paralegal hours spent locating details or citing data. Ideally, lower legal costs and standardization will decrease fixed costs which benefit the market by opening up the ecosystem for more complicated deals.

Tokenizing Back Office Benefits: The back office, or the administrative and operational support for the front office, can greatly benefit from the adoption of digital assets and blockchain-based systems. Instead of holding cash on the balance sheet, a digital representation of cash offers a return. For example, digital money market funds may become more like cash equivalents or treasury ETFs. Some low volatility securities or stablecoins can also provide a treasury-like return. Efficiencies can be gained in:

- collateral management, which is a process to reduce credit risk
- treasury management, optimizing cash flow and short-term liquidity
- securities lending
- account or portfolio balancing
- repo markets with interest paid by the minute or hour as opposed to by the day

- servicing transactions, which are currently paper-based and rely on analysts to input and check data. Payments and processes could be automated, and credit information made available.
- subscriptions, increasing efficiencies, allowing for more subscriptions without increasing headcount.

For example, margin calls could be programmable using digital currencies and smart contracts, especially considering that the global market never closes. The current clearing and settlement process involves many intermediaries and many steps which can add counterparty risk, expense, error, and increased time to settle. Digital assets offer efficiencies and blockchain can offer atomic settlement. Most counterparties to clearing and settlement, including SWIFT and DTCC, are incorporating digital assets into their ecosystems.

Impediments to Tokenization Adoption

There are several issues standing in the way of adopting tokenization in traditional finance:

Cost of innovation: No doubt about it, there is a cost to innovate, but traditional finance institutions can learn from the cryptocurrency industry's 15 years of experience, leveraging what's already been built and what has worked, thereby aiding traditional capital markets. For those brave first movers, there could be trillions of dollars of value to unlock.

Currently, most of the traditional digital asset deals that are brought to market are digital twins, where the deal is recorded on the blockchain but it is also created in the traditional format and all of the traditional counterparties are in play. This is like a hedge to see how the deal can be done as a digital asset but backed by the comfort of old-school execution. Digital twins make transactions more expensive, but many look at it as the cost to innovation with the recognition of what the true benefits are. There are additional legal and tech fees incurred to create the deal in a digital form, making early deals costly as digital asset proof of concept deals. Cost efficiencies will, however, be recognized when a program is rolled out and the benefits can scale.

For some industries, first mover adoption creates a clear winner, but then, look at AOL, Yahoo, and Google – the clear winner, yet not the first mover.

In 2017, Vanguard announced a partnership with enterprise blockchain provider Symbiont for investment data as well as proof of concepts in modeling out an asset-backed securitization and completing a foreign exchange-forward contract. While the exposure and proof of concept deals helped Vanguard experience blockchain-based digital assets, it is not known if they have benefited financially from the early exposure.

Similarly, JPMorgan has spent millions of dollars as an early mover in blockchain technology with their private blockchain Onyx, internally experiencing cost benefits from increased efficiency and speedy transactions. JPMorgan runs multiple programs using Onyx, including repo transactions, so the specific cost benefit is not made public and yet its existence has been shared. They do expect that using tokenized collateral for their intraday repo market will save the bank $20 million a year.[24]

In the world of banking, there is no personal incentive for innovation. There appears to be more downside than upside for individuals. Running a proof of concept project using a new technology with inconclusive monetary return would require employees to wager their bonuses, which is a substantial portion of their compensation, on the success of the project. Similarly, a technology expense for an unknown monetary return is a career risk that a CEO or top executives at public companies, where performance is reviewed on a quarterly basis over earnings calls, is a risk they're probably not interested in taking.

Familiarity in communication and user experience: At times, there is a language barrier between Hoodies and Suits. Some of what the Hoodies have created is not altogether different from traditional rails, but the lingo is different. Familiarity in digital assets will expand in both the communication and the user experience, but it will take time and effort. Here are some terms that Suits need to learn:

wallet: similar to a traditional account but it holds funds of crypto assets, with functionality similar to a traditional bank or investment account

key: not a physical key but similar to a password

gas: the cost of the transaction

hash: similar to a transaction record, it has 64 characters that serve as a record, locating and tracking the transaction

token: a digital unit of value, which could be a commodity or a security

staking: similar to an interest-bearing account, but you are technically lending your deposit

Terms that are the same for both Hoodies and Suits are exchanges, derivatives, fear of missing out (FOMO), futures, hedging, and KYC/AML.

For many blockchain projects, the user experience of blockchain products is pretty rough around the edges. While users are accustomed to a smooth and attractive online experience for checking their bank account balances, some of the blockchain products are more focused on behind-the-scenes functionality than user friendliness. As the industry progresses, traditional finance experiences will be found in DeFi, so users signing into accounts or buying bonds or private assets won't need to know the functionality of blockchain, consensus mechanisms, or validators. Clients will appreciate the more seamless experience they receive when buying and selling and even lending securities.

Interoperability: As they begin to recognize the benefits of blockchain, institutions are working to build their own private blockchains with their own code and standards. Both the buyer and the seller need to be able to use the same blockchain or, minimally, the blockchains must communicate with each other to buy, sell, or transfer digital assets. Interoperability is increasingly important as more and more companies create their own private blockchains.

Think of blockchains as railroad tracks or electrical outlets. In Europe, each country has the same type of railroad tracks; they're even the same as the Chinese rail system. However, in the former Soviet Union, the standard rail tracks are wider. As a result, trains can't seamlessly connect from track to track between the countries without a fix on the train's wheels.[25] Similarly, Americans have to pack adapter plugs for their electrical devices to work in Europe. In digital assets, wrapping a token or using a bridge allows them the functionality to be recognized on different blockchains.

Interoperability will reduce friction, and users will benefit from the different applications or securities or bonds on the different blockchains and blockchain protocols. Though cross-chain bridges have been created to bridge between two different chains, they've been vulnerable to hacking.

Antiquated systems and integration: Digital transformation is harder than it sounds. The systems of many banks and financial institutions are built out on antiquated systems using old programming languages, such as COBOL or Fortran, which were popular in the 1960s. While improvements have been made to the systems, they're generally layered over legacy systems. That's because financial regulation requires record retention so systems have been built on top of and not necessarily upgraded.

There are still old-school, ultra-high-net-worth families that appreciate the old way of doing things, and one large asset manager admitted to accepting written checks for fund investments. But this is time-consuming and requires more man hours than accepting a wire or an instantaneous stablecoin transfer.

Institutions integrating or adding in a new way of doing things could take 12 to 24 months to get through risk and compliance departments. Change takes time.

Multinationals have been pouring billions of dollars into upgrading systems and digital transformation. To fully embrace digital assets and even basic APIs, an application programming interface which allows different computers, systems, and companies to speak to each other, companies' systems need to be compatible with today's technology, which is always evolving. It is tough for large companies to keep up.

Custody issues: Custody, which refers to where the asset is kept, is important to protect investments from theft or loss. Digital assets are stored in wallets, but there's a lack of digital asset custody solutions that deliver on confidence, accessibility, security, and scalability that institutions require.

Digital asset securities can be held at a qualified custodian; however, there are few that are approved as qualified custodians. In recent years, many startups have provided solutions but it's difficult for a one hundred-year-old institution, a fiduciary, to choose a company without substantial history and capital to custody assets. Regulators are currently examining digital asset-qualified custodians and working with the industry for a solution that provides confidence.

Prepare for the Upgrade

Traditional finance is not disappearing. It's being upgraded. There is an in-between stage now, and the change won't be a giant leap, but more of a gradual adoption. Frustrated by finance's slow adoption of digital ledger technologies, *Forbes* declared in late 2023 that tokenization was "failing," and a lack of trust in crypto markets was to blame. But that's a short-sighted take on the inevitable. It is a marathon not a sprint.

What's certain is that we are in an upgrade, and it's important to understand where we've been and where we're going.

6

Incremental Wins in Wall Street's Pre-Season

"The secret of change is to focus all of your energy, not on fighting the old, but building on the new."

– Socrates

In the spring of 2023, three American banks failed. Silvergate Bank, which had catered mostly to cryptocurrency companies, including failed FTX, reported a $1 billion loss for 2022 and shut its doors.[1] The next day a run on the bank began to bring down Silicon Valley Bank (SVB), which catered mostly to tech start-ups with accounts larger than the FDIC-backed minimum of $250,000. Worried that their money wouldn't be available, customers cleared out their accounts to the tune of $42 billion in a single day, and soon, the bank went under.[2] Crypto-friendly Signature Bank soon became the third regional bank to fail that week.

In his annual letter to investors, BlackRock CEO Larry Fink called the collapse "a classic asset-liability mismatch." With more than $200 billion in assets, Silicon Valley Bank ranked sixteenth of all US banks. Signature Bank held $110 billion, placing it within the top 30 banks. The key issues included the bank's investment in US Treasuries and the rise in interest rates. When the banks were forced to sell Treasuries to meet customers' withdrawals, they were forced to sell large quantities at a discount.

If these banks had been open to investing in digital assets backed with short-term investments in a '40 Act SEC-registered US Treasury Fund, would the bank have had greater liquidity and price transparency? Given a deep enough market, perhaps the sales would not have been as discounted, and customers wouldn't have been as shaken. In the next generation of finance, will a run on the bank be a thing of the past?

When it comes to digital assets, Wall Street and traditional finance are in the pre-season warm-up. In fact, BlackRock's Fink saw the value of digital assets, declaring in 2022, "I believe the next generation for markets, the next generation for securities, will be tokenization of securities." Eventually, tokenized digital assets will be traded as commonly as traditional financial products without anyone noticing they were built using blockchain technology. But first, the early innovations, which can be costly and time-consuming, are being developed.

The New Age of Digital Assets

Experts in tokenization sometimes cite how it took email 30 years to reach mainstream adoption, while digital assets will be implemented far faster. Deloitte's 2021 Global Blockchain Survey declared the 2020s a "new age of digital assets," and two-thirds of respondents believed that digital assets would "serve as a strong alternative to or outright replacement" for fiat currencies within a decade.[3] Some say that tokenization has been part of the financial system for centuries anyhow, with stock certificates representing a token of ownership. Digital tokenization takes finance to the next level.

What's new is blockchain technology, which as previously discussed can speed up asset trading to instantaneous settlement from T+2, trade plus two days, while cutting out some of the intermediaries and reducing costs to trade by moving ownership representation onto the blockchain. But traditional finance doesn't move fast. Finance is one of the most heavily regulated industries, and the US Securities and Exchange Commission and other regulators tasked with the job of protecting investors continue on their mission. After fraud and volatility caught their eye, regulators began cracking down on crypto in 2017.

Estimates peg the growth of the digital asset space at $102 billion by 2027 – nearly doubling from 2023 – and some of finance's biggest institutions are already participating by investing in blockchain and developing digital asset projects.[4]

Citibank is even more bullish on tokenized asset trading, estimating that volume will reach $5 trillion by 2030, according to CNBC.[5] Bank of America meanwhile estimates that half of Fortune 100 companies have launched digital assets projects since 2020.[6]

An early mover in institutional distributed ledger technology (DLT), R3 held a record raise in 2017 backed by 40 financial institutions, including Barclays, BNP Paribas, BNY Mellon, Citi, Deutsche Bank, Wells Fargo, Royal Bank of Scotland, Societe Generale, TD Bank, and UBS. R3 co-founder Todd McDonald said they "started the company backwards," asking banks what they needed to bridge the gap between traditional finance and decentralized finance. R3 worked with the banks' input to develop Corda distributed ledger technology to assuage those "originally threatened by blockchain [by providing] a way to capitalize on the benefits of the technology, while maintaining or advancing their market position," reports CoinDesk.[7]

The permissioned chain continues to launch pilot programs with financial institutions to advance DLT institutional adoption.

Institutional Building Blocks

Traditional finance has been laying the institutional building blocks for digital assets. Fidelity Investments Chair and CEO Abby Johnson sees the long-term benefits of investing in digital assets, telling the audience at Consensus 2022, "The industry can really play a bridge role, because we've got this established business . . . we have to connect the two." She added, "Anything that trades on a blockchain versus anything that trades through the legacy world of settlement . . . there's nothing that's the same."[8]

In fact, the *Wall Street Journal* called Fidelity the "mafia behind big crypto," the place where "the most prominent players in the digital assets industry cut their teeth."[9] They even made plans to offer bitcoin in 401(k) accounts.

When blockchain-based funds were introduced in 2022, the *Wall Street Journal* noted that private-equity firms were launching them "despite crypto's collapse."[10] Blockchain-based traditional finance structures are not crypto investments. They are an enhancement of a traditional structure.

Tokenization of real-world assets continues to grow. Binance reported in 2023 that the tokenized US Treasuries market was valued at over $600 million with a yield over 4 percent,[11] and the market size was expected to grow.[12]

Decrypt observed, "Traditional finance moving into crypto at the same time as they increasingly adopt its underlying technology for tokenization may be part of an emerging trend in finance."[13] Institutions are noticing what startups are doing with traditional assets and building technology themselves as institutions are the eight-hundred-pound gorilla. Take the startup Ondo Finance, for example. The Ethereum-based asset manager launched a tokenized fund in early 2023 that allowed both institutional and retail investors outside of the United States to access traditional US Treasuries and bank demand deposits in a digital format for the first time. With a market cap of almost $158 million, the firm had the largest market share of tokenized assets on Ethereum. Imitation is the most sincere form of flattery and, potentially in this instance, profits.[14]

There are many different sectors in finance for which the industry is implementing the benefits of blockchain. Traditional finance has been and will continue to build their digital asset offerings. Let's dive in.

'40 Act Funds

Shortly after the Great Depression ended, Congress enacted the Investment Fund Act of 1940 ('40 Act) to regulate US investment funds with the goal of decreasing conflicts and protecting investors.[15] The act gave the SEC power to regulate US-registered investment companies and trusts, requiring more disclosure. Fund categories include:

- open-ended mutual funds
- closed-end funds or interval funds
- exchange-traded funds
- unit investment trusts

Tokenization of '40 Act funds can add to general efficiencies, cost reduction, improved compliance, increased transparency, automation, and potential liquidity. Tokenized shares represent ownership and can be issued, transferred, and redeemed on the blockchain. Experienced fund managers are diving in.

Franklin Templeton: "You don't make it for seventy-five years if you haven't been able to innovate along the way," Franklin Templeton's CEO Jenny Johnson said. "And so I actually do think it's part of our DNA as a firm."[16] With $1.5 trillion of assets under management and clients in 160 countries, Franklin Templeton has stepped up as a pioneer in the digital asset space. Approved by the SEC, their '40 Act Franklin OnChain US Government Money Fund (FOBXX) is a mutual fund that invests all but 0.5 percent of the fund in US government securities that may be fixed, floating, and variable rate securities. It also involves repurchase agreements that are collateralized by US government securities or cash. The investment in short-term US Treasuries aims to keep the price pegged to $1 USD while maintaining capital and providing a yield. The fund makes Franklin the first institution to offer a US-registered '40 Act fund on a blockchain for both processing transactions and recording share ownership. By October 2023, it had surpassed $300 million in assets. The timing was perfect to provide liquid treasury investment options that sell at market value potentially alleviating the kind of hit that SVB had taken.

Initially launched on the Stellar blockchain and subsequently added to the Polygon network, a layer 2 on the Ethereum blockchain, FOBXX uses blockchain to process transactions, and the fund's transfer agent maintains records on a proprietary system integrated on blockchain.

Both blockchains are public, and while risk and compliance departments may voice concerns about privacy on public chains, they offer greater interoperability and security. FOBXX is designed for compatibility with other blockchains, and investors can purchase shares of the fund online or on Franklin Templeton's proprietary Benji app, which allows users to browse select cryptocurrencies as well. The app supports hot and cold wallets – think of them as accounts – and one share is represented by one BENJI token, which can be viewed as the digital share. The forward-thinking of developing a Benji app appeals to the next generation of investors who want access to their investments on their smartphones.

Franklin has other blockchain initiatives including their Blockchain Fund, a $20 million tokenized blockchain venture fund launched in 2021. Two years later, the firm registered a private equity fund called the Franklin Templeton Blockchain Fund II with the SEC, targeting institutional investors who wish to invest in private equity opportunities with a minimum $100,000 investment. Franklin Templeton highlights the pathway for long-term company visionaries. Franklin Templeton's Head of Digital Assets Roger Bayston wrote in the firm's 2023 report that "digital assets are poised to 'grow up' right before our eyes."

WisdomTree: With a reported $96-plus billion of assets under management, WisdomTree,[17] which self-identifies as a "global financial innovator,"[18] has long been a pioneer in finance, launching their first exchange-traded funds (ETFs) in 2006 and now providing digital asset offerings. Their goal is to be a leader in "the best structures and executions" in financial services, including digital assets.[19]

WisdomTree's first blockchain-based fund, Short-Term Treasury Digital Fund (WTSYX), which tracks the Solactive one- to three-year Treasury index, was approved by the SEC in September 2022. Nine more tokenized funds, all of which invest in traditional assets, received the green light later that year. Though the blockchain does record the transfer of ownership, WisdomTree has also used a transfer agent, and the funds have had custodians and administrators as well. The firm utilizes two public blockchains for issuance: Stellar and Ethereum.

WisdomTree's Head of Digital Assets William Peck told Markets-MediaGroup, "We asked ourselves what will have the impact on ETFs that ETFs had [on] mutual funds. The next forefront of innovation is blockchain and distributed ledger technology."[20] Once again, it's about the technology that the Hoodies created, and the Suits see its value.

One of their innovations is a blockchain-native digital wallet called WisdomTree Prime™. Like Franklin Templeton's BENJI, it allows investors to buy select crypto assets, such as bitcoin and ether, and WisdomTree funds on an institutional app.

abrdn's: As one of the largest asset managers in the UK, abrdn teamed up with Archax, a UK-regulated digital asset exchange, broker, and custodian, to tokenize a sleeve of the GBP 16 billion Aberdeen Standard Liquidity Fund money market fund[21] using the Archax Tokenization Engine to mint its token.[22] They used the Hedera Hashgraph DLT, allowing a minimum $5,000 investment for the tokenized shares.

Russell Barlow, Global Head of Alternatives at abrdn said, "We made the investment into Archax because we see the future for financial markets lies with leveraging new technologies, such as Web 3.0 and DLT." Abrdn's Chief Executive Stephen Bird told Reuters, "Blockchain technologies are inevitably going to form a big part of the future of financial markets."[23]

Ondo Finance and Arca Labs: Startups Ondo and Arca are run by founders who bridge the gap between the Hoodies and Suits. Each has created a digital US Treasury fund that follows KYC/AML requirements and has traditional counterparties.

Founded by a Goldman Sachs associate in his twenties, Ondo Finance set out to make institutional-grade financial products and services available to everyone, in part by offering tokenized US Treasuries through their Ondo Short-Term US Government Bond Fund (OUSG).[24] It's a tokenized version of BlackRock's short-term US government bond ETF that runs on both the Ethereum and the Polygon networks. Partnering with institutions like BlackRock and PIMCO for their fund investments adds credibility to the startup, which also offers the Ondo US Money Market Fund (OMMF) and Ondo High Yield Corporate Bond Fund (OHYG). At the time of this writing, Ondo had plans to offer a yield-generating stablecoin alternative and a lending marketplace. Ondo gives investors outside the US access to US Treasury markets and money market funds.

Arca Labs launched the Arca US Treasury Fund in 2020 as a registered '40 Act fund on the Ethereum blockchain. The fund is invested in short-term US Treasuries and cash or cash equivalents. The digital share of the fund, ArCoin, is tradeable peer-to-peer and via an alternative trading system 24/7/365. The fund retains a $1 USD net asset value, though it pays accrued interest quarterly. Monthly redemptions are also offered.[25] The clever benefit of the '40 Act US Treasury is the option of generating yield in a liquid cash equivalent format. These are not stablecoins, but low volatility securities that pass through KYC/AML.

"Albeit ahead of its time, the Arca US Treasury Fund, which tokenizes a portfolio of US Treasuries under the Investment Company Act of 1940, is one of the financial instruments we will all look back at as groundbreaking and brilliant at the same time," Jerald David, president of Arca Labs, said. "At this point, DeFi is really just replicating traditional finance in a decentralized way. This is a proof of concept with the real innovation yet to come."[26]

The world of tokenized '40 Act funds will only grow given the expected approval for ETFs and the demand for tokenized low volatility securities.

Tokenizing Private Equity

Asset managers are seeing the opportunity to grow AUMs by offering tokenized private equity (PE) funds. As discussed in Chapter 3, the large pension funds, insurance companies, sovereign wealth funds, and endowments have a set portfolio limit for PE and are approached by all the big players to invest. Chapter 7 highlights the changing wealth and cultural dynamic affecting finance. The opportunity is "democratizing access" by tokenization and allowing more retail investors to participate, opening up an opportunity previously reserved for institutions, while allowing asset managers to grow AUM.

KKR & Co. Inc.: In April 2023, global investment giant KKR's new co-CEOs announced plans to double earnings in the next five years as co-founders Henry Kravis and George Roberts step down after 47 years of stewardship. The company has grown through acquisition, but they are looking at multiple avenues for expansion.

Enter tokenization. KKR was the first large asset manager to tokenize a flagship fund. An institutional innovator, KKR tokenized part of its $4 billion Health Care Strategic Growth Fund II (HSCG II) on the Avalanche blockchain.[27] KKR worked in partnership with Securitize, a digital asset securities firm, to tokenize a sleeve of the private equity fund and offer it to investors as an SEC Reg D 506(c) private placement. The offering is available to investors with a minimum net worth of $5 million. Though the typical retail investors can't partake, the minimum $100,000 investment for KKR's tokenized fund is lower than the $25 million minimum that some asset managers require.[28]

Dan Parant, co-head of US private wealth at KKR, explained, "A tokenized fund will allow individuals to invest smaller amounts than would be required of institutions and provide a smoother process for monitoring transactions and vetting investors through Securitize's digitized onboarding process, as well as greater potential for liquidity."[29]

Hamilton Lane: Founded in 1991, alternative investment manager Hamilton Lane, which boasts over $850 billion of assets under management or supervision, has expanded access to funds in both the US and the Southeast Asian markets through tokenization, accessing global boundaries opportunities more seamlessly.[30]

Hamilton Lane's private market report for 2023 highlights private market performance outperforming the public market defining "clear areas" of opportunity. The study also identified that more private investors are choosing private markets more than ever before. Securitize CEO Carlos Domingos highlighted, "Private equity has outperformed the S&P 500 by 70 percent over the past twenty years, but that performance has mostly been enjoyed by major institutions, sovereign wealth funds, and university endowments. Individual investors can begin accessing these opportunities, too."[31]

In laying the groundwork to expand private market access in the United States, Hamilton Lane announced tokenized access to three flagship funds in partnership with Securitize. The first tokenized access fund was the Equity Opportunities Fund V, which closed with commitments of $2.1 billion, including tokenized access through a feeder fund with partner Securitize on the Polygon Network. For the digital asset investors, the minimum investment dropped from $5 million to $20,000.[32]

The second fund offered was Hamilton Lane's Senior Credit Opportunities (SCOPE) Fund, targeted at yield-seeking investors with floating-rate, senior-secured loans. Offered through Securitize and on Polygon, it invests in privately held company assets in sectors such as healthcare and information technology. Its tokenization opens up opportunities for more investors, as the minimum investment is lowered from $2 million to $10,000.[33]

In late 2022, the firm teamed up with Figure to launch '40 Act-registered funds that run on the Provenance Blockchain using Figure's Digital Fund Services platform. Its Private Assets Fund (PAF) is the first-ever '40 Act fund focused on the private markets. Benefits include convenience, cost savings, and access.[34]

The firm also partnered with Asia's digital marketplace Alta in 2023 to allow expanded access to alternative private market assets in Southeast Asia.

Apollo Global Management: In 2022, private equity firm Apollo Global Management partnered with the first federally chartered crypto bank and custodian, Anchorage Digital, to hold digital assets for its clients.[35] Apollo also partnered with Figure Lending, LLC to transfer ownership of digital mortgage loans using the Provenance blockchain, a first for the industry. The transactions were expected to reduce friction, risks, and costs in mortgage lending. What's more, Apollo announced plans to launch a tokenized private equity fund on the Provenance blockchain.[36]

To guide the firm in this new direction, Apollo, which manages about $500 billion in assets, hired former JPMorgan Chase executive Christine Moy to head its digital assets and data programs.[37] These partnerships set the stage for how established financial giants can work with regulated digital asset banks and fintech firms. The process was designed to reduce "transaction friction," making it easier for investors to access private-market funds.[38]

Apex Group: One important aspect to tokenized funds is finding counterparties that will work with digital assets that bridge traditional and crypto. One group that is ahead of the curve is Apex Group within Apex Fund Services. They are focused on the digital ecosystem and invested in Tocan, a differentiated digital onboarding platform that offers a "frictionless subscription and onboarding process."[39] Apex works with native digital funds focused on trading digital assets or representations of real assets on chain. They also provide fund administration for tokenized funds and crypto funds depending on jurisdiction.

"Our view is that we want to deliver a platform for where the industry will be in 3, 5 and 10 years and not just build to meet today's requirements," said Georges Archibald, Global Managing Director at Apex Group, Ltd., adding that "digital infrastructure, blockchain technology, and data has been pivotal in that journey."[40]

Fixed Income

Recognized as an excellent use case for efficiency, fixed income instruments have been targeted for pilot programs around the world. Many of the fixed income issuances to date are digital twins, when a digital replication of the traditional structure and paperwork is created. Most transactions are not yet settled on-chain, but the increase of stablecoins and comfort with regulations will change that. Here are examples of institutional use cases:

The Vanguard Group: The second largest asset manager with more than $7 trillion AUM, Vanguard was an early mover investigating the space.[41] In 2020, they mapped out asset-backed securitization, replicating end-to-end transaction flows on blockchain in collaboration with BNY Mellon, Citi, and State Street.[42] In 2023, Vanguard completed an FX forward trade with partner State Street.

Though Vanguard Chief Investment Officer Greg Davis had called cryptocurrencies a "special asset lacking intrinsic value,"[43] the firm invested in the crypto mining sector in 2023, buying 10 percent of Marathon Digital Holdings and Riot Blockchain. By mid-2023, Vanguard owned more than a half-billion dollars of stock in bitcoin mining.[44]

Redwood Trust: China's state-owned Bank of Communications issued $1.3 billion of residential mortgage-backed securitization (RMBS) in 2018 using blockchain technology that allows all participating parties of the loan to track assets.[45] Soon, blockchain-backed RMBS came to the United States when Redwood Trust, a leading REIT, priced a $449 million securitization using Stellar, a public blockchain.[46] This was a first in the US non-agency RMBS market, and it provided users with more frequent reports on loan level payments, shortening the report cycle from monthly to daily.

Figure Technologies and Saluda Grade: Fintech Figure Technologies has originated over $6 billion of HELOCs for 85,000 borrowers using blockchain technology, which has proven faster and more cost efficient, boasting 150 basis points in savings. In total, Figure has transacted almost $30 billion of multiple loan types on Provenance.[47]

Back in 2020, Figure announced it completed a digitally native loan sale to Saluda Grade in seconds, not the standard weeks. Today, both companies have published DBRS Morningstar-rated digital HELOC securitizations. Figure Technologies came out with the first AAA-rated deal, the $236 million FIGRE 2023-HE1 asset-backed securitization, followed by a Saluda Grade–sponsored rated securitization, including Saluda Grade Alternative Mortgage Trust 2023-FIG3.[48] Including rating agencies credit review adds an additional layer of institutional acceptance and paves the way for other asset classes to follow suit.

The World Bank: In a groundbreaking issuance in 2018, the World Bank launched a $110 million ASD two-year bond issued on an Ethereum-based blockchain called the bond-i.[49] A year later, a second $50 million ASD Kangaroo bond was issued.[50] The bank used the Commonwealth Bank of Australia as well as other institutional partners for both issuances.

In 2023, the World Bank initiated the first issuance of digital securities settled through the Euroclear Digital Securities platform raising 100 million euros for a three-year digital bond for sustainable initiatives.[51] Euroclear is responsible for trillions of dollars of valued securities globally and is compliant within the European Union. Citi acted as the issuing and paying agent, TD Securities acted as the dealer, and Euroclear Bank acted as the central securities depositor. The transaction was issued on R3's Corda DLT platform.[52]

BBVA: An early mover in 2018, the Spanish bank BBVA was the first global bank to issue a corporate loan on blockchain.[53] The €75 million loan used DLT, which decreased the negotiation time from "days to hours." Together with Mitsubishi UFJ Financial Group and BNP Paribas, BBVA piloted a €150 million syndicated loan using blockchain in November of that year.[54]

BBVA continues to use innovative technology in many different countries for different financial instruments. They have issued Spain's first blockchain-registered, regulated bond, spearheaded by the Inter-American Development Bank (IDB), which issued a two-year, $10 million blockchain-based bond.[55] BBVA served as a digital custodian for the blockchain-based project. The tokenized bond was listed on the Spanish stock exchange, BME. Other avenues for exploration include client crypto investing, wallets, and custody.

Societe Generale: In 2019, this French investment bank issued the first digital bond, a deal valued at 100 million euro, on a public blockchain. The French firm also completed the first financial transaction settled with a central bank digital currency (CBDC), and its SG-FORGE division granted a loan to its mother company by borrowing DAI stablecoins from MakerDAO.[56] The bank said, "This experiment opens the way to on-chain refinancing markets serving as an example of how real money asset owners can leverage decentralized finance to create new avenues for borrowing."[57] In 2023, SocGen was licensed to receive and transmit crypto orders by the Autorité des Marches Financiers, France's version of the SEC.[58]

European Investment Bank: One of the more active banks in blockchain innovation is the European Investment Bank (EIB). "The EIB's role as the EU public policy bank goes beyond acting as an ordinary bank. We promote innovative and disruptive solutions," Ricardo Mourinho Felix, EIB Vice-President, said. "This new financial tool will provide additional capital flow that the EIB will invest in projects with global impact."[59]

In 2023, the EIB issued its first sterling-denominated £50 million digital bond out of Luxembourg via HSBC tokenization platform Orion. The Luxembourg legal framework was used for this floating rate instrument.

In late 2022, EIB launched Project Venus through Goldman Sachs, Santander, and Societe Generale with a €100 million bond on GS DAP. Tokenization cut the settlement time from five days to T+0 – settling in less than 60 seconds. Some of the benefits include peer-to-peer transactions and cutting out intermediaries, thereby lowering costs.

In 2021, the EIB launched a €100 million, two-year bond where the issuance of money was completed with CBDC in partnership with Banque de France.

ABN Amro: In 2023, ABN Amro issued a €450,000 bond on the Stellar public blockchain on behalf of an aircraft parts company. The firm's Chief of Strategy and Innovation Edwin van Bommel said, "Thanks to the blockchain, it's highly efficient and very client-friendly."[60]

Repo and Securities Lending

Since the early 1900s, the repurchase agreement, or repo, and securities lending market, now worth more than $4 trillion, has remained the foundation of the financial system. A repo is short-term borrowing collateralized by liquid government securities, such as Treasuries, which are later bought at a premium. Typically, investors buy repos on an overnight basis and sell them back the next day at a slightly higher price. Running repos on distributed ledger technology can reduce costs and risk. They can also price interest in increments less than 24 hours.

JPMorgan: Formed in 2020, JPMorgan's Onyx Digital Asset business launched the world's first bank-led blockchain platform for trading digital assets, focusing on traditional assets such as US Treasuries and money market funds.[61] Through Onyx, borrowing rates can be reduced by more than half compared to traditional credit funding, reports *Forbes*.[62] Plus, the platform offers near instantaneous payment settlement with minimal operational involvement. "For example, a client may want to borrow $1 billion for 3 hours and we can use smart contracts to automate delivery versus payment at the right times using precise terms," Tyrone Lobban, head of Onyx Digital Assets & Blockchain at JPMorgan, commented. "There is no middle or back office processing."[63]

CoinDesk reported that JPMorgan has processed nearly $700 billion in short-term loan transactions through the Onyx blockchain Quorum, a permissioned version of Ethereum. Some of the clients who have used the Onyx repo service include BNP Paribas, DBS Bank, and Goldman Sachs. Lobban told CoinDesk, "We think that tokenization is a killer app for traditional finance."[64]

Broadridge: A global fintech company, Broadridge issued a white paper in 2022 that predicted a crypto evolution phase from 2025 to 2030 marked by digitization of securities, such as equities and bonds. Meanwhile, the firm launched a distributed ledger repo platform that allows the transfer of ownership via smart contracts.[65] Broadridge said they conduct $70 billion of blockchain repo trades per day. The firm asserts that "senior leadership should be embedding a defined crypto and digital asset strategy into their overall corporate strategy. That initiative should start immediately."[66]

Broadridge Financial Solutions launched its own distributed ledger repo (DLR) platform called VMWare Blockchain, providing a market to executives and settling repo transactions. The platform reportedly used distributed ledger technology and smart contracts to enable real-time securities mobility in the repo market. Within two years, it was averaging a trillion dollars a month in volume. Even Swiss bank UBS completed a cross-border intraday repo transaction on Broadridge's DLT platform. It's a process that gave UBS "the ability to dramatically lower risk and operating costs and see enhanced liquidity," Broadridge's head of digital innovation, Horacio Barakat, told The Asset.

Stablecoins

The Federal Reserve published a 2022 paper entitled "Stablecoins: Growth Potential and Impact on Banking" that stated, "Among the various scenarios, a two-tiered banking system can both support stablecoin issuance and maintain traditional forms of credit creation. In contrast, a narrow bank approach for digital currencies can lead to disintermediation of traditional banking but may provide the most stable peg to fiat currencies."[67]

Stablecoins are the backbone to the digital asset ecosystem. They are unofficial programmable money with similar advantages of cryptocurrency but without the volatility. While Chapter 2 covered different types of stablecoins, this chapter identifies institutions that offer stablecoins. But they're not traditional stablecoins, which have yet to be used outside of the individual bank's ecosystem.

JPM Coin: Building the next generation of finance, JPMorgan created a digital representation of depository receipts that could be used as a transfer token of value within the institution. It allows for instant transfer, liquidity funding, and cross border payments, and it reflects value. It is a blockchain-native "cash equivalent." Extended to corporate client payments. The stablecoin allows banks to lend assets while keeping them on their balance sheets. The result is reduced liquidity risk and settlement times as short as hours instead of days.

Citi Token Services: To make client payments more efficient, Citi launched an internal cash management system for clients called Citi Token Services. It can provide cash management services on a 24/7/365 basis, which is important for trade finance.

"Digital asset technologies have the potential to upgrade the regulated financial system by applying new technologies to existing legal instruments and well-established regulatory frameworks," said Shahmir Khaliq, Citi's Global Head of Services. "The development of Citi Token Services is part of our journey to deliver real-time, always-on, next generation transaction banking services to our institutional clients."[68]

In 2018, Citi published a report stating, "Structural issues challenging today's capital markets could be solved by the creation of a new type of registered investment token that embeds smart contracts into a blockchain." They have participated in numerous proofs of concept for tokenization and back office settlement. Citi launched a new digital assets unit with crypto trading capabilities in 2021.

The firm estimates that the market for tokenization will reach $4 trillion to $5 trillion by 2030, with the bulk coming from debt and real estate and the rest in private equity, venture capital, and securities (see Figure 6.1).

Societe Generale-FORGE Stablecoin: In 2023, Societe Generale-FORGE launched the first institutional stablecoin, CoinVertible (EURCV), which is pegged to the euro and runs on a public blockchain.[69] It's designed to bridge the traditional financial system with digital assets. The firm claimed that the institutional-grade stablecoin,

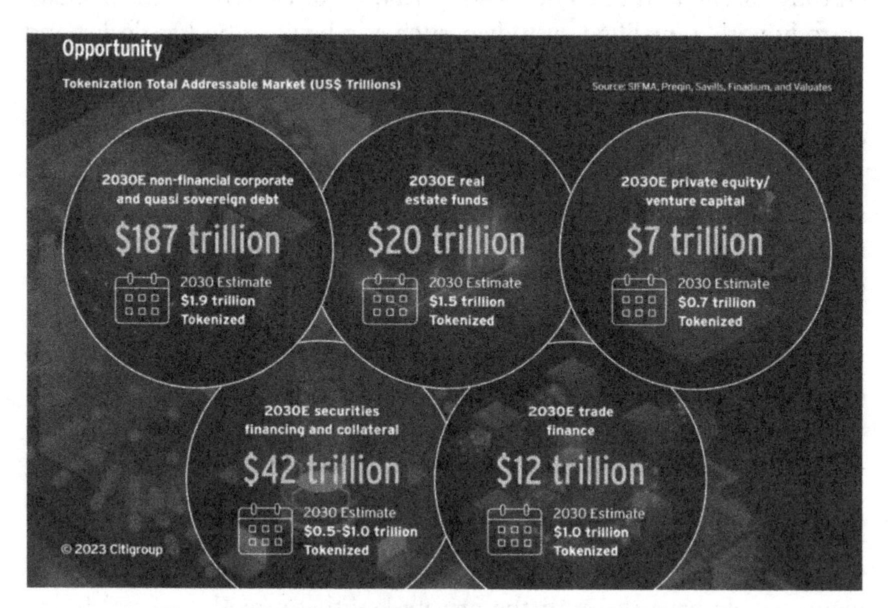

Figure 6.1 Tokenization Total Addressable Market
Source: Citigroup

offered on Ethereum, offers investors the "benefits of digital assets, such as efficiency and security, while reducing the volatility associated with many cryptocurrencies."[70] The firm says CoinVertible provides a secure legal structure, liquidity, transparency, and interoperability. At its launch, it was available only to institutional clients onboarded with KYC/AML processes.

Custody

In 2023, the SEC proposed regulations that would make it more difficult for digital asset firms to be registered as qualified custodians and work alongside registered investment advisors. While a decade-old rule requires SEC-registered investment advisors to use qualified custodians, the regulatory group also published an accounting rule that required all digital assets held in custody to be included on the balance sheet.[71] Many custodial entities feared this would mean they would need to set aside capital to keep digital assets in custody, but the Basel Committee found otherwise.

The Safeguarding Rule would regulate the investment advisors' custody of client assets. The existing rule requires advisors to maintain custody with a qualified custodian, such as a bank or broker dealer, and these advisors are subject to surprise asset audits. But this leaves a question about whether the rule would apply to assets that aren't securities, such as cryptocurrencies.

The new rule would require all client assets be held in custody accounts, thereby targeting not just crypto, but precious metals, art, or real estate, among others. The rule would also require banks to keep their clients' assets separate to protect them from the bank's insolvency, likely causing the costs of custody to rise dramatically. Plus, the rule would regulate contractual terms between advisors and custodians. The result could block investments in certain digital assets in the United States.

It's a reflection of the SEC's focus on the safekeeping of digital assets by advisers. It expands the existing Custody Rule, which applies to "funds and securities" to expand to include "other positions held in the client's account."[72] While traditional assets would be held in exclusive physical possession or control, digital assets present a problem: How many people have access to the private key that provides access? International law firm Perkins Coie noted, "As a practical matter, therefore, it will be important for digital asset qualified custodians to ensure that they are sufficiently involved in private key signing mechanisms to help detect and prevent unauthorized transfers."

Bank of New York Mellon: The world's largest custodial bank launched its own digital asset custody platform in late 2022, citing demand for tokenized investments by more than 90 percent of institutional investors.[73] The bank's 2022 survey found that 41 percent of institutional investors held crypto assets in their portfolio and an additional 15 percent expect to hold digital assets in the next two to five years.[74]

BNY Mellon launched its Digital Asset Custody platform, allowing select clients to hold, transfer, and issue bitcoin and ETH. America's oldest bank, BNY Mellon teamed up with digital asset technology specialists Fireblocks and Chainalysis to develop the platform. The *Wall Street Journal* called it a "broader acceptance of the once-fringe digital currency." Roman Regelman, chief executive of the bank's asset-servicing and digital businesses, told the *WSJ*, "Digital assets are becoming part of the mainstream,"[75] and the bank's 2021 report shared that investors were demanding the infrastructure for digital assets.

But the venture may hit a regulatory roadblock – the SEC's Staff Accounting Bulletin 121 (SAB 121), which requires custodians of digital assets to record them on their balance sheets.[76] It would mean holding capital against digital assets, an expensive proposition, hurting the business case. Still, the bank continued to expand digital asset services, including custody and clearing, implementing blockchain, and tokenization.

Fidelity: Fidelity's Digital Assets division has begun offering custodial services, including transferring, buying, or lending digital assets and holding them on their digital platform, promising to focus on "how – not if – digital assets will become part of the financial industry's future."[77] Fidelity was also granted a UK license for digital asset custody and trade.[78]

The company announced institutional crypto capabilities beginning in 2022,[79] allowing investors to buy, sell, and transfer bitcoin and ETH. Fidelity announced a first-of-its-kind investment account, the Digital Assets Account, which allows employees to invest in digital assets within their 401(k) accounts. The benefits include account diversification, secure custody, and dollar cost averaging in a tax deferred account that helps manage risks. Fidelity had long been a proponent of crypto, calling bitcoin a "superior form of money"[80] that the firm considered a good entry point for traditional investors to get into digital assets. In a paper called, "Bitcoin First,"[81] Fidelity cited six attributes of bitcoin that showed it outperformed gold and fiat currencies: durability, divisibility, fungibility, portability, verifiability, and scarcity. Its only weakness, said Fidelity, was its short track record.

State Street: State Street's digital asset services provide tools including custody, administration, tokenization, and payment for DLT, crypto, CBDCs, blockchain, and tokenization.[82] At the 2021 launch, most of State Street Digital's asset programs involved tokenization and not crypto trading. The bank views tokenization as providing the ability to create new asset classes that will become mainstream, explaining, "The reason blockchain is so attractive is at its heart, blockchain verifies and confirms ownership as well as value in a way that is both immutable and seamless." State Street Digital is also working to provide digital asset custody and fund administration. They have partnered with many industry players on different pilots, including Paxos and Credit Suisse for same-day settlement.

State Street has been vocal about the SEC's guidance notes on digital asset custody services. In 2022, the head of State Street Digital said, "So, for every dollar of crypto we custody, we've got to reserve a dollar of capital on a balance sheet. So, I'll leave it up to you guys to do the math."[83]

Northern Trust: After the FTX collapse (see Chapter 4), Northern Trust's Global Head of Regulatory Product, Natalie Berkecz, said, "We need to change the narrative of 'another month, another crypto crisis.'"[84] Northern Trust took a stance that the digital asset industry was ripe for regulation.

The asset management firm co-launched a crypto administration firm in 2021 and created the Digital Assets and Financial Markets Group to help its investors enter the crypto market. The firm's president of Asset Servicing, Pete Cherecwich, told *Forbes* that the company was intentionally focusing digital and traditional markets together, as their "clients are increasingly interested in the development of digital markets and investing in digital assets alongside allocations to more traditional asset classes, such as equities, fixed income, alternatives, and private assets."[85]

The firm created a Digital Assets and Financial Markets group in 2022, focusing on both digital and traditional markets in one effort. "Traditional and digital markets already coexist and the boundaries between the two will only continue to blur over time," said Cherecwich.[86] Northern Trust also invested in Zodia Custody, an institutional grade crypto asset custody solution based in London, to complement their suite of offerings.[87]

Foreign Exchange

According to the 2022 Bank for International Settlements (BIS) triennial survey, every day, $2.2 trillion is subject to settlement risk in foreign currency exchanges.[88] That's why distributed ledger technology is being considered as a solution across the globe. In 2023, UBS and UK-based NatWest joined the Finteum intraday platform, a DLT that enables quick and low-risk settlement of foreign currency exchanges, reducing the amount of high-quality liquid assets needed as reserves.[89]

In December 2021, State Street, Symbiont, and Vanguard completed their first live trades for foreign currency-forward contracts on a DLT.[90] The goal was post-trade workflow automation, which reduced counterparty credit risk.

HSBC and Wells Fargo, too, began using blockchain to settle bilateral foreign currency trades in less than 3 minutes, reducing exposure and settlement risks.[91] In Australia, the first foreign exchange translation on a DLT served as a live pilot for the country's central bank digital currency when crypto fund managers DigitalX and TAF Capital traded eAUD against stablecoin USD Coin.[92]

The Federal Reserve Bank of New York at the time was "optimistic" that blockchain could enable "faster, simultaneous, and safer cross-border payments."

Carbon Credit Market

Carbon credits, or offsets, allow companies to emit a certain amount of carbon dioxide or other greenhouse gases, and the carbon market lets investors and companies trade excess credits. A set number of carbon credits are issued each year via "cap-and-trade," with limits, or caps, set by regulators. To stay under the cap, some companies trade credits. Now, blockchain is helping to facilitate carbon credit trading.

Northern Trust launched a blockchain-based carbon credit platform that allows institutional buyers to trade tokenized carbon credits directly with project developers.[93]

Australia and New Zealand Banking Group Limited launched the first use-case of carbon credit trading under Australia's CBDC pilot program, tokenizing credits and purchasing them with a stablecoin.[94]

The World Bank launched a project on blockchain to tokenize carbon credits for crypto investors.[95] It's a way to redirect increased interest in NFTs toward climate control projects. Blockchain's inherent transparency reportedly prevents people from selling each carbon credit to more than one buyer.

Other Active Players

As banks continue to find ways to make blockchain technology work for them, some big players are coming on board with digital asset offerings:

Goldman Sachs: The firm introduced the Digital Asset Platform on the Canton privacy-enabled blockchain and in the DAML smart contract language in 2023 with a focus on digital bonds. Goldman cited four main benefits: improved speed and efficiency, cost reduction, increased transparency, and accessibility.[96] In a 2021 report, the firm posited, "It is likely that blockchain technology will be as high-impact in the future as the internet has been over the past several decades."[97] Goldman Sachs has participated in numerous digital asset pilots or transactions including underwriting Figure Technologies HELOC securitization. Also, Goldman Sachs has their own node on JPMorgan's Onyx blockchain, and has access to tokenized intra-day repos.

Morgan Stanley: CEO James Gorman said, "I don't know what the value of bitcoin should or shouldn't be, but these things aren't going away and the blockchain technology supporting it is obviously very real and powerful."[98] Morgan Stanley, the first major US bank to offer bitcoin funds to its existing clients with at least $2 million in assets, also invested in the Series B for Securitize.[99] They similarly invested in NYDIG and R3, both ecosystem investments in the digital asset space. The firm noted in a 2022 research report that the development of regulation to crypto's ecosystem made it less decentralized.

These identified examples of institutional building blocks of digital assets aren't an exhaustive list. There are many other companies that are building, with even more innovation happening outside of the United States. In a few years, the functionality and use of digital assets and blockchain technology will no longer be newsworthy, because the technology will be the engine for the financial system.

In fact, by the summer of 2023, nearly three-quarters of institutions were actively engaged in digital assets, up from just under half the year before, a Citi Securities Services survey found. It depends on which side of the business they're on. "The sell side see tokenization benefits for listed equities and public debt. In contrast, institutional investors are interested in the tokenization of private equities and debt, hoping to see liquidity improvements."[100]

PwC agreed in its 2023 Digital Asset Predictions report, which predicted that "a few forward-looking legacy financial institutions will likely be among the real winners of the digital asset space." The firm cited the cause of the crypto winter as human, not technological, failures, and predicted that customers may demand "trusted, blue-chip names" to usher them into the digital asset era.

What's certain is that tomorrow's investors and finance players will come to expect the technologies and benefits of digital assets just as Wall Street's pre-season is coming to an end.

7

How Tomorrow's Investors Will Expect Change

"Okay, Boomer"

– Generation Z

In 2021, young day traders on Reddit's WallStreetBets forum openly mobilized and drove up the stock price for GameStop, a video game store popular with Millennial and Generation Z Hoodies, by more than 5,000 percent over the course of a few weeks. It was a modern twist on a "pump and dump," when traders collude to inflate a stock's price, typically by spreading false information, and then profiting by selling their shares at the inflated price. Or was it? Proving stock manipulations by small-time traders has been difficult.

It was, however, one of the largest increases in an individual stock price in the history of the New York Stock Exchange. In the subreddit where people discuss trading opportunities, the group noticed that hedge funds had taken a short position on GameStop stock – a bet that the stock's value would decrease. So the Redditors started posting recommendations to purchase GameStop shares, driving up the price dramatically, forcing Wall Street firms that had bet on a lowering stock price to lose billions of dollars in their portfolios.

As one of the subreddit moderators put it, "How'd you guys manage to win so big it made these old guys drown in their tears?" He added, "Wall Street no longer dismisses your presence anymore. The smart ones know that you guys do things differently and will adapt in ways to accommodate you and how you, as the next generation, want things done. You should all be proud of yourself. Your time is now."[1]

Meanwhile, GameStop's market capitalization skyrocketed from $3 billion to $25 billion in just one week. Hedge funds were forced to close out their short positions and buy GameStop shares at the higher market price – while losing millions. Then, the National Securities Clearing Corporation required the CEO of online investing platform Robinhood, Vlad Tenev, to prove he had adequate on-hand liquidity. He halted trading of GameStop and negotiated the requested deposit to their clearinghouse for settling and trading stock from $3 billion down to $700 million.

The young Redditors who orchestrated what will no doubt be just the first coordinated stock surge of its kind called it a push-back against "crony capitalism" – Wall Street. With Robinhood's average user just 31 years old – younger than the networked computer firewall – it's a sign of how the future of investing will be affected by younger generations of investors, who tend to put their money into socially responsible causes, investments they relate to, and, in this case, sticking it to hedge fund managers. They rely less on financial advisors and migrate to alternative sources and alternative investments, such as crypto and the alternative investment options digital assets will create.

The GameStop pump-and-dump is a sign of things to come and a sense of the generational changes already under way.

American Generations

The Greatest Generation:	born 1901–1925
The Silent Generation:	born 1926–1945
Baby Boomers:	born 1946–1964
Generation X:	born 1965–1979
Millennials:	born 1980–1994
Generation Z:	born 1995–2012
Generation Alpha:	born 2013–2025

Why Do Generational Shifts Matter to Finance?

In the opening scene of 2015's *The Big Short*, a Baby Boomer is credited (or vilified, depending on how you look at it) for popularizing the securitization of finance. Salomon Brothers' bond trader Lewis Ranieri is introduced as the creator of mortgage-backed securities (MBS) in the late seventies, which led to a revolution in home borrowing, decreasing the cost of financing. Similar to a bond, an MBS is backed by a collection of home loans, essentially putting banks in a mediator position between homebuyers and investors.

As Ryan Reynolds narrated in the movie, "The money came raining down . . . Pretty soon, stocks and savings were almost inconsequential . . . and America barely noticed as its number one industry became boring old banking."

Unfortunately, Ranieri's creation laid the structural foundation for the 2008 financial collapse and the Great Recession, when the housing market collapsed. It was a Suits failure in order of magnitude, displacing some 10 million homeowners and doubling the unemployment rate, making it the worst financial crisis since the Depression. A decade after the crash, he expressed regret to the *Wall Street Journal*, "I'm the guy who played a central role in this home thing and I regret it because . . . it got abused beyond everybody's imagination."[2]

But he was just one Boomer that affected how finance and the economy work. Investopedia even named the generation's influence the "Boomer Effect," defined as the influence that "the generation born between 1946 and 1964 has on the economy and most markets."[3]

The Boomers came of age at a time of relative postwar economic prosperity. They benefited from lower housing costs and interest rates and easy credit, allowing them to buy houses and stocks. As they reached retirement, they voted for public spending on social programs that benefited them, such as Social Security and Medicare, and they accumulated wealth at unprecedented levels.

This single, behemoth generation had an outsized effect on the economy and on finance. Though they were pioneers in online banking, a third of them still like to visit a bank branch and many of them still use the drive-through window. But as they leave the labor market and downsize their homes, the shift to younger, more tech savvy generations is having its own effects on finance, beginning with the Great Wealth Transfer.

The Great Wealth Transfer Will Change Finance

The Baby Boomers amassed approximately $84 trillion of wealth that they are starting to transfer to their heirs (see Figure 7.1).[4] This Great Wealth Transfer will see more than half of the nation's wealth change hands in the coming years.[5]

Over the past thirty-five years, the total household wealth has grown roughly 550 percent or almost 16 percent on a straight line basis. The *New York Times*[6] reports that the Boomers benefited from price growth in the financial and housing markets over the past few decades. Once the wealth is transferred, Millennials, now in their thirties and forties, and Generation Z, in their teens and twenties, will become even more important to Wall Street, Main Street, the economy, and the political climate.

This transfer of wealth could create large swings in economic policies that affect older Americans as the balance of power shifts younger. Reports Deutsche Bank Strategist Jim Reid, the shift could include harsher inheritance taxes, less income protection for pensioners, higher taxes, and other wealth redistribution policies unfavorable to older Americans. The younger generations may wind up benefiting from their parents' and grandparents' economic situations as they take over the lion's share of wealth. Yet it's important to note that not all Millennials will gain from the transfer of wealth, which won't be passed down equally.

The New Pig in the Python

In 2022, Millennials, Generation Z, and Generation Alpha made up more than half of the US population with approximately 180 million people (see Figure 7.2).[7] Millennials now outnumber Boomers, once the "pig in the python" generation – the enormous cohort that pushed its way through our economy – who once didn't trust anyone over thirty and now are in retirement or nearing it.

For these younger workers, technology is their native tongue, whereas older generations had to learn tech as a second language. These newer generations don't have to program their grandparents' flashing VCR clock. They probably don't even know what a VCR is. They likely don't remember when Netflix, launched in 1997, mailed DVDs to our mailboxes, or when Google launched in 1998, back when the oldest Millennials began to graduate from high school.

Millennials are starting to accumulate wealth.
Unfortunately for them, the amount and rate of
accumulation is significantly behind older generations.

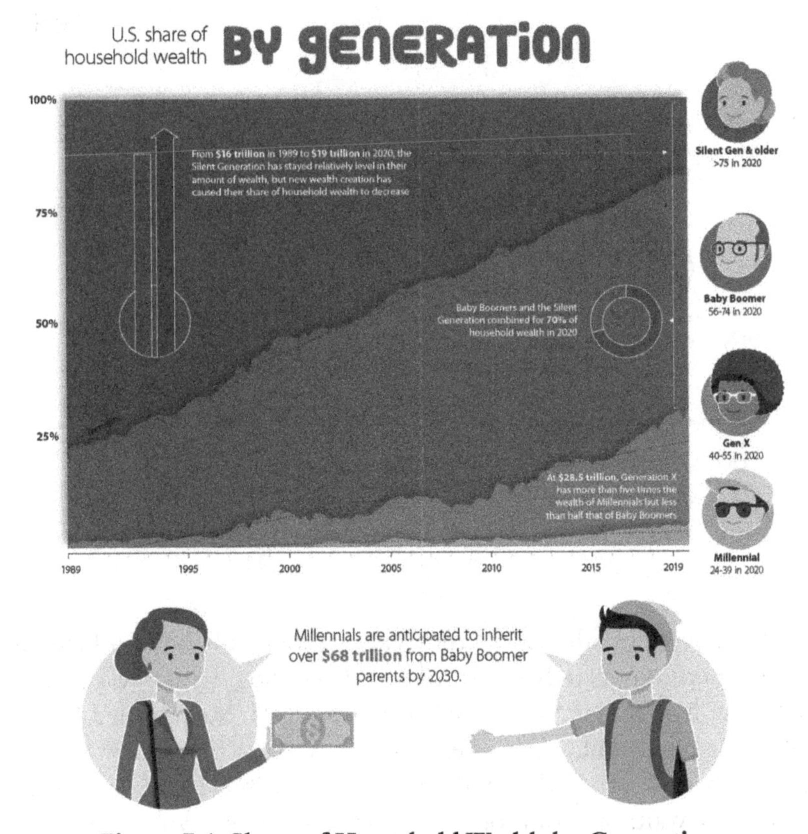

Figure 7.1 Share of Household Wealth by Generation

Source: Visual Capitalist / https://www.visualcapitalist.com/charting-the-growing-generational-wealth-gap/

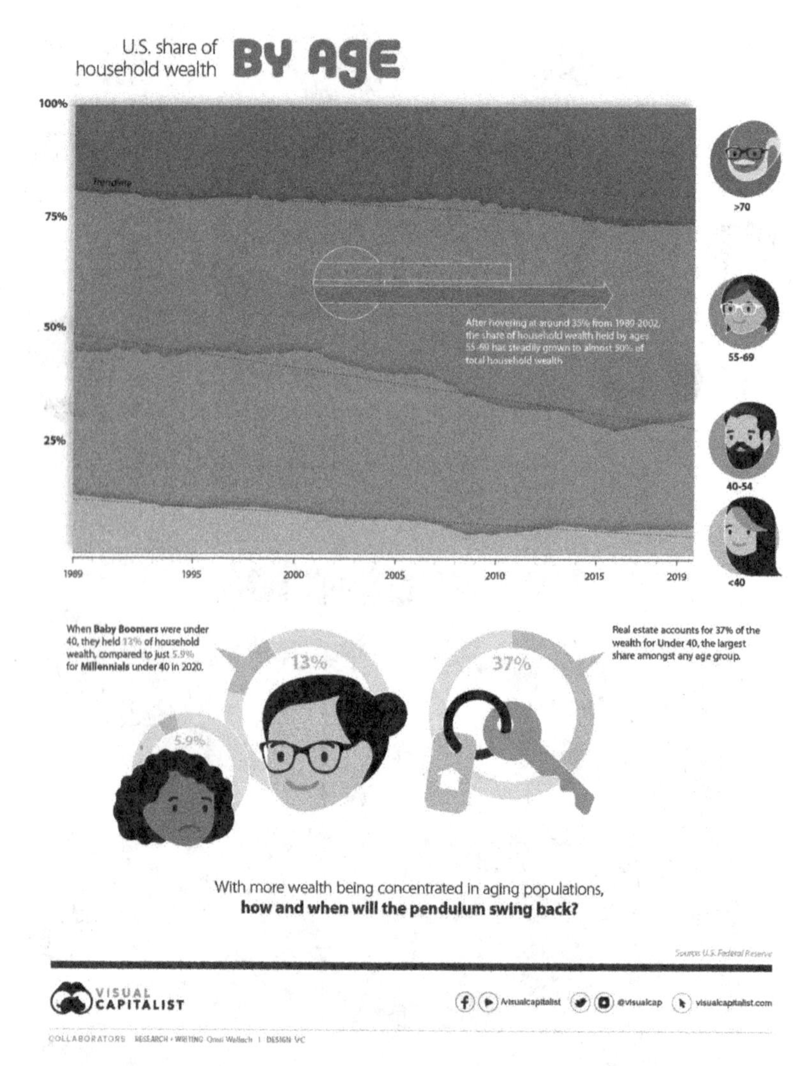

Figure 7.1 (Continued)

They were unaffected by the death of social media dud Friendster in 2003 and only briefly spent time on Facebook, which was launched by fellow Millennial Mark Zuckerberg in 2004. Surrounded by technology as teens and, some, even since they were born, they were and are the babies and kids on iPads at the family restaurant, on a car drive, in a waiting room, or on an airplane. They don't remember a life without it.

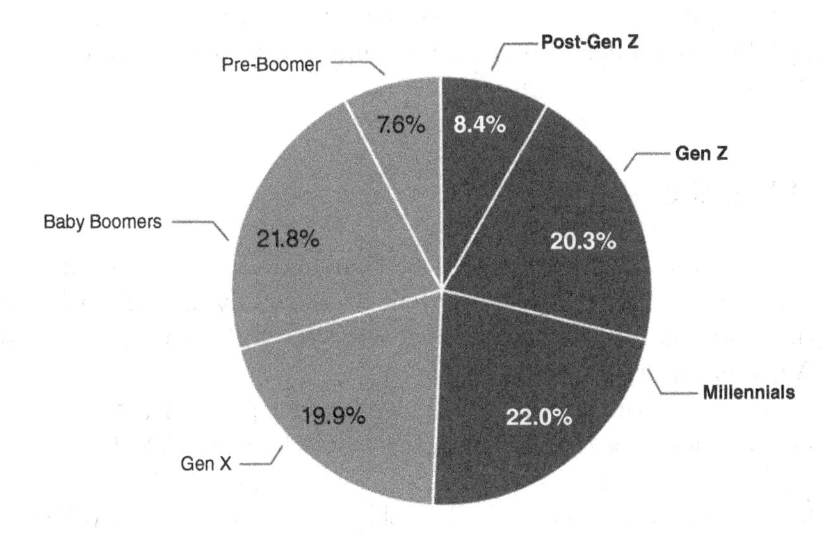

Figure 7.2 Share of US Population by Generation
Source: Brookings Institute/ https://www.brookings.edu/articles/now-more-than-half-of-americans-are-millennials-or-younger/

By the time the oldest of Generation Z were in elementary school, two-thirds of US adults owned a cell phone.[8] Less than a decade later, more than half of the population used smartphones,[9] essentially handheld supercomputers with exponentially more power than NASA's Apollo 11 guidance computer.[10] It's this access to and reliance on technology that shapes a different perspective on finance and investment for the three youngest generations, who are the investors, business leaders, and decision-makers of tomorrow. For them, the only constant is change.

These generations have a different perspective and shifting values from their parents and grandparents. They have an increasing distrust of institutions, a disdain for income inequality, and increased financial awareness, thanks in part to the supercomputers in their pockets. Combine that with their push for socially responsible investing, a desire for a more diverse portfolio of alternatives, and a generally shorter attention span. In fact, more than 75 percent of young people confess to reaching for their phones to occupy their attention, compared to 10 percent of Boomers.[11]

The future of finance is beginning to look very different, and it's being driven by how the younger generations view money and investing. Understand that, and you understand how to prepare for the future of finance.

Millennials

Born between 1980 and 1994, their childhood coincided with John Lennon's death, the US boycott of the Moscow Olympics, Ronald Reagan's and Bill Clinton's presidencies, the Rwandan massacre, and the O. J. Simpson trial.

Their formative years included plenty of political and economic turmoil, including the Gulf War, the Lewinsky scandal, Y2K, the 9/11 attacks, the War on Terror, the Dot-com bubble, WorldCom, Enron, the subprime mortgage crisis, the collapse of Bear Stearns and Lehman Brothers, the Great Recession, the Madoff scandal, and Presidents Bush's and Obama's eight-year reigns.

The volatility and chaos of the era informed their views on investing and spending. Wage stagnation and record levels of student loan debt have affected their ability to save for the future. They are less likely to own a home, with fewer than half paying for mortgages compared to nearly 70 percent of Generation X and more than three-quarters of Baby Boomers.[12] Homeownership among young adults has declined in 95 percent of US cities as fewer Millennials marry and then have children later, housing prices and interest rates increase, and wages stay stagnant.

Yet Millennials are more on track to save more for retirement than Boomers and Generation X, reports the *Wall Street Journal,* mainly through 401(k) plans.[13] Meanwhile, the Millennials grew up during a time of great technological growth, starting with the internet and email. As kids, they went from cassettes to DVDs to digital music, and from home phones to Blackberries to iPhones/smartphones, and phone calls to text messaging. From dial up to Wi-Fi, Nintendo to Xbox.

Technology quickly changed the way people interacted, communicated, and behaved, affecting society's, and the Millennials', behavior. As the first global generation of the Internet age brought together by connectivity, they could pull up information 24/7/365 on their phones or laptops, never touching a microfiche at the library.

Most Millennial billionaires made their money as founders or first employees of technology companies that gave the world something new. From Facebook to Telegram to Airbnb to Snapchat to Coinbase, each company's founder leveraged technology to expand on a Millennial generation trait. Many have expanded ways for the world to connect, increasing communication, creating experiences, and providing access.[14] This will be expanded on further as it directly ties with investments and digital assets in traditional finance.

Sometimes raised by "helicopter parents," Millennials have been defined as the "Me, Me, Me Generation," the cohort that owns selfie sticks, counts social media followers, and grew up watching reality shows starring narcissists. They were raised to believe in themselves; in their world, everyone gets a trophy.

Yet Millennials are the most educated generation, with nearly 40 percent earning a bachelor's degree, compared to 3 in 10 Gen Xers and about a quarter of Boomers (see Figure 7.3).[15]

They remain adaptable, global, and individualistic. According to Dr. Jean Twenge, a psychology professor at San Diego State University, who wrote *Generation Me*, "As far back as we have measures, and both as teens and young adults, Millennials are the most optimistic and self-confident generation in history."[16] What was earlier called entitlement comes across now as confidence, which has helped the generation climb the corporate ladder.

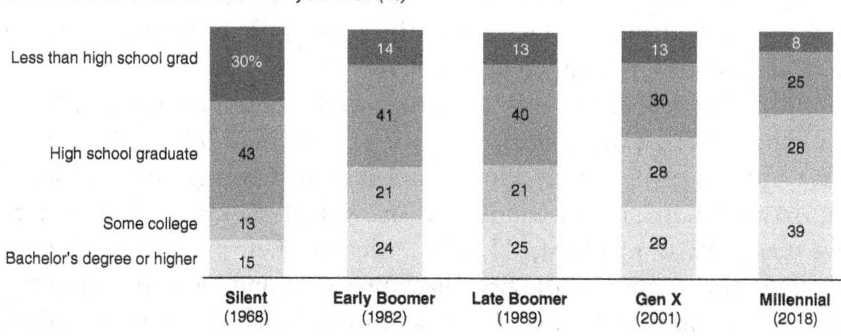

Note: Figures may not add to 100% due to rounding "High school graduate" includes those who have a high school diploma or its equivalent, such as a GED certificate. "Some college" includes those with an associate degree and those who attended college but did not obtain a degree. The educational attainment question was changed in 1992. For Boomers and Silents, "high school graduate" includes those who completed 12th grade (regardless of diploma status) and "bachelor's degree or higher" includes those who completed at least four years of college (regardless of degree status).

Figure 7.3 Millennials Are Better Educated Than Prior Generations
Source: Pew Research Center

Millennials are self-assured and hard workers who spend their money on travel,[17] experiences, and home goods.[18] They are known for the following traits:

- highest education rates
- value experiences over things
- embrace change and exhibit adaptability
- individualistic
- less formal social interactions and communications
- prioritize work-life balance, value their health, exercise, and eating healthy.

They are the perfect generation to bridge the Hoodies and the Suits as they lead the charge for change in finance.

Generation Z

Next in line to run the world is Gen Z. By 2034, this generation will overtake Millennials as they are expected to peak at 78 million strong. Who are GenZ?

Tell a "Zoomer," those born around the turn of this century, something that they find out of touch, and they're likely to respond, "Okay, Boomer," even if you're not one. Raised largely by Generation X, Gen Z is a force with a very different way of thinking. They were born into technology and push companies to increase their tech options while increasing their environmental action as well.

Born between 1997 and 2012, their childhood coincided with the founding of eBay, the collapse of Barings Bank, and 9/11. Their peers were victims of the Sandy Hook mass school shooting, some endured Hurricanes Katrina and Sandy, and many had classes on Zoom during the COVID pandemic. Headlines during their primary years have included the election of the first Black president and Donald Trump, the January 6th insurrection, and several climate-related events, including wildfires and record-breaking land and sea temperatures.

They have experienced increased civil violence and climate change, and more school shootings than any other generation. No other generation has had to practice school lockdowns for active shooters like Generation Z.

Their formative years coincided with several high-profile events in finance, including Occupy Wall Street, the Bitcoin white paper, inflation, and the housing bubble.

Technology defines most of their lives: social life, entertainment, shopping, and education. As a result, they are the most tech-savvy generation yet, experiencing as children the introduction of YouTube, X (formerly known as Twitter), Snapchat, self-driving cars, Chat GPT, ecommerce, Fortnite, Roblox, Pokémon Go, TikTok, Reddit, Discord, gaming as socialization, streaming, and smartphones. They typically don't remember prime-time TV or home phones.

They've been called the "Social Media Generation" for the new social scene and the "Lockdown Generation," both for school shooting lockdowns and COVID restrictions. Here are some traits common among "Zoomers":

- They spend their money on electronics, technology, and health and wellness.
- They are tech-oriented, socially anxious, value-driven, and environmentally minded, with two-thirds surveyed willing to spend more on a product that is environmentally friendly and 82 percent expressing concern for the planet.
- They expect the efficiency of operability.
- They're a global generation comfortable with worldwide content and communication.
- They look to live and work with their values aligned.
- They spend less time face-to-face and more time online – a 17 percent increase during the pandemic[19] – which has led to higher levels of social anxiety, depression, fear of missing out (FOMO), and poor body image.
- They report higher levels of social media usage with teenage screen time increasing to 8 hours and 39 minutes per day.[20]
- They are waiting longer to get a driver's license if at all, preferring the convenience of Uber.
- More than three-quarters report attending a protest for racial equality.[21]

Gen Z has been defined as value driven and idealistic, in search of independence, financial freedom, and purpose. They have proven to be compassionate and strive for a work-life balance. McKinsey called Gen Z "communaholics" who prize "uniqueness."[22] In the workplace, this generation is more likely to find a job with a company that aligns the corporate values to their own.

For accomplished GenZ businesspeople, look to the world of technology, gaming, and influencers. The world of celebrity has changed from TV and movie stars to online streamers or e-gamers. They are the generation of the social media influencer, with TikTok star 18-year-old Charli D'Amelio raking in $17.5 million in 2022 and Australian esports gamer ana (aka Anathan Pham) earning $6 million by playing video games.[23]

GenZ is a force with a very different way of thinking.

Generation Alpha

The first fully 21st century generation, Gen Alpha, born between 2013 and 2025 to Millennial parents, are the kids of today and the clients of tomorrow. The oldest are only in elementary school. One historian calls them "Polars"[24] to represent both the political polarization they're being born into and the melting of the polar ice caps.

As babies, they've been handed iPads – 61 percent of the generation own a tablet – and have been exposed to social media earlier in life than any other cohort. Growing up on Minecraft, Fortnite, TikTok, Snapchat, and Discord, they will likely adapt to technologies even faster than Gen Z. For them, the most advanced tech is the norm,[25] and they'll demand it into adulthood. Algorithms shape their actions, and they'll expect customized digital experiences. The pandemic, meanwhile, served only to reinforce their reliance on digital communication.

In short, says the *Atlantic*, Gen Alpha is the most technologically advanced and the wealthiest yet.[26] Though they are still just children, expectations are that they will be:[27]

- family-focused, in part from the pandemic
- climate advocates due to increased climate catastrophes
- inclusive and diverse
- dependent on technology with more experience in screen time and to audio content, cementing their role in a digital future
- individualistic, educated
- wealthier than previous generations

How the New Workforce Affects the Economy

By 2016, Millennials had become the largest generation in the workforce, representing 35 percent of all workers.[28] Companies have begun to see them as the most powerful generation for marketers to target.

Together with Generation Z, they led the Great Resignation, quitting their jobs at higher rates during the pandemic years than other generations.[29] They are known to job hop, moving on average every three years,[30] which may seem misguided but has increased their salaries with each job move. Millennials are comfortable challenging the status quo and proposing new ideas.

Both Millennials and Gen Z have reported higher burnout rates and experience less engagement in the workplace or with coworkers.[31] A Gallup poll found that most young workers don't feel a close connection to their coworkers, manager, or employer.[32]

Generation Z is just as likely to leave a higher paying job for something more interesting. They generally don't care for longevity in the workplace, changing jobs on average every two to four years. However, with the evolving labor landscape, jobs are less secure than they were when older generations were starting out some 30 or 40 years ago, with few retention benefits.

Three-quarters of managers have reported that Gen Z is difficult to work with, citing a lack of motivation and calling them "easily distracted" and "easily offended."[33] Yet Gen Z workers also come off as innovative, adaptable, and unafraid to challenge the status quo. Remember, the oldest Gen Zs entered the workforce only recently, and many started their careers during the COVID-19 remote work wave, so they haven't yet experienced the same workplace training as other generations did at their age.

The younger generations seem to be more entrepreneurial, with more than three-quarters of Millennials and Gen Z aspiring to be their own bosses, compared to 63 percent of older generations.[34] They sometimes make money in alternative ways. In 2023, the 10 top influencers made over a million dollars per social media post promoting products. Today with technology, social media, remote work, and online retail, there are lucrative opportunities outside of corporate life.

With strengths including transparency, communication, and working as a team, Millennials have high expectations for themselves and their teams. *Harvard Business Review* reported that Millennials can change company culture for the better, and a focus on autonomy would well suit their Gen Z charges, who value purpose over paycheck. In the era of "quiet quitting," where employees do the bare minimum while looking for a new job, this is more important than ever. Workplace flexibility, which requires trust of productivity without losing the company's communication and culture, is crucial.

As corporate managers, Millennials and Gen Z will likely have the open mindset and tech savvy to adopt digital assets. They will recognize the benefits for both the clients and the company.

So we have a large cohort of entrepreneurial young and younger workers who value work-life balance about to receive a windfall of family wealth. What does this mean for finance? It's important to understand the trends in investing 5, 10, and 20 years down the line. The tides are changing, and Millennials and Gen Z are changing them.

The Evolution of Finance Continues into the 21st Century

Finance is not new, and it is not broken. It has developed over time as business leaders optimized, refined, and upgraded to meet investor demands. The World Bank traces the earliest banking activity back to 8000 BC, and the first banks date back to Mesopotamia around 2000 BC with lending, credit, and deposits.[35]

The first bank in the United States was founded in 1791, and what is now the New York Stock Exchange evolved from a small group of traders in 1792 to the world's largest stock exchange, with brokers trading directly. Centuries later, the telegraph, telephone, and fax changed the face of trading. NASDAQ launched in 1971 to offer automated trading, and high-frequency trading started in 1983.

Finance in the 21st century has changed significantly. The term "paperwork" is going the way of the term "pay phone," virtually unrecognizable to these generations. The world is becoming digital, and printers and fax machines have become redundant. Structured finance and securitization have decreased the cost of borrowing. Credit and borrowing facilities are much more available than they were previously. Digital payments and online banking are the norm now. Apple Wallet, Google Wallet, PayPal, Venmo, Cash App, and Zelle have made carrying cash unnecessary. Checks can be deposited, accounts can be opened, and fraud can be reported all from the banking app on your smartphone. No more waiting in a long queue for an operator or standing in line at the bank. Fees are decreasing. The next generation of both Hoodies and Suits will continue to innovate and demand more efficient structure.

Generational Shifts in Financial Information

These next generations are getting the majority of their financial information and education through free access channels from influencers on YouTube and other social media platforms. In fact, Generation Z is nearly five times as likely to get financial information from social media than older generations do.[36] No wonder there's a new term: "finfluencer," a social media influencer that shares financial tips and advice. They have power and followers. The World Economic Forum estimates the market size for the finfluencers creators' economy at $104 million.[37] Compare TikTok influencer @marktilbury's 7 million followers to @fidelity's and @blackrock's thirty thousand each, as of mid-2023.

A UK study reported that 85 percent of Gen Z gets financial education from social media, whose top finfluencer is Millennial Humphrey Yang, a former Merrill Lynch advisor with 54 million followers across TikTok, YouTube, and Instagram. Millennial Tori Dunlop, author of "Financial Feminist" and advocate for empowering women in personal finance, has some 27 million followers. Gen Z's top finfluencer is Taylor Price, "GenZ financial activist" and Savvy app creator with more than 21 million followers across platforms. She says she sets out to "end the 'silent' pandemic of financial illiteracy."

A report by FINRA and the CFA focused on Gen Z investing behaviors highlighted that GenZ get their financial information and education from social media sources. A majority turn to YouTube followed by other searches, internet communities, or social posts (see Figure 7.4).

Yet not all influencers have the finance credentials required to share financial advice. What's more, finfluencers make money by promoting products and/or selling courses that could potentially create a conflict of interest. That doesn't seem to matter to most of their audience, who trust those with the most followers. Despite the heavy reliance on social media, 51 percent of Gen Z investors rely on their family as the end resource.[38] As a result, the final investing decisions are generally discussed IRL (in real life) with a trusted person.

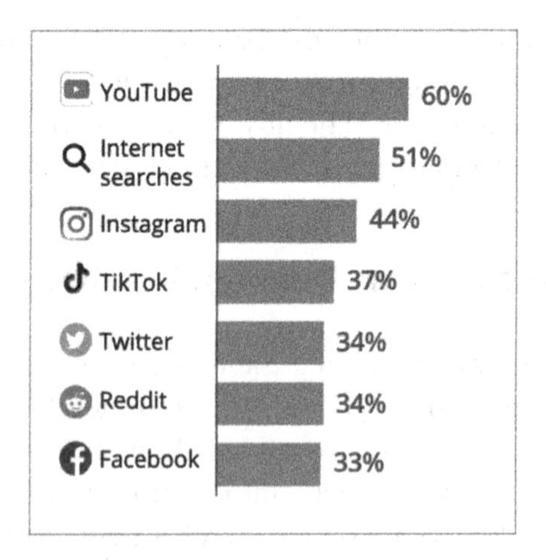

Figure 7.4 Top Sites Gen Z Investors Use to Learn about Financial Topics and Investing
Source: FINRA/CFA

Millennials and Gen Z prefer investing on apps rather than meeting with a financial planner. With the apps, they can trade on a mobile device or laptop, anytime, anywhere without speaking to anyone.

Founded in 2013, finance app Robinhood's mission was to "provide everyone with access to the financial markets, not just the wealthy." As of May 2023, Robinhood reported 23 million accounts with some 11 million active users. The average user age is 31 with 8 in 10 under 35, and half are first-time investors. On average, users checked their Robinhood app seven times a day in 2020.[39]

No-fee platforms like Robinhood, Stash, and eToro have already had a huge effect on large brokers, such as E-Trade, Fidelity, and Charles Schwab, which now, too, offer no-fee trades.

Still, as these generations build or inherit more wealth, they will likely migrate to a trusted financial advisor for financial advice, but that advisor is unlikely to be the same type their parents had.

A recent study by FINRA and the CFA found that a quarter of Gen Z began investing before age 18, with 56 percent reporting owning investments.[40] What's striking is the composition of their portfolios:

- 55 percent own cryptocurrency, which can be purchased on an app via mobile technology for a small investment capital, with a high, though volatile, potential return profile

- 41 percent own stock
- 35 percent own mutual funds
- 25 percent own NFTs
- 23 percent own ETFs

A *US News and World Report* survey of 9,500 Zoomers found that the number one public-owned brand investment for this group was Starbucks (SBUX), followed by Chipotle Mexican Grill (CMG), and Nike (NKE),[41] making next gen investors the most likely frequent consumers of their products. This climate-friendly generation believes that company investments should be tied to corporate responsibility, and each of these companies has a corporate social responsibility pledge that appeals to Gen Z. Yet Gen Z has voiced a lack of trust in the stock market.

One study found that 83 percent of Gen Z and 66 percent of Millennials have invested in Environmental, Social, and Governance (ESG) investments, and 79 percent of Gen Z and 68 percent of young Millennials have made sustainable investing a priority.[42] One issue with alternatives is the lack of availability of options. Given the current nature of private assets, they are hard to access and illiquid, which is something blockchain technology can address. It is yet to be seen if the importance of ESG investing is tied to idealistic youth and changes with age and more life responsibilities.

Today's technology offers new opportunities in finance, with the upgrade helmed by the next generation of investors and business leaders. In fact, changing demographics and technological advances have led to notable changes during this century.

These generations are important to understand when considering the future of finance in 5, 10, and 20 years. They are the majority of the US population, and they will one day hold the majority of the US wealth and already make up the majority of the workforce.

These generations are natively digital, tech savvy, and expect efficiency. They don't accept the status quo and are open to change. They rely on social media for research. They invest in cryptocurrencies and are open to investing in digital securities.

They will also be the future leaders of the board, the banks, asset managers, and clients. The tides are changing. Go with the tide.

8

The Building Blocks of Securities

"Life is not always black and white, it's a million shades of gray."
— Ridley Scott

If you want to make big returns, you should have spent your pandemic lockdown investing in . . . Minions-themed LEGO sets.

No, really.

These LEGOs are the same colorful building blocks invented in Denmark in 1932 as toys for children; only now, they've become a tradable investment. Take, for example, the LEGO Minions Kung Fu Training set, retired in 2022. Its value has increased by 40 percent as of this writing, trading on eBay with an average annual growth of nearly 20 percent.[1]

According to a study published by Research in International Business and Finance, "Toys prove to be better investment than gold, art, and financial securities."[2] The secondary market for retired **LEGO** sets has grown by 11 percent annually, outperforming investments such as stocks, bonds, art, and wine.[3]

It's a simple supply and demand consideration. LEGO retires a set, reducing supply, and then demand rises in the resell market. One LEGO collector, who has a room full of unopened LEGO sets, told the *Wall*

Street Journal that he typically sees a 150 to 250 percent return on his investments, and that he has spent upwards of $65,000 so far.[4]

For more on LEGO investing, BrickEconomy.com is "a comprehensive guide to LEGO economics, market values and trends" and supplies expected annual growth on LEGO sets.

But are collectible LEGO sets a commodity or a security? The Howey Test can help determine what constitutes an investment contract and therefore, what's a security – or not. A security holds monetary value and can be traded, but an investment can only be regulated as a security if it passes the Howey Test's criteria, as established from the 1946 case *SEC vs W.J. Howey Co.*:[5]

1. It involves an investment of money. This means money is exchanged.
2. It's in a common enterprise where the investor's fortunes are tied to the efforts of a third party. For instance, when profits and losses are shared or there's joint ownership.
3. There's an expectation of profit on a passive investment. The investors don't need to perform a service to expect a return.
4. It's derived by the effort of others.

So is an investment in LEGO a security, a commodity, or just a toy? Why does this matter? When the Hoodies' technology, which brings efficiency, potential liquidity, and broader access to financial markets, meets the Suits' recognized regulatory environment, how will traditional finance scale? Will all tokenized assets become securities even if the underlying asset is not a security? Finance regulation can't be gray. It has to be black and white.

Former Chief Legal Officer for dYdX Trading and current Polygon Labs CEO, Mark Boiron, believes that crypto's decentralization has helped issuers avoid violating securities law, citing "sufficient decentralization," a phrase introduced by the SEC's William Hinman. Boiron wrote that if an investor reasonably expects profit from the "uncoordinated efforts" of many people, the protocol should be considered sufficiently decentralized.[6]

Protecting investors and penalizing fraudulent activity allows the United States to maintain its dominance as the world's largest economy. Regulators, the SEC, and the Commodities and Futures Trading Commission (CFTC) have a difficult and thankless job.

What Is a Security?

In the nail-biting 149th Kentucky Derby, Mage, who had 15 to 1 odds, pulled ahead on the outside off the turn in the last 10 seconds to win the race. Go Mage! Interestingly, Mage's ownership was fractionalized. Four hundred investors held 25 percent of Mage's ownership through a Reg A+ investment, allowing retail investors to participate in the otherwise hard-to-access world of racehorse ownership. Though this security issuance was not tokenized, in time, racehorse investors may hold digital assets as ownership structures, which would likely allow for less friction on transfers. That means that a horse could technically be a security.

Under the Howey Test's criteria, stocks, bonds, mutual funds, limited partnership interests, and investment contracts are securities. Securities generally have a higher level of regulation because they are offered to the public retail investor, who the SEC has deemed as lacking a financial education. Securities can be complex and require a higher level of understanding than commodities or loans.

Securities laws are important to ensure that issuers provide accurate and sufficient information and disclosures to the public so they can make informed investment decisions. Issuers are not allowed to provide false or misleading information or performance guarantees.

Regulation requires sales and trades to go through a registered broker dealer. In addition to KYC/AML, broker dealers must exercise diligence when making investment recommendations to retail investors.

What Is a Commodity?

The Financial Industry Regulatory Authority (FINRA) defines commodities as a basic good, such as cattle, gold, oil, and wheat.[7] They're an economic good, a mass-produced, unspecialized product, and they're regulated by the CFTC.[8] Commodity investments can be direct exposure or they could be in futures, which is a legally binding agreement for a set price and quantity in the future.

Many invest in gold as a hedge against inflation. Though gold has short-term volatility, it typically offers long-term appreciation (see Figure 8.1). While there's no utility value in gold, it's held for its intrinsic value, and some 27 million ounces are traded daily, according to CME Group.[9] Gold is a commodity.

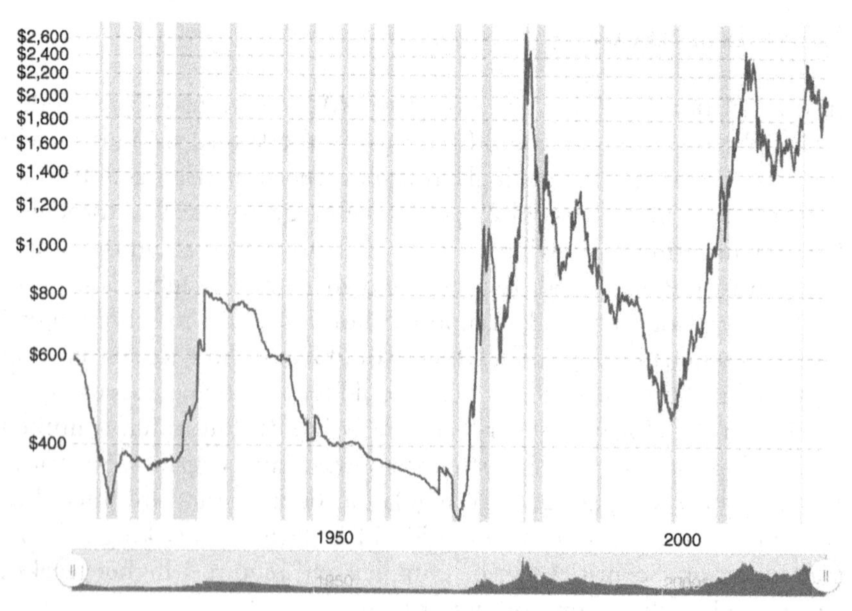

Figure 8.1 Gold's Price over One Hundred Years, Adjusted for Inflation
Source: Macrotrends

Why isn't gold a security? Though gold involves an investment of money with a reasonable expectation of profit, it's not reliant on the efforts of others, a Howey Test criterion. But what about gold miners? Through their efforts, the total gold supply has increased 2 percent year on year through 2022. Does the investment in gold rely on them passively, or does the increase in the supply of gold decrease the investment value?

What about wheat, corn, and soy agriculture futures? Does the future price of agriculture rely on the work done by the farmer who grows and maintains crops? Does that make them passive investments? These are defined as commodities, so no, they are not securities.

The most actively traded future, oil, which is part of the $5.3 trillion oil and gas market, is defined as a commodity. Miners assist in the oil industry as well, contributing to the available supply. It's a limited resource and the primary source of energy production.

Collectibles like LEGOs, art, cars, wine, and sports trading cards are also commodities. They have other utility, but no one person or enterprise creates value for them and no value is derived from another party. An auction house or marketplace can bring people together, but it doesn't add to the "market value' "or what the market perceives it to be on purchase. Therefore, they are not defined as securities from the Howey Rule.

What about Debt Instruments: Loans?

According to Cornell Law School, a loan is "a form of debt where one party agrees to lend money to another."[10] Debt refers to monetary amounts owed and a loan is a structured agreement of one party to lend to another.

Though loans are financial instruments, they are not considered securities. Transfer or acquisition of securities requires working through a broker dealer and are subject to more onerous regulation. Loans can be transferred or acquired directly between parties though settlement may take days to weeks.

In the case *Reves v. Ernst & Young*, the Supreme Court explained that multiple types of notes are *not* securities under federal securities law, and even if a loan doesn't squarely fall into one of the mentioned categories, a note still will not be deemed a security if it bears a "family resemblance" to any of them.

Loan participations and syndications are generally not securities but can at times be viewed as investment contracts. Participations and syndications are in essence a fractionalized loan where a portion is sold to or financed by typically institutional bodies. To determine if these loans are securities, four questions must be asked:

1. Are the loans for commercial purposes or investment purposes?
2. Is the lending for speculative or investment?
3. Has it been advertised as an investment?
4. Is it governed by another regulator body?

If issuing the loan is deemed for commercial purposes or if it's governed by another regulatory body, it is generally not deemed a security. It seems the more participants involved and the less institutional they are, the more likely a loan is deemed a security that's regulated under securities law.

Why is this important? Syndicated loans can be similar to tokenized or fractionalized loans. Will introducing technology to the loan market make the instruments securities and therefore subject to more burdensome regulation? It seems that including retail investors in the offering may make it more likely to be deemed a security.

Blockchain-based debt instruments using smart securities can automate bonds and decrease friction, saving time and money. It seems that institutional grade digital debt assets that are not offered to retail investors could still be viewed as syndicated loans. Time will tell.

What about Bonds?

Bonds, which are issued by a company, government, or municipality to raise money, are securities. They can also be offered for structured product pools and backed by pools of mortgages, student loans, or credit card receivables. The investor purchases the bond, and the issuer agrees to pay them back the face value plus interest for a certain period of time.

While publicly issued bonds are registered securities, privately issued bonds are generally a 144A exemption transaction and are not registered with the SEC. Infrequently traded to fewer investors, they are not listed on a public exchange. Rule 144A limits future buyers to qualified institutional buyers (QIB), which are companies or sophisticated investors that manage a portfolio of $100 million, not retail buyers. If a bond were to be tokenized and fractionalized, allowing a more accessible pool of retail investors, it is expected that the bond would still be a security and subject to securities regulation.

What Does This Mean for Tokenized Products?

Would tokenized private assets be securities even if their underlying asset is a commodity or a loan? Syndication vs. tokenization? What about fractionalization? Would creating a programmable digital asset be considered a security?

When referring to tokenization, we are assuming the ownership and value transfer take place on-chain. The increased efficiency added with the new technology still abides by existing securities law.

It seems that if the target investor is retail, it is likely it would be a security with regulation to protect the end investor. If the structure is institutional in nature, it may stay the same definition it is today. This all seems less gray and doesn't seem to be the technology defining the investment, but the intent, collateral, structure, and target investor.

There are nuances to the current securities law and technology applications that need to be ironed out. While regulators have the unenviable position in determining the next iteration of technology applications in traditional finance, they will create clarity for the Hoodies and Suits to build, structure, and apply by understanding the goal posts.

9

Here Come the Regulators

"I am a patriot. I want America to win. Thoughtfully embracing bitcoin and digital assets is how we win."

– US Senator Cynthia Lummis

After a successful IPO in April 2021 requiring registration with the SEC, Coinbase (NASDAQ: COIN) reached a market cap of $18 billion. Two years later, the SEC filed suit against Coinbase for "operating its crypto asset trading platform as an unregistered national securities exchange, broker, and clearing agency," claiming it made billions of dollars unlawfully.

Around the same time, the SEC accused the largest global cryptocurrency marketplace, Binance, and its founder, Changpeng Zhao, for operating an "unregistered broker, exchange, and clearing agency."[1] Binance had accounted for almost 70 percent of the crypto market trading by 2022, amounting to billions of dollars a day. Binance had claimed to have restricted US investors' access to Binance.com. In turn, Binace.us was launched for the US market and US investors, but the SEC alleged that the two entities were not truly separate. Then in 2023, the US Commodity Futures Trading Commission (CTFC) filed suit against Binance, claiming they had transacted in illegal off-exchange derivatives in "digital assets that are commodities, including bitcoin, ETH, and litecoin for persons in the United States."

Setting the Stage

The issue is how regulators look at cryptocurrencies as either commodities or securities. While a professor at Massachusetts Institute of Technology, Gary Gensler, who'd later become SEC Chair, said, "Over 70 percent of the crypto market is bitcoin, ETH, litecoin, bitcoin cash. Why did I name those four? They're not securities. Three-quarters of this [digital asset] market are not securities." But as SEC Chair, Gensler changed his tune, refusing to comment in his testimony before the House Financial Services Committee about whether ETH was a security or a commodity in the eyes of the SEC.

As SEC Chairman Gensler, he told the crowd at the Aspen Security Forum, "Right now, we just don't have enough investor protection in crypto. Frankly, at this time, it's more like the Wild West." He called crypto an asset class that's "rife with fraud, scams, and abuse," and he worried that if the SEC didn't take a stance, investors would end up hurt. He said that crypto was being offered and sold as securities, and securities must be registered with the SEC.

This was years after the unregulated ICO boom and its subsequent bust that saw billions raised for blockchain and crypto start-ups, only to flop a few years later. In late 2017, the amount of funds raised by ICOs topped $1.5 billion, but by the end of 2018, funding had all but dried up (see Figure 9.1). Some 80 percent of ICOs had been identified as scams that year, and more than one thousand crypto projects were reported "already dead" by TechCrunch. NASDAQ CEO Adena Friedman meanwhile warned that ICOs were really securities offerings that could either become something interesting or "become the Beanie Baby phenomenon."

At issue was (and is) the lack of oversight of the crypto market because many cryptocurrencies, NFTs, or other financial assets were launched that fit within the definition of a security. For instance, the investor is passive and expects an increase in value. When we talk about investing in cryptocurrency, that sounds like a security, and if an asset is a security, it must be registered with and regulated by the SEC or meet an applicable exemption. Though not all seem to fall into this criteria.

Crypto can fall outside of the definition of securities because it's decentralized, so there are no intermediaries helping investors derive profit, and market factors drive the price, rather than issuer actions or marketing (see Chapter 8).

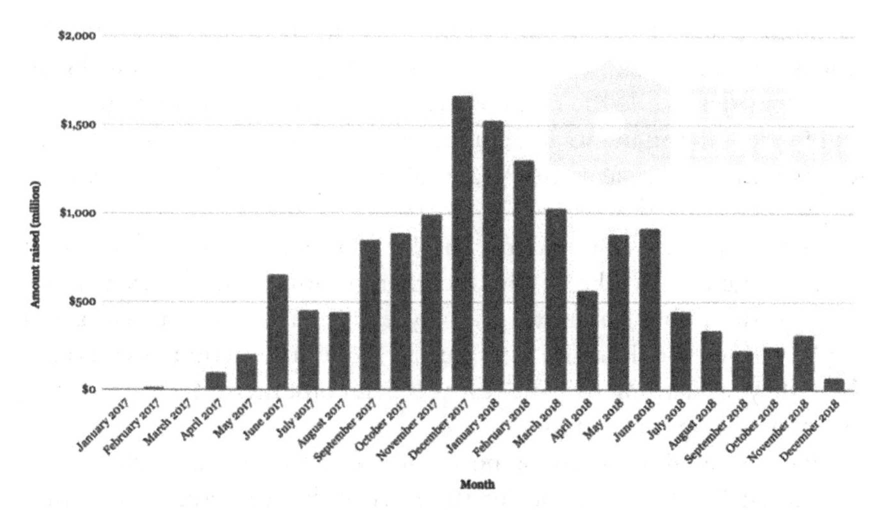

Figure 9.1 ICO Funds Raised
Source: The Block

But ICOs are a different story. In a 2018 speech called, "Beaches and Bitcoin," SEC Commissioner Hester M. Peirce said that cryptocurrencies are unlikely to be considered securities, but tokens used in ICOs might be, because they're sold to raise funds. She wondered, though, what they became after the ICO:

> *"Are they still securities, subject to all the regulations that follow securities into the secondary market? Or are they something else? A commodity? A currency? Something in the nature of a Chuck E. Cheese token?"*

While the IRS is clear that the conversion of digital assets is a taxable event, the SEC still isn't quite sure whether they are ever or never securities, and the collapse of Sam Bankman-Fried's FTX (see Chapter 4) caught their attention. They've announced lawsuits and settlements with several crypto firms for offering unregistered securities to investors.

Chairman Gensler agreed with his predecessor, Jay Clayton, who had told the US Senate, "I believe every ICO I've seen is a security." He added, "I want to go back to separating ICOs and cryptocurrencies. ICOs that are securities offerings, we should regulate them like we regulate securities offerings. End of story."

When it comes to digital assets, there is a lack of regulatory clarity. Obviously, it is clear that blockchain is not bitcoin; however, the technology does add new rails to the current financial system, and the regulatory rails cross between the two – cryptocurrencies and digital asset securities. While the cryptocurrency ecosystem is facing regulatory hurdles, it's important to remember that crypto is a proof of concept for institutional digital assets. As a result, much can be learned from the crypto regulatory discussion.

Alex Strzesniewski, founder of DeFi protocol AngelBlock, told Cointelegraph, "It's like a schoolteacher berating you for giving the wrong answers but failing to give any explanation beyond that. I also don't believe that the SEC does, in fact, have jurisdiction over everything they're claiming to." The fear was that consumer interest in crypto investments might take a hit.

It's a clear illustration of how hard it is to regulate fast-moving innovation. While regulation for the internet has centered around privacy, net neutrality, and cybercrime, proposed crypto regulation is based mainly on finance, and the finance industry is heavily regulated in the United States.

Yet even with oversight by regulatory bodies such as the Financial Industry Regulatory Authority (FINRA), the industry has seen its share of fraud and insider trading. Not only were Bernie Madoff's Ponzi scheme funds legally subject to regulations, but he also happened to be the chairman of NASDAQ, flying under the radar – until he wasn't.

Crypto remains largely unregulated and volatile. Though digital asset commercials were so prevalent at the 2022 Super Bowl, it was dubbed the "Crypto Bowl," the industry's prices tumbled, and several top companies went bankrupt later that year.

The path to digital asset adoption has been paved with regulatory murkiness. The lack of regulatory clarity increases risks and curbs engagement in blockchain technology by institutions. It's true that regulation has always been reactive, not proactive, which makes it truly difficult to roadmap innovation. Yet the best way to build smart regulation is to work together with the regulators, educating without over-regulating a technology that is still innovating.

Meanwhile, major institutions are putting money behind blockchain and implementing ways to use the technology in-house and for client deals. Big banks, including Citibank, Goldman Sachs, JPMorgan, Morgan Stanley, and Societe Generale, and asset managers such as Apollo, BlackRock, KKR, Northern Trust, State Street, and Vanguard, are just a few of the builders and first movers in the future of more efficient finance.

Some view digital assets as a new asset class. That's because Bitcoin, NFTs, and other cryptocurrencies don't fall into a historically defined asset group. In fact, "digital asset" is a broad term that includes traditional securities in digital form. For example, equity, private funds, private placements, debt, and even money market funds are digital assets – existing asset classes in digital form. Regulatory issues over custody, trading, and classification straddle both worlds.

Digital assets are traceable, with an indisputable record ownership, a trait that's viewed positively by US regulators. Similarly, digital securities have KYC/AML whitelists built in, ensuring that the investors are known and approved while simultaneously making loss or theft impossible. Investors can benefit from the added efficiency of blockchain as well, with decreased counterparty risk, speed of transactions, and access to information.

This is a good time for the Suits to enter the picture to work with the powers that be for smart regulation, and they have already. *Fortune* reported in 2022 a "talent exodus" from Wall Street to crypto that would accelerate, likening it to the Dot-Com boom. Yet that was before the bankruptcies and SEC crackdown, before Bankman-Fried was convicted of fraud, before the founder of crypto exchange Thodex was sentenced to 11,196 years in a Turkish prison for crimes, including fraud.

A Word from the Experts

The best and brightest legal minds in the industry offered to kindly share their thoughts on industry questions, issues, and solutions ahead. Commenting are a hoodie-wearing Suit, a commodities lawyer, and a securities lawyer.

Jason Allegrante is chief legal and compliance officer at Fireblocks, a software solution that allows institutions to hold crypto-assets and engage the ecosystem. His prior experience includes Davis Polk & Wardell, LLP and the Federal Reserve Bank of New York. He holds his BA and a JD from Columbia University. Here are his thoughts on constructive digital asset regulation given the current environment:

> *The emergence of blockchain technologies poses a fundamental challenge to legal and regulatory frameworks that have been in place for decades. Although these challenges are not limited to financial services, this is the area where the tension has been felt most acutely in the early days of adoption and into the present.*

At root, this challenge pitted those with a vision of decentralization and the "sovereign citizen" against the legal and institutional status quo – a legal world order literally built on the assumption of the need for intermediaries. These disagreements were not necessarily born of bad faith on either side, but they were clearly expressions of different visions, with decentralizing viewed as an inherent good on one side and, at worst, an attempt to evade money laundering rules and disrupt incumbents.

How to resolve this inherent tension? Different jurisdictions have taken different approaches, each with its own risks and rewards.

The easiest and perhaps most prevalent approach to date is to do nothing. There are certainly advantages, including for entrepreneurs who are permitted to build unencumbered. However, we also know this tends to lead to failure and consumer harm, sometimes on a mind-boggling scale. In the long run, this model does not seem entirely tenable at more mature stages of ecosystem development.

A middle approach has been adopted by some. Where this has been tried, an attempt is made to draw digital assets into the regulatory perimeter by insisting there are workable analogies to existing rules. The United States is a particularly stark example of the difficulty of doing this, not least because it has become obvious that the technology – decentralized and without intermediaries – is fundamentally incompatible with certain major aspects of the legacy framework.

A better approach still – although not without risks – is that taken by the EU with MiCA [Markets in Crypto-Assets Regulation] and, increasingly, other jurisdictions interested in taking a leadership role. This approach treats a digital asset as a digital asset and, potentially, unlocks innovation. To date, however, these frameworks have also been prone to not going far enough in the direction of innovation. It remains to be seen how much more successful they can be than the middle ground alternative.

What does the future hold? Nothing less than the potential to remake multinational law in ways both anticipated and wholly unanticipated. It is fairly obvious, for example, that multinational organizations are taking an interest. It is impossible to say what will result from lawmaking from incumbent interests, but it is more likely than not that we are on the cusp of a shift in the global regulatory environment not seen since the financial crisis of 2008–09.

It's clear that digital assets, cryptocurrencies, and blockchain open a more global financial world.

Next, we learn about how the antiquated legacy legal framework was constructed decades before the rise of technology. Today's technology is upgrading money, investments, and the transfer of value which is highly regulated. It brings us back to the main question: How can regulators best regulate innovation? Let's dive in deeper. Two esteemed legal experts have shared their thoughts.

Kari Larsen is partner and co-head of Willkie Digital Works, at Willkie, Farr & Gallagher LLP. Her prior experience includes the CFTC regulatory body; Perkins Coie, LLP; Reed Smith, LLP; McDermott Will & Emery; and General Counsel at LedgerX. She holds a BA from Binghamton University and a JD from American University. Kari is an expert on commodities law.

Tiffany J. Smith is a partner at WilmerHale, where she is co-chair of the Blockchain and Cryptocurrency Working Group. Previously, she worked for M&T Bank. She holds a BA and a JD from George Washington University. Tiffany is an expert on securities regulatory matters.

Annelise Osborne:

What should the regulatory definition of a digital asset be? Does there need to be a regulatory distinction between digital asset securities from digital asset commodities?

Kari Larsen:

It's complicated to determine a clear and straightforward regulatory definition for a digital asset as they are varied in characteristics, purpose, structure, style of offering, and sales. I commend the efforts untaken so far by legislatures and regulators attempting to do so.

Regardless of the complexity, it is evident from current market ambiguity that there must be a clear regulatory distinction between digital asset securities and digital assets that are commodities at a minimum. As a digital asset ultimately is just an entry in a ledger, it can represent virtually anything, including real world assets, but also rights, services, financial obligations, identity, and other real world or digital characteristics. As with tangible assets, not everything that may be transacted in digital commerce is necessarily appropriately regulated by the SEC or CFTC (or at all). But with regulators using enforcement actions to craft regulatory obligations, additional regulatory clarity is clearly necessary to allow business growth in the US.

The securities and commodities legal and regulatory regimes represent distinct regulatory frameworks governing different financial instruments, participants, and markets. For example, securities laws tend to focus on ensuring disclosure, transparency, fair trading practices and other investor protections, with a strong focus on retail customer participation. The commodities and derivatives legal regime tends to focus on the trading of physical goods or raw materials like agricultural products, energy resources and metals, and the derivatives contracts having such commodities as the underlying foundation. The participants are mostly end users hedging their market risks having a deep understanding of the products or sophisticated investors and speculators. The commodities and derivatives regulatory regime, overseen by the US Commodity Future Trading Commission, is designed to supervise the trading and delivery of these instruments, to foster quality standards and market resilience, and to protect market users from fraud, market manipulation and other market abuses. The CFTC generally is very supportive of innovative products and technology that buttress those goals.

While both regimes attempt to maintain market integrity and protect investors, they differ significantly in scope and style of regulatory requirements. The securities law regime is more prescriptive regarding exactly what is required, particularly with respect to retail investors, while the commodities/derivatives regime offers "Core Principles" designed to provide those regulated by it with some flexibility in how they comply. Digital asset market participants would need to be able to clearly understand where a particular digital asset and/or digital asset transaction falls within the financial regulatory framework in the United States in order to prepare for a compliance regime or develop procedures for digital asset activities. Driven by the current Chair of the SEC Gary Gensler, the SEC's current regulation-by-enforcement regime (see response below) is unfortunately only adding confusion to the market with its very aggressive stance. In addition, not all courts are in agreement with the SEC's positioning, resulting in sometimes conflicting and unclear results for market participants, with little opportunity (or a lengthy wait) for further guidance.

I also would note that there is precedent for different regulators having specific non-overlapping jurisdiction with respect to the same or similar assets. For example, the Dodd-Frank Wall Street Reform and Consumer Protection Act classified certain index derivatives as securities and others as commodity derivatives, depending upon the components of the relevant index. Treasury and the CFTC split jurisdiction over currencies, depending upon the type of offering. Even Howey, the often-cited precedent for the definition of what is an investment contract, recognized that the investment contract was a security, but that didn't necessarily affect the classification of the oranges themselves, or the orange groves, as commodities.

The Digital Asset Market Structure Discussion Draft, which was generally well received by the industry, is a respectable start in attempting to create a distinction between when a digital asset may be a security and when one may be a commodity and also seeks to define the concept of decentralization to provide further clarity for classification.

Tiffany J. Smith:

There is no uniform definition of "digital asset." Instead, most regulators in the US use different definitions. For example, in the context of custody guidance, the SEC defined a digital asset as "an asset that is issued and/or transferred using distributed ledger or blockchain technology ('distributed ledger technology'), including, but not limited to, so-called 'virtual currencies,' 'coins,' and 'tokens.'"[2]

The CFTC as well as certain state regulators generally view digital assets as a form of currency and use terms and definitions reflective of this view. For example, the CFTC views assets like BTC as a "virtual currency" and defines the term as "a medium of exchange, a unit of account, and/or a store of value." The New York Department of Financial Services (NYDFS) similarly uses the term "virtual currency," and defines it as "any type of digital unit that is used as a medium of exchange or a form of digitally stored value."[3]

The definitions of digital assets or virtual currencies do not differentiate between stable or volatile assets. Instead, the definitions focus on the use of blockchain/DLT (SEC) or the fact the asset is a medium of exchange (CFTC and NYDFS). Based on these broad definitions, it seems that stablecoins can be included within these definitions, but some regulators have a separate definition of stablecoins. For example, in a Congressional Research report,[4] *stablecoins were defined as "digital financial instruments that use technology underpinning cryptocurrencies but attempt to eliminate the volatility by pegging their value to a stable asset. There is current pending legislation that would regulate stablecoins separately from other digital assets. Specifically, in August 2023 the House Financial Services Committee approved the "Clarity for Payment Stablecoins Act of 2023" which would create a regulatory framework for the issuance and oversight of payment stablecoins. Notably, this bill is separate from the bill passed by the Financial Innovation and Technology for the 21st Century Act, which would provide a framework for digital assets generally.*

Annelise Osborne:

Does there need to be more clarity regarding digital asset securities vs. securities transactions involving digital assets?

Kari Larsen:

Absolutely. And this is currently under scrutiny in a number of lawsuits. For background, currently, the SEC generally is categorizing digital assets as "investment contracts" under the Howey test. The Supreme Court defined an investment contract as a contract, transaction, or scheme whereby a person invests money in a common enterprise with a reasonable expectation of profits to be derived from the efforts of others. SEC v. W.J. Howey Co., 328 US 293 (1946) [emphasis added].

In its complaints, settlements, and general discussion involving crypto assets under the investment contract framework, the SEC started to use the term "crypto asset securities." In doing so, the SEC is essentially advancing the theory that a digital asset, in and of itself, is an investment contract and therefore a security. The SEC staff has also cited digital asset secondary market trading as supportive of this interpretation. However, while digital assets may be the subject of an investment contract, prior investment contract case law does not support the notion that the asset, in and of itself, will necessarily constitute an investment contract.

This interpretation is not necessarily gaining traction outside the SEC itself, as both judges in the recent Ripple Inc. and Terraform Labs decisions reasoned that a digital asset – when considered in isolation – is not an investment contract. Just as the oranges in the seminal Howey case did not constitute securities, digital assets themselves do not automatically constitute securities. There also are a handful of SEC no-action letters which provide some guidance on selling tokenized products without implicating investor contract status under Howey. However, given this ambiguity, legislative guidance on the distinctions between investment contracts and underlying non-security assets and providing guardrails to issuers and developers would be greatly appreciated by market participants.

Annelise Osborne:

What are some of the larger issues that you see and how do you recommend we solve them?

Kari Larsen:

One significant issue that the digital asset industry tends to face is a branding issue, which may be marked by a lack of mainstream understanding and a perception of high risk. With the SEC and CFTC both primarily pursuing a "regulation by enforcement" strategy at this time, and that new markets generally are susceptible to significant fraud due to a lack of general public understanding of the products and markets, the public is mostly hearing bad news regarding digital assets. This has not been helped by some of the initial players in the space being somewhat hostile to banks and regulation in general, as they perceive cryptocurrency usage as a method to reduce or eliminate the reliance on intermediaries in financial transactions. In addition, despite its potential to revolutionize finance, the extreme volatility and periodic use of digital assets for illicit activities have contributed to a level of skepticism among the general public. It sometimes feels that the industry has yet to rebrand from the early days of bitcoin being a means of engaging in nefarious activities via Silk Road, which was shut down a decade ago.

This branding issue is also exacerbated by certain digital asset market participants that promise investors exceptional rates of return and high yield, but ultimately scam or "rug" the participants in those projects. Various industry members have discussed publishing market guidance and have even attempted to self-regulate crypto-asset market participants, but this is a challenge without legislation providing clarity and delegating authority and enforcement powers to a self-regulatory organization.

Moreover, solving the branding issue has to begin with education and thoughtful regulation. For example, if the general public and regulators have a better understanding of the industry, and the breadth of the solutions being attempted by developers in this space, then people may be more willing to try and participate in the market legitimately, and not just as a get rich quick scheme. Additionally, many institutional players as well as retail investors would be less skeptical of the industry if thoughtful regulations were enacted, providing guardrails and certainty to digital asset products, resulting in larger and more familiar names engaging with the market. The approval of a spot bitcoin ETF may further support a rebranding as it creates more traditional products that will promote robust participation by more traditional investors.

The biggest issue I see is the lack of regulatory clarity. The SEC claims most crypto assets are securities, but the securities registration framework is not fit for the purpose for crypto. As a result, if the SEC brings an enforcement action against a crypto market participant, that market participant either has to settle the charges and discontinue the activity (since there is no way to lawfully continue it) or decide to litigate with the SEC, which is very expensive thus practically only an option for larger companies. Considering stablecoins, and adding banking and payments regulatory regimes to the mix will further muddy the regulatory waters.

Annelise Osborne:

What about tokenization of real-world assets? How do we navigate the regulatory regimes for the underlyings and does that bring those tokenized products into the securities regulatory regime?

Kari Larsen:

Offerings of tokenized real world assets are increasingly common. Tokenization may lead to more efficient clearing, reconciliation, and settlement processes, intraday financing, global trade solutions, and simpler and more secure delivery of real world assets or title to such assets.

However, in the US, it is important to conduct a securities analysis on the underlying asset and the effect of tokenization. Any tokenized security will be treated as a security, and all issuers of tokenized securities and intermediaries dealing with the tokenized securities must comply with all laws and regulations applicable to traditional securities. The SEC has to date been unwilling to materially change any existing regulatory requirements to accommodate these products and, if anything, has made it more difficult for these products to trade. For example, broker-dealers that offer custody of tokenized securities cannot custody other types of securities (or non-security crypto assets like BTC). Also, transfer agents still need to keep ordinary master securityholder records and these records control over the state of any blockchain.

With respect to tokenizations of non-security assets, like non-security real world assets (RWAs) themselves (e.g., orange groves, gold bars, art), tokenized RWAs can be sold as investment contracts, thus triggering securities regulatory requirements. Given the SEC's enhanced focus on crypto products, sellers of tokenized RWAs have to take more care in the marketing of these products than RWAs themselves. But it is common to sell and transfer ownership of RWAs that are maintained with a custodian via a document of title or warehouse receipt. These instruments are typically not deemed to be investment contracts unless the seller advertises that the value of the RWAs will increase based on the seller's efforts (e.g., in selecting a profitable arrangement of RWAs and finding a market for the RWAs). There is significant case law dealing with whiskey warehouse receipts and certificates of title to precious metals that will be instructive on these issues. However, the issuer must comply with the provisions of UCC Article 7 to offer a valid document of title.

Courts may view instruments that are not compliant with UCC Article 7 as something else entirely, and this may lead some courts to deem these products to be investment contracts or another type of security (e.g., transferable share, certificate of interest or participation in a profit-sharing arrangement). In particular, courts will consider whether the token is redeemable for the associated RWAs and/or fractionalizable. Case law regarding securitizations will be instructive in this analysis. In short, at least initially, the structuring and contracts concerning tokenization of RWAs will have to be carefully structured and involve proficient legal analysis.

Annelise Osborne:

Are institutions comfortable utilizing DeFi? What does the future of DeFi look like in the United States?

Kari Larsen:

It's difficult to generalize and say institutions are comfortable utilizing DeFi. However, I do think there are some institutions that have highly sophisticated digital asset teams that use DeFi comfortably and are developing their own protocols. Some institutions are analyzing the potential of DeFi protocols for multiple purposes, such as lending, clearing and settlement, and ledger and other back office solutions.

One potential future of DeFi could see the DeFi protocol front ends being subject to some form of regulation. Front ends are the most popular way to access and interact with DeFi protocols today, and include a web-based graphical user interface with forms, buttons, and other visual components that enable users to perform various actions within a DeFi protocol. This may be a simpler first step towards integrating DeFi into regulatory regimes.

Annelise Osborne:

Will US entities move offshore more substantively to access these markets and products?

Kari Larsen:

Yes, and it's been happening for years. There is a significant viewpoint that the regulatory uncertainty in the United States has resulted in talent (e.g., developers) and businesses relocating offshore so that they can build and operate with more confidence, and without the threat of regulatory enforcement. In my personal experience, particularly this year after the collapse of FTX, I've assisted a number of clients open non-US offices for certain activities, if not move their businesses out of the US altogether.

For example, the British Virgin Islands, Bermuda, Cayman Islands, Ireland, the UK, Singapore, and others have tried to establish themselves as digital hubs for those seeking to build and operate compliant digital asset business in non-US jurisdictions.

Annelise Osborne:

Is there anything else you would like to share about digital asset/blockchain regulation?

Kari Larsen:

We are still early. Although it may not feel like it, we are still in the early days of the development of this technology and asset class.

Regulation is a significant undertaking, and new legislation even more so, especially when it involves an industry and asset class as complex and novel as digital assets. For example, traditional concepts are challenged by "decentralization." What should a regulatory definition of decentralization mean? What should it look like? Given the nuances native to the industry, legislators and regulators alike should be exerting time and resources to better understand the industry, technology, potential risks, and potential solutions potentially collaborating with academia to further education efforts. Legislators and regulators also should be conducting extensive conversation with a wide variety of market participants and only then subsequently put forth thoughtful legislation, followed by thoughtful regulation.

The last thing we should want is to disadvantage the United States relative to other countries that are positioning themselves as digital hubs and welcoming this industry. The United States must ensure that it is not losing talent, successful businesses, the drive to innovate and market presence by stifling growth of this industry. We will lose more than just our standing in the world with respect to this wave of technology. The technology evolution on many fronts is coming fast and furious and we should be strongly supporting those innovating in this industry as well as those working on the next technology developments to ensure the US continues to be on the cutting edge.

Annelise Osborne:

How do we protect investors while embracing new technology?

Tiffany J. Smith:

My view is that the best way to protect investors is passing tailored digital asset regulation designed to address the unique risks of digital assets. Certain regulators like the SEC take the view that most digital assets are securities and therefore these assets should comply with the securities regulatory framework. However, this framework does not take into account the differences in digital assets and traditional assets, or the fact that the federal securities laws are designed for operating companies, not crypto protocols/networks. For example, when a traditional asset is registered, the issuer must provide information, including audited financials and information about the officers and directors, and describe its business. Most token projects are designed to be decentralized and not under the control of a person or group of persons, so it may not be possible to identify the issuer. Assuming an "issuer" can be identified, in addition to the registration requirements for information that cannot be provided by the issuer, most importantly the registration requirements do not address topics that would be viewed as "material" to a purchaser of a crypto asset like the governance rights of the crypto asset (token), the cybersecurity of the network, or general information design.

Annelise Osborne:

How do you see the path to institutional digital assets progressing?

Tiffany J. Smith:

I believe more institutional investors will be open to digital assets once we have regulatory clarity and a framework to register crypto assets. Most institutions are licensed/registered with various government agencies and either cannot receive the permissions/authorizations from their primary regulator to engage in crypto activity or do not want to risk being involved in activity that is viewed as violating the law. For example, entities that are regulated by the federal prudential regulators (Federal Reserve Bank, Office of the Comptroller of the Currency, Federal Deposit Insurance Company) must seek permission from their regulator before engaging in crypto activities.

Annelise Osborne:

Do you believe there are other jurisdictions outside the United States that have regulated responsibly while allowing for innovation? What can we learn from them?

Tiffany J. Smith:

I am not an expert on non-US regulations but do know that jurisdiction like the EU (MICA), Singapore, and Bermuda have adopted crypto-specific regulations. While not perfect, these regulations allow companies to create crypto products and services without the threat of enforcement action. These regulations also have resulted in US companies seeking licenses and opening operations in these countries. One example is the license that Coinbase recently received to operate in Bermuda.

Annelise Osborne:

What do you see as the path to success on digital asset custody regulation?

Tiffany J. Smith:

It's a tall order, but the various regulatory agencies (e.g., banking regulators, SEC, states) need to come together and create uniform standards. Currently, each regulator has separately addressed custody from its perspective and has not coordinated with other agencies. For example, the SEC issued guidance regarding the custody of digital asset securities for broker-dealers, and separately issued a proposal rule addressing the custody of digital assets by investment advisors.

Annelise Osborne:

Can you comment on the adoption and regulation of stablecoin?

Tiffany J. Smith:

Today most stablecoin issuers are regulated at the state level as money services businesses or trusts. These regulations do not address key items important to stablecoins, like stablecoin reserve requirements, so there has been an effort to pass more comprehensive legislation. The House Financial Services Committee introduced the Payments Stablecoins Act of 2023. If passed, this bill will provide a regulatory framework for fiat-based stablecoins.

Annelise Osborne:

Do you see a regulatory path forward for digital dollar or CBDC projects?

Tiffany J. Smith:

I do not think the US will move forward with a digital dollar or CBDC in the near future. Amongst other issues, there are privacy concerns with the US government having the ability to view each purchase of consumers. In reality, this can be addressed, but this has become a large gating issue even among legislatures that are largely in favor of crypto regulation. This concern is key because the Treasury does not have authority to issue a CBDC, it needs specific authorization from Congress.

In addition, with the creation of comprehensive stablecoin regulation, it is not clear that a CBDC/digital dollar is necessary. My projection is that the stablecoin regulation passes and the various government agencies closely monitor how the stablecoin market evolves before deciding whether to move forward with a CBDC.

Annelise Osborne:

Does digitizing a loan make it a security? How do you see this affecting the debt market and digitized debt market moving forward?

Tiffany J. Smith:

It is possible that "digitizing" a loan would create an investment contract, a type of security. Critically, an investment contract can be created from any type of underlying asset, even a non-security like a loan. In the past, the SEC has taken the view that loan marketplaces like Prosper[5] *were creating securities.*

Because digitizing or tokenizing existing financial products and real-world assets has tremendous potential, there is interest in providing clarity so this market can develop. For example, Congressman French Hill noted in an interview that there is interest in passing legislation for tokenizing assets.[6]

Annelise Osborne:

Where do you see the best applications of digital asset securities given the current regulatory environment?

Tiffany J. Smith:

One of the best applications of digital asset securities is tokenized private placements. If these offerings are initially issued as tokenized, the offering memorandum requires the necessary disclosures regarding the tokenization, so the question of whether tokenizing an existing security creates a new security is avoided. There's also a use case since, historically, private placements are illiquid. Using blockchain technology as a secondary market platform can be created so purchasers can easily find each other and seek liquidity if necessary.

Annelise Osborne:

How do you see the trading of digital asset securities advancing?

Tiffany J. Smith:

As noted above, regulatory clarity is needed for the trading of digital asset securities to truly advance. One of the key benefits of blockchain technology is that it can replace the various intermediaries in a transaction. Today, the SEC is still insisting that digital asset market participants use the same intermediaries used in traditional securities transactions (e.g., clearing agencies) although blockchain technology makes them unnecessary. In order to truly move forward and recognize the benefit of blockchain technology the SEC has to be more open to recognizing the differences in digital securities versus traditional securities.

Annelise Osborne:

How can the industry help regulators in the process of streamlining digital assets for institutions?

Tiffany J. Smith:

The industry can help regulators streamline digital assets for institutions by engaging with regulators and explaining the use cases, potential, and value. The various regulatory agencies have published numerous requests for comments on regulating the digital asset market, and the industry should participate and share their views.

Blockchain innovation benefits companies, countries, economies, investors, and regulators. The United States is the superpower. We will come around.

10

Don't Be Afraid of Change

"Change before you have to."

– Jack Welch

Long before cryptocurrency brought changes to finance, the music industry went through a revolution. The same year that Sony released the first model of the Walkman, a portable music device that played cassette tapes that you had to flip over manually, a 23-year-old British kid named Kane Kramer had an idea: What if you could transfer music onto a portable device using telephone lines? This was before everybody had personal computers on their desks, before people could dial up into the internet, and about 20 years before the invention of the iPod.[1]

Kramer envisioned a device smaller than the Walkman that would store music digitally on a memory chip. It would have a display screen, which users would navigate with their thumbs. It would make any recorded song available, and you'd never again have to flip a cassette tape to hear more music.

Kramer imagined a digital music central service where consumers could load up their devices with songs. They'd not only be located in music stores, but in vending machines in places like gas stations, supermarkets, and bars, a sort of iTunes store, only in person. Production costs would plummet, translating to lower prices for listeners and greater distribution for artists. This, even before the compact disc had even been invented.

So Kramer patented his idea and built a prototype device with a techie friend. They called it IXI. They even got financial backing from Paul McCartney. But there was a problem: It could hold just three-and-a-half minutes of music – barely longer than Elvis Presley's "Heartbreak Hotel." The world's first MP3 player failed to impress the industry, and the infrastructure to support it was never built. Unable to raise the $320,000 to renew patents, Kramer shut down his company, and the technology became public property.

Then in the late nineties, an offshoot of the Korean company Samsung released an MP3 player, but it didn't go over well at a tech conference, because, explains one executive, "No matter how the Korean staff tried to explain what an MP3 player was, people didn't understand why they needed such a device because they could listen to music with CDs or cassettes . . . most people didn't take it seriously."[2]

When a second MP3 device hit the market, the Recording Industry Association of America sued the company that made it and lost. Without that case, there might not even be MP3 music at all. Yet the device never took off. Then in 2001, Apple released the first iPod with a user friendly interface that made it easy to navigate the thousands of songs the device could hold. Suddenly, consumers understood the value of digital music stored and played on a small device.

In 2008, Apple gave Kramer credit for his invention – and a free iPod for his trouble. The tech giant went on to sell some 450 million iPods until it discontinued production in 2022[3] after demand fell as people stored more and more music on their smartphones.

The moral of the story? Technological advances are inevitable, consumers want what they want (until they don't want it anymore), and good ideas have a way of coming to fruition with or without you. Digitizing happens, and there's no sense fighting it.

Digital Assets Are Here to Stay

It's easy to dismiss digital assets as another crypto Ponzi scheme but that would be a mistake. By 2022, more than half of the top 100 banks by assets under management had invested in cryptocurrency and/or blockchain-related companies, reports Blockdata.[4] Nearly a quarter were building custody solutions, "despite being very vocal about how bad Bitcoin supposedly is" and saw the "importance of having a strong strategic position in the crypto economy."[5]

The 2022 KPMG Banking Industry Survey of 100 senior executives found that 92 percent reported that their banks provided or planned to provide digital assets, and 85 percent said the same about digital wallets.[6]

That the ideas came from the Hoodies is hard for Suits to come to terms with, but traditional finance is filled with good ideas shaking up the status quo. For instance, America was in the middle of a recession in 1982 when Michael Bloomberg introduced an innovation that would endure well into the 21st century, the Bloomberg Terminal, which provides real-time financial data and trading tools.[7] Traders take it for granted now, but before this dual-monitor computer system, the stock market wasn't automated.

"Bloomberg was this new startup that was nimble, that was experimenting, that was battling against the Goliaths of the time," Marguerite Gong Hancock, executive director of the Computer History Museum's Center for Entrepreneurs, told *Fast Company* in 2015.

In the 1990s, the Bloomberg system was networked for privacy, security, and speed, and today, it provides more than 320,000 subscribers worldwide financial news, real-time quotes, and research tools.[8] It has competition in the Thomson Reuters system, which offers Eikon software, and lower-priced products such as Capital IQ and FactSet.[9]

It's a great example of a startup shaking up the financial industry for the better. Sometimes, though, innovation comes from big financial institutions, like when Bank of America mailed little pieces of plastic to customers in California in 1958, offering a $500 line of credit,[10] effectively inventing the modern credit card. Before the "Fresno Drop" mailing, consumers had to save up their money to buy something expensive, or put items on layaway, paying in installments before they were allowed to take possession of the item. Credit cards changed all that.

Then there's the ATM. When the first automated teller machine was installed in the wall at Chemical Bank in Rockville Centre, New York, in 1969, an ad to promote the new cash machine promised, "On Sept. 2, our bank will open at 9:00 and never close again!" The earliest ATMs could only dispense cash; they couldn't accept deposits, transfer money between accounts, or check balances, much of which can be done today on a cell phone from just about anywhere. Yet customers adopted ATMs because they liked the idea of no longer standing in long lines for a bank teller.

At first, banks resisted. As *Wired* reported, banks "worried that customers would reject the machines, or that reducing face-to-face interaction with customers would lose opportunities to sell customers other bank services."[11] But customers loved ATMs, and now, they're not only located in banks, but also in supermarkets, convenience stores, bars, gas stations, casinos, hotels, and cannabis dispensaries.

More recently, some industry experts have feared that mobile banking and cashless shopping would kill the ATM, not to mention the bank branch, but that hasn't happened, even as ATM fees reach a record high near $5.00 a transaction.[12] That's likely because nearly 60 percent of consumers still make at least some cash purchases, according to a 2022 Pew Research Center study.[13] But those consumers skew older, with 71 percent of bank customers 50 and older reporting keeping cash on hand, just in case, compared to less than half of people ages 18 to 49.[14]

These are all examples of innovations in finance that meet customers where they are. Mobile payments apps are another good example. Long before you could tip your hairstylist or transfer cash to your college kid with an app on your phone, consumers used checks, credit cards, and cash. Then came PayPal, a digital wallet that allowed electronic payments that were quicker than paper and cards. By 2006, PayPal had 100 million end-user accounts; in 2023, that number was 435 million – more people than the population of America.[15] PayPal typically charges a 2.9 percent fee plus $.30 for transfers.

Venmo was founded in 2009 and was acquired by PayPal five years later. Its social features allow users to comment and share information on their transactions. There are no fees for transfers made with a debit card, prepaid card, or bank account, but Venmo does charge a 1 percent fee for instant transfers. Zelle, on the other hand, is owned by seven of the country's largest banks, among them Bank of America, JPMorgan Chase, and Wells Fargo. Launched in 2017, it allows users to transfer money from their bank account to others via the app. Zelle doesn't charge a fee, but some banks may charge for sending or receiving money via Zelle.

These examples of technological advances in traditional finance have the same components that tokenizing has today:

- improved technology that increases efficiency, speed, and more
- consumer interest

- higher adoption rates by younger users
- interest among large financial institutions

Changes are here already. It's important to adapt.

The Age of Disruption

This is the Age of Disruption, or so says the 4th Annual AlixPartners Disruption Index, which found that three out of four CEOs say their companies face high rates of disruption – and that they're not ready for it. One of the greatest disruptions of our time is technological change, and most companies – 94 percent of growth leaders – are investing in new technologies to keep up.[16]

But humans don't like change. Even monkeys are better at change than we are. A 2019 study of both humans and monkeys discovered that it took humans longer to accept and adapt to new strategies than it took the monkeys. *Psychology Today*[17] cited four reasons we resist change:

1. We prefer to avoid uncertainty.
2. We don't want to feel incompetent.
3. We don't like to feel controlled by others.
4. Change is uncomfortable and requires effort.

Our brains are wired to stay in its comfort zone because that saves energy. It likes to feel certain, and new things, such as new technologies and new methods, aren't certain to us. *Psychology Today* reported, "While the financial markets of 2008 showed once again that the future is inherently uncertain, the one thing that's certain is that people will pay lots of money to at least *feel* less uncertain. That's because uncertainty feels, to the brain, like a threat to your life."[18]

When we feel threatened, we feel fear, and the chemicals in our brains kick in the autonomic nervous system, which typically leads us to respond in one of three ways: fight, flight, or freeze. This natural reaction made sense when we faced threats like animals that wanted to have us for lunch hundreds of thousands of years ago, but it makes less sense in the context of our modern lives.

The amygdala is designed to draw on memories to fuel fear, which is designed to protect us. So if your experience with digital assets is reading headlines about the likes of Sam Bankman-Fried, no wonder you're skeptical, if not fearful, of this particular change.

Plus, change is more work, and you've already got plenty of work to do. But, says *Harvard Business Review*, "Leadership is about change," adding, "To overcome inertia requires a sense of safety as well as an inspiring vision."[19]

It's hard to feel safe when changes happen so quickly, and these days, change is lightning fast. During the US Patent Office's entire first decade in the late 18th century, 229 patents were granted – about the same number the agency grants every seven *hours* today.[20] When personal computers arrived about half a century ago, they weren't very powerful or ubiquitous. Now most of us carry around little computers with access to nearly all the world's information in our pockets. People used to write checks to pay friends back for their portion of dinner out, and now they just Venmo cash on an app.

Change happens, and traditional finance is beginning to bridge from a centralized world using fiat currencies to blockchains with smart contracts and digital assets that provide users with more control and ownership. It is a marathon not a sprint.

McKinsey says that organizations and early adopters of Web3 will offer "significant value."[21] Benefits cited include faster transaction settlements, operational costs savings, accessing democratization, enhanced transparency, and cheaper, more nimble infrastructure.

The concerning part, says Bain & Company, is that 60 percent of senior executives at financial institutions believe that Web3 will disrupt activities historically performed by banks and that change will occur within five to six years.[22] But there's hope.

"Banks are well placed to capture these opportunities because of their history of complying with regulations, their strong risk management and KYC abilities, and the trust that they have earned with many customers," Bain & Company reported in late 2022.[23]

The truth is that Web3 and digital assets are at our doorstep and on the verge of exploding in popularity as more and more companies and people adopt blockchain (see Figure 10.1). As *Forbes* put it, "Ready or Not, Web 3.0 Is Coming. Bold Banks Can Seize the Opportunity."[24] The areas that *Forbes*'s Finance Council sees as having potential are places where banks already excel: consumer data collection, compliance practices, problem-solving for consumers, and forging strategic partnerships with consumers and vendors. What's more, banks can be the go-between for crypto and regulators; the Hoodies and the Suits.

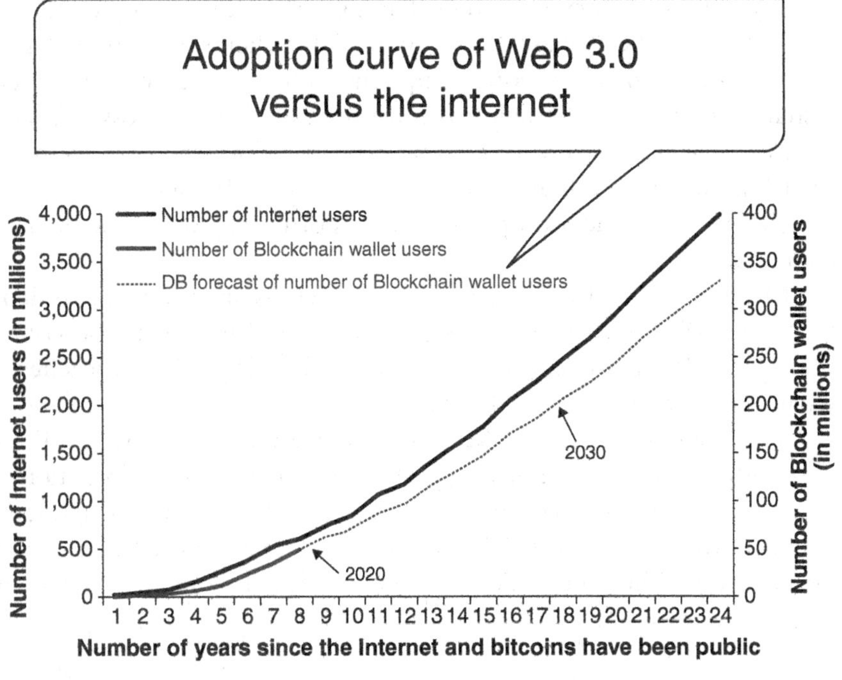

Figure 10.1 Adoption Curve of Web 3.0 versus the Internet
Source: Adapted from Deutsche Bank

In an opinion piece for the *Wall Street Journal,* Goldman Sachs CEO David Solomon said, "I still see blockchain as a promising technology if allowed to innovate under the right conditions. Under the guidance of a regulated financial institution like ours, blockchain innovations can flourish."[25]

When it comes down to it, digitizing and tokenization address the needs of customers, and if banks offer what customers need, they'll stay. For years now, Bank of America has received more deposits from its mobile application than it does at its bank branches.[26] Deloitte reported in its 2024 Banking and Capital Markets Outlook, "Open banking initiatives that give customers more control of their finances are gaining steam in many parts of the world."[27] Technology is providing opportunities for customers in ways never seen before, and "many will be willing to switch accounts and diversify their relationship across multiple platforms with a tap on their smartphones."[28]

If you build it, they will come. Citi's Global Head of Digital Assets, Ryan Rugg, told Coinbase, "We recognize that clients want multi-bank, multi-jurisdiction, cross-border liquidity. They don't want a siloed system; they want to be able to move liquidity freely across a multitude of banks and to streamline that operational process and optimize their liquidity across their markets."[29] No wonder 90 percent of major North American and European banks reported exploring blockchain technologies.[30]

Meanwhile, the daily trading volume of stablecoins is now equivalent to the world's 22nd largest sovereign currency.[31] More than 100 countries are exploring or piloting CBDCs,[32] and by 2021, NFTs reached a staggering market value of $41 billion.[33]

That $600,000 of that went to the sale of a GIF of a cat with a Pop-Tart body is irrelevant. Annoying perhaps, but irrelevant. There's money to be made and new ways to make it. Scoff at the Hoodies if that feels good, but they have unleashed technologies that have brought change to finance. Now's the time to decide if you're going to embrace change or fight it and miss out.

11

Finance's Imminent Upgrade

"There's a way to do it better. Find it."

–Thomas Edison

In 1962, ABC television network aired its first color broadcast, the animated sitcom *The Jetsons*, depicting a typical Space Age family in 2062. The Jetsons lived a life filled with aspirational technology, where the show's writers envisioned many technological advances, including robots for household help, video calls and conferencing, smart watches, tablet computers, voice-activated smart home appliances, 3D printing, jetpacks, and flying cars.

Though the Hoodies are still working on the jetpacks and flying cars, the rest has already become a reality through Apple Watches, Roombas, Zoom, Facetime, iPads, Alexa and Siri, smart refrigerators, and 3D printers. Even individual air travel is available in self-flying planes.

This is traditional finance's Jetsons' moment. How will finance change in the next 5, 10, and 20 years? What will it be like in 2062? We're already starting to see glimpses of how the world is evolving from fiction to fact.

Where Finance Stands Today

On the forefront, a new technology has emerged that makes finance and securities more efficient and faster and increases trust and decreases risk. Blockchain technology born with the launch of the cryptocurrency bitcoin with the intention of disintermediating the banks has actually become a tool for the benefit of the banks and traditional finance.

Today, blockchain technology is maturing. The past 15 years have laid the groundwork toward creating digital assets and programmable securities that are regulatory compliant with similar structures to traditional securities. Institutions are creating live use cases and pilot programs. We are working toward the inflection point.

There is a changing investor demographic, increased demand for investments, and a large-scale distribution of wealth on the horizon. This change is apparent in the markets and indicators. Digital assets and blockchain technology will provide the expected efficiency that this dynamic generational shift embraces and expects.

Finance is already changing. Banking is now done on apps, and funds are wired into accounts instead of mailed by check. The few checks still written can be deposited using an app on your phone. Even bank accounts can be opened online, reducing the reliance on physical bank branches.

Electronic payment apps like Venmo and Zelle have reduced the reliance on cash. PayPal wallet and Apple Wallet allow purchases of goods and services with the click of a button or the tap of the phone. In the world of "cash is king," we no longer need to hold fiat cash.

The retail opportunities are gaining steam, offering benefits to individuals while commercial opportunities are currently being ironed out. New technology offers payments with 24/7/365 access, making "banking hours" soon to be a phrase of the past. Business-to-business payments are undergoing changes. For instance, Citi's recent campaign focuses on liquidity, capital financing, and cross-border payments made possible by the new technology (see Figure 11.1).

Apps aren't just for payments, but also for investing. Robinhood, E-Trade, and eToro are among the first movers with big asset managers now offering apps, and big name traditional finance firms have followed suit, including Charles Schwab, Fidelity, Franklin Templeton, TD Ameritrade, and Vanguard. The asset managers see that digital accessibility is

Figure 11.1 Citi AD
Source: Citi

important, efficient, and the future. Opportunities for more types of investments that digital assets offer is next.

Finance of Tomorrow: Emerging Trends

Blockchain and DeFi have created new trading instruments and financial networks once considered impossible. And this is just the beginning. It's our Jetsons moment.

Much of the innovation will occur behind the scenes, with user experience similar to what is available today – easy to use and comfortable for corporate and individual clients. However, the performance and efficiency will be enhanced to a higher standard, with more functionality.

There are eight emerging market trends in development that will become commonplace in financial markets in the next 5 to 10 years:

1. **Digital money, including stablecoins and CBDC**
2. **Tokenization of asset classes, including new alternative investments classes**
3. **Ownership of investment collateral**
4. **Digital identity**
5. **Utility benefits in securities**
6. **Merging of traditional finance with decentralized finance to form institutional DeFi**
7. **Data, data, data**
8. **Automated/autonomous finance**

The emerging trends will be accompanied by five business shifts that include:

1. **New large players emerge from startups**
2. **Asset managers will drive change**
3. **Refocusing revenue lines by banks**
4. **Expansion of retail investors of the investment universe**
5. **Transformation of wealth management and private banking**

Eight Emerging Trends of Financial Markets

The biggest change will be more efficient financial rails as the backbone of the financial system. People will no longer talk about blockchain but will instead recognize and use the increased efficiency and opportunity found in systems, process, securities, investments, and money. Our path to get there includes a number of upgrades.

1. Digital money becomes mainstream.

Money, in whatever form – bills, notes, gold, shells, and soon to be code – is the foundation of the financial system. Soon, forms of digital money will be commonplace. While credit cards were once a new alternative to cash or bank notes, they are now the payment of choice for many, allowing us to avoid the need to carry cash and permitting us to float the charged expense until the monthly payment is due. Similar to cash, a physical credit card is no longer required for some purchases, because consumers can pay with Apple Pay or Google Pay wallets, linked to a credit card, from their cell phones. The credit card company charges the seller fees and may charge the buyer fees. Many retail establishments are no longer even accepting cash. Will cash money soon become obsolete?

The move from fiat cash-based systems to digital money, electronic money that relies on computers, code, and internet connectivity, has already started. According to *Harvard Business Review*, "over 97 percent of the money in circulation today is from checking deposits – dollars deposited online and converted into a string of digital code by a commercial bank."[1]

The continuance of the digital money trend started to gain traction with bitcoin and led to the launch of hundreds of other cryptocurrencies, which have proven to have volatile prices. From an institutional and retail use perspective, stablecoins will become more mainstream.

Stablecoin crypto assets have had limited use cases within traditional finance; however, that will change. Already, PayPal's stablecoin, PYUSD, (see Chapter 3) offers a large user base of 435 million people an alternative payment option in a wallet familiar to them. In 2022, almost $7 trillion was transacted involving USD-backed stablecoins,[2] greater than that of both Mastercard and PayPal. USDC and Tether have proven out the use case for stablecoin generally through noninstitutional channels, but traditional companies are taking note and recognizing the benefits. In December 2023, S&P issued a stablecoin stability assessment on existing stablecoins highlighting institutional recognition.[3]

The US Federal Reserve issued guidance in 2023 for state banks to launch or engage with stablecoins,[4] requiring them to first obtain a non-objection letter. This shows federal recognition and may help bank stablecoins become more readily available. How will these differ from banknotes issued in the late 1800s and early 1900s that were later consolidated into federal notes in the 1930s?

Bank stablecoins haven't been created as of yet but bank settlement tokens have. They have proven to be beneficial for internal processing and settlement, but they haven't yet lived outside of their greater ecosystem. Two examples include JPMorgan's JPM Coin, which is based on depository receipts that can be used internally only as a settlement token, and Societe Generale's CoinVertible stablecoin, which is available only to qualified institutional investors within their ecosystem. Banks are working to create stablecoins for external uses to be a medium of exchange.

Should individual banks issue currency? That is the job for central banks, and central bank digital currencies (CBDC) or digital dollars will become commonplace. In fact, sovereigns and municipalities in countries that make up 98 percent of the global economy, including the US Federal Reserve, are exploring their use.[5] A digital dollar is embraced by many, though it has a few roadblocks to overcome, both regulatory and commercial. China launched a digital yuan that boasted transactions equivalent to $250 billion USD by end of second quarter 2023.[6] It's expected to eat into the market share of private pay companies AliPay and WeChat, which had accounted for 94 percent of transactions or $16 trillion in value.[7]

CBDCs bring up potential privacy concerns as digital money can easily be tracked. Not everyone wants Big Brother tracking every purchase. Privacy technology is being developed that will be able to act as a privacy buffer. CBDCs also change the ownership structure as digital currencies can be held by individuals in digital wallets, whereas fiat currency is generally held by the banks in accounts. This could decrease money held within the banking system, which would decrease bank lending capabilities. However, with all the clever Suits out there, this could be structured around and resolved.

Digital money will make the world go round faster and more efficiently.

2. Tokenization of asset classes including new alternative investments classes.

The next large-scale shift on the horizon is the expansion and tokenization in the investment market. Tokenization of financial instruments will broaden the opportunities for investments, adding efficiency to existing classes and creating new financial instruments, such as private funds, bonds, loans, and alternatives. The Federal Reserve acknowledges the benefits, "Among the benefits of tokenization, lowering barriers to entry into otherwise inaccessible markets and improving the liquidity of such markets are the most prominent."[8]

Tokenized traditional structures in the private markets, which are almost double the size of public markets, will be commonplace. Between 2000 and 2020, the number of publicly listed companies decreased from 7,810 to 4,814, limiting opportunities for retail investors who don't have access to private markets. Institutional private equity funds and money market funds have been tokenized, while tokenization of real-world assets has started, opening up a new world of access and potential liquidity of alternative investments. Groundwork has been laid to tokenize debt instruments with mortgages, home equity lines, corporate bonds, municipal bonds, and structured finance securitizations.

Portfolio optimization will change from historical norms to include more alternative assets as the wealth paradigm and demand have shifted. The demand for alternatives has increased, especially with both high-net-worth families and the younger generations. Tokenization of investment assets will allow for a new diversification of investing.

For example, investors will be able to long or short assets in specific geographic regions, industries, or vertices more granularly. They could focus on real estate investments in one market, such as Nashville or Tampa, or short a market if they anticipate a downturn in a sector or region such as Los Angeles or Stamford. The digital nature allows investors to trade in and out with less friction. This type of investing is not available today. REITs offer real estate equity exposure, but it is typically specific to property types, not regions and not flexible.

Traditional structures, even company equity, and new structures linked to payments, royalties, or securitizations as well as gaming, brands, art, music, and others, will be created. Brian could invest in his favorite movie series. Rory could invest in his favorite video games. Adina can invest in her favorite city or her favorite NFL player's contract. Investments may become more fragmented and allow for more diversification.

As the ability to buy, hold, and trade them becomes seamless, certain sectors will grow quickly. Infrastructure providers are working on interoperability and connectivity. Custodians are working to accept digital asset securities and debt instruments.

Digital assets can help increase liquidity for illiquid assets by providing a format for trading on digital asset exchanges or ATSs. Of course, liquidity assumes there are active buyers and sellers to create a market. Liquidity is not guaranteed. Large issuances are more likely to be liquid with more potential buyers and sellers. Smaller alternative assets provide a benefit in diversification; however, due to the smaller nature of the investment, potential liquidity could be limited.

Standards, which are important for industry adoption, will be developed and set for tokenized digital assets. Experience, pilot programs, and interoperability will determine optimal structures. Tax and legal structures will also be addressed.

3. Ownership of investment collateral will become important.

Cryptocurrencies and digital assets change the dynamic of ownership of money and securities. For example, when Nate holds his money in a bank, the bank has the right to lend that money to someone else. Nate benefits because he doesn't have to keep his bills under the mattress, and his bank gives him a low interest rate to hold the money. The bank benefits by lending the money out at a higher rate.

When Jamie holds a cryptocurrency in his crypto asset wallet, he maintains custody and ownership. He can in turn then lend out the cryptocurrency to someone who could pay him interest directly. In this instance, Jamie doesn't keep dollar bills in his mattress because he is holding his money in a digital wallet and he makes a higher interest rate on his money by cutting out the bank. Jamie has become the bank.

Crypto financing allows parties to obtain instant liquidity while keeping custody of their assets. Chris wants to hold on to the 10 bitcoins she owns because she believes the value may increase, but she also wants to take a loan out against them for money to use today. She can use the collateral and borrow the value of 5 bitcoin at a rate of, say, 5 percent, a solid rate, given the current environment. Also, Chris benefits from any appreciation for all 10 bitcoins as well as any returns from the borrowed proceeds she put to work. Similarly, digital asset securities will provide the same opportunities as the market grows.

The ownership dynamic of the digital assets opens up never before available opportunities, and this market will grow and morph. Multiple types of digital asset securities will serve as collateral lent out or borrowed against, and its appreciation adds a new level to traditional structures. This will be exciting to watch.

There are, however, risks for the responsibility of your own crypto asset wallets, including potential loss of access, theft, and hacking. That's because the FDIC does not back these wallets like they do bank accounts. Also, bad actors use phishing and hacking to steal in the digital world.

That said, digital wallets can offer a wider range of uses and services than traditional banks can. Also, per regulation, digital securities are sold only to whitelisted parties, so ownership is always known. The digital security can't be traded to someone not on the whitelist, and it is easily tracked. Therefore, digital securities cannot be generally stolen. Other crypto assets, like bitcoin, can because it is not a security and does not require the whitelist for trading. Digital asset transfers leave fingerprints, and so cryptocurrencies have been recovered. However, increases in privacy technology could make traceability more difficult.

In the future state, the user experience for holding assets traditional or digital is expected to be similar to what it is today for most users, with institutions holding assets for clients. Aunt Linda doesn't want to hold her own digital asset securities and lend or borrow against them. But Uncle Gus does want to hold his assets in a digital wallet to personally trade, lend, and borrow. There will definitely be more optionality than there is today and all within a regulated environment.

4. Digital identity will be solved.

The first iteration of digital identity, which is a digital file specific to the individual representing personal information, will be solved. Digital identity will be useful in many different forms. Globally, 850 million people don't have a form of identification,[9] including a birth certificate. Outside of our humanitarian goodness, this matters to finance people because identity affects financial regulations for KYC/AML.

Financial institutions are required to know who their customer is by confirming their identity, thus ruling out or decreasing the risk for an association with identity theft, illegal activities, or financial crimes. The money, too, needs to be checked for any possible links to illicit activity or money laundering.

Many companies are working on solving digital identity, but it can't be resolved through a lone wolf approach. Too many counterparties are involved. When it is solved, the inefficient manual KYC/AML process can be scaled especially with the expectation of more retail investors participating in opportunities.

If someone is running a broker-dealer and accepts a bad actor customer or dirty money, they risk going to jail. Would they trust another company to adequately perform KYC/AML when the penalty is still jail time for them? What about shifting the liability?

Consider air travel. Global Entry and TSA Precheck are federal programs that perform background checks on individuals allowing them to travel in a pre-cleared manner. Clear is a private company offering biometric verification systems at airports to similarly pre-approved travelers. There could be a digital identity Global Entry program run by a financial regulatory body or a private entity working with regulators to perform KYC/AML in finance. This could shift the burden of incarceration for KYC/AML away from broker-dealers.

There are many use cases. Digital identity will also assist in identity theft, health records, driving ability, citizenship, and age verification, among others. Currently, identification is paper based. We can do better. Privacy can and will be protected through digital channels so personal information isn't shared. The development and refinement of zero knowledge proofs will aid in privacy protections.

5. Utility benefits in securities will become available.

Tomorrow's investments will offer perks or utilities, compliant with regulations, in addition to their purchase of a publicly traded stock. What does this mean? The utility benefits will be a boon for brands, including collectibles, increasing communication with more loyal customers, soliciting feedback, and offering early product sales to investors or access to discounts.

An added utility benefit could be valuable to both the companies and the investor. Companies could better engage their investors, including feedback loops and customer loyalty. Customers would benefit from the perk or value, the customer experience, and additional revenue for the invested asset. This isn't limited to public companies or equities.

Think of American Airlines (NASDAQ: AAL) giving investors frequent flier miles or automatic upgrades. Or Mastercard (NYSE: MA) waiving the annual credit card fee or offering loyalty perks for its investors. Or Amazon (NASDAQ: AMZN) providing Amazon Prime memberships to investors.

Business-to-business investors could also benefit. The utility could include a fraction of a discount on goods or services, governance utility, or additional access. Could the utility have value and be traded? Yes, if supplied as a token, the token could be traded or bartered.

After a rocky few years of stock volatility, AMC Entertainment Holding Inc. (NYSE: AMC) announced shareholders perks, including free popcorn at their theaters.

In another example, owners of the Aspen Coin can get complimentary upgrades at the Aspen St. Regis Hotel and other benefits, offering a broader value than just the security itself.

Celebrities and sports teams are already embracing the digital assets' benefits, including community building by developing fans and working to create loyal customers. Among the possible offerings are collectibles, access to fan events, or celebrity meet-and-greets. For celebrities, these utilities could be offered with ticket sales or as investments in a share to a certain song or album royalties. For sports teams, the benefit could similarly be offered to season ticket holders, investors, or to individual players who may securitize income streams.

Game investors could receive game skins, early access, game credits, or conference events. A publishing house company could offer investors early access to expected best-sellers. Internet company investment could offer discounts or additional benefits. Transit bonds could come with metro cards. Real estate investments could offer detailed research, data, or networking opportunities. Home decor companies could offer online design consulting. Clothing companies could offer first access to new lines, fashion show tickets, discounted merchandise, or sample sales. Food company investments could offer recipes and sample snacks testing.

Regulators are looking at utility benefits and the transferability as a potential transfer of value and thus, as a potential security.

6. Merging of traditional finance with decentralized finance to form institutional DeFi.

Decentralized finance has created the next generation of finance. Some developments are similar to traditional finance, and some are different. At its core, DeFi decreases or eliminates fees charged by intermediaries and allows for peer-to-peer transactions, which are faster, better, and cheaper. Why would traditional finance fail to strive to promote faster, better, and cheaper transactions?

True, many traditional finance players are the intermediaries that DeFi is structured to cut out. However, banks and financial institutions provide many services that won't be replaced in the short term because of regulations, fiduciary responsibility, and customer service. There is time to benefit and new opportunities will emerge.

There will be a gradual merging of many traditional and DeFi developments, starting with the institutional and retail adoption of digital assets and leading to applications with more efficient rails and structures. In turn, traditional finance will mimic opportunities provided by the DeFi technology and the financial system, only it will be regulated. We are seeing glimpses of it already with the banks, asset managers, and financial players that are working to embrace digital assets.

Efficiency in lending and staking will occur. Derivatives and more complex structures will benefit most from this technology, leading to complex innovations. Perpetual swaps, for example, as well as atomic swaps, staking, instant settlement, 24/7/365, digital escrows, automated margin calls, and liquidation will be prevalent. Open-source sharing communities will be of a permissioned or private nature, respecting personal information with new privacy applications. Governance tokens will evolve to traditional finance.

Yet, decentralized autonomous organizations (DAOs) without a governing body are still questionable for traditional finance. In a DAO, one person is not in charge, and everyone has the same weighted vote. However, a DAO is similar to a cooperative, which has existed for centuries, and MakerDAO[10] has proven successful within DeFi. How DAOs develop within traditional finance remains to be seen.

Between the Hoodies and the Suits, we will find efficient, novel, and regulatory compliant structures that the market embraces creating institutional DeFi. The future is so bright, we will need virtual reality glasses that allow us both hindsight and foresight.

7. Data, data, data will have value.

Data is an economic asset because it can provide an economic benefit. According to NASDAQ, the world creates 2.5 quintillion bytes of data[11] every day, and that data has value. In fact, data is today's gold, with an estimated global value of $3 trillion USD. Data derived from digital assets and blockchain will add to the daily creation of data and deliver the data clean.

Data has been a monetary windfall from social media companies and can be a quantifiable asset for financial firms. For example, Bloomberg sells financial data, netting an estimated $12 billion in revenue in 2022. Data has value.[12]

Artificial intelligence and machine learning are based on data, which is used to measure risk in the market, credit, or operations to pricing, arbitrage opportunities, and hundreds of other examples. Predictive models are generated from data as are all financial models. Customer data can lead to providing new services and creating innovative business lines.

How is this an emerging trend of financial markets if data is already being used? Poor data has a cost of approximately $13 million USD a year to individual companies, equating to trillions of dollars in aggregate. Blockchain and the digitization of financial instruments does provide useful and economically advantageous data that will be owned by financial institutions using the digital technology in the private and permissioned chains. Public blockchains offer public data. More and better data will be provided from financial and commercial applications. The real-time pricing data, risk data, and credit data that blockchain can provide will be a boon for any company and industry.

"We saw the opportunity to use blockchain to improve the speed and accuracy of some of the slowest sloppiest data from real world private asset data," Patrick O'Meara, chairman and CEO, Inveniam Capital Partners, said. "The real world's data has gaps, opinions, and typos, and what the blockchain sees could easily not correspond to reality . . . So blockchain helped the data by giving it provenance and privacy."[13]

8. Automated finance will become commonplace.

In our technology-driven world, blockchain added to artificial intelligence (AI), machine learning, and data will enable automated and even autonomous finance. Following the likes of the self-driving car and self-flying plane, finance can be automated and parts can be autonomous.

Financial automation is defined as "the utilization of software and other technology to automate financial tasks that have historically been performed manually." In finance, manual tasks include many back office functions of reconciliations, preparing financial statements, record management, data entry, data management, and budgeting. Finance is a spreadsheet of numbers and conditions that can be codified as programmable and, therefore, automated.

Similarly many front office functions can be automated. Front office manual functions include creating financial models, pitch books, research, competitive analysis, managing accounts, and more. Servicing of securities can be automated as can much of the manual entry and process. This will decrease costs, errors, and time, which ideally leads to increased profits and scalability.

"End-to-end AI processing with 100 percent confidence on as much as 80 percent of non-electronic invoices means lower error rates, less manual intervention, and greater cost efficiency," reports *Harvard Business Review*. "Therefore, all functions don't need to be automated to recognize the benefit but why not use technology and efficiency that is presented."

AI is a foundation when discussing automation, but blockchain technology allows the automation to flow into finance. Blockchain offers transparency, privacy, and trust, while AI offers scalability and efficiency. Blockchain's programmable smart contracts can automate payments, securities, and flows. Blockchain can help automate trade finance, supply chains, fund administration, settlement, transfer agents, and much else.

Only three academic studies were discovered on blockchain and autonomous finance. One discusses the benefits of payments of integrated project delivery allowing all parties to control and track financial transactions using smart contracts. Another highlights an autonomous blockchain-based check-clearing program developed that addresses duplication, forgery, and other issues more efficiently and effectively. The third shows the benefits of automation on compliance and regulation.

Here is your chance to get ahead of the curve.

Five Business Shifts from Emerging Trends

With the dynamic financial market, players will adapt and sectors will change.

1. New large players emerge from startups.

Innovation is difficult to drive at large institutions due to bureaucracy, risk and, let's be honest, independent Hoodies' talent.

Look at the top data companies. The behemoth IBM hits as number one, helped by its status as the top global technology company. However, it is closely followed by companies that were 1990s tech startups, Amazon and Google. And that is for data. As of June 2022, Amazon held almost 38 percent of online shopping and has outstanding monopoly charges filed by the Federal Trade Commission. For 2022, Google received 58 percent of its revenue from the $162 billion it made in search advertising. Neither of these largest data companies derive the majority of their revenue from data. They are large, multifaceted players that emerged from the 1990s tech boom. Similarly, we will see an emergence of new market-leading companies.

Winners in the digital assets world will be those startups that have figured out how to monetize revenue lines from digital assets and will likely be infrastructure based. The largest US public companies in digital assets are exchanges, financial companies, and mining companies. The large future players are builders of the ecosystem and may not yet be public. There is no prediction as to who the companies are, but here are possible examples:

Coinbase: Founded in 2012, Coinbase launched with the "radical idea that anyone, anywhere, should be able to easily and securely send and receive bitcoin." The company developed into the largest cryptocurrency exchange in the United States. Coinbase (NASDAQ: COIN) went public in 2021 with a valuation of $85 billion, and in late 2023 hovered at around $20 billion. The current lower market cap is influenced by regulatory concerns, market dynamics, and consumer sentiment. The SEC has filed suit against Coinbase for selling unregistered securities. Stay tuned.

Circle: Founded in 2013, Circle began as a peer-to-peer payment technology company and now manages the second largest stablecoin, USDC. Their investors include BlackRock, Fidelity Investments, and Goldman Sachs. According to Crunchbase, funding rounds for Circle total $1.12 billion with the 2022 funding round valuation of $7.7 billion.[14] An IPO is reportedly in consideration. As stablecoin gains more importance in both the traditional and digital ecosystem, Circle is poised to be a winner.

Fireblocks: Founded in 2018 and structured as a software company, Fireblocks allows companies and institutions to securely hold cryptocurrencies as a "digital asset security platform."[15] They have raised $1.23 billion in funding rounds from investors, including Bank of NY Mellon, General Atlantic, and Sequoia Capital. In January 2022, the company was valued at $8 billion at the closing of their Series E, boasting $2 trillion in assets transferred.[16] (Company valuations typically come out only during capital raises.)

Other Bets: Companies creating interoperability between blockchains and rails into institutions' antiquated tech systems are a behind-the-scenes product that could be a behemoth opportunity. Layer 1 and Layer 2 technologies also have opportunities to win if the Hoodies and Suits mindset is there as well as recognizing complementary potential growth avenues. Typically service companies have difficulty scaling, but remember that both Uber and Airbnb are service companies that created an innovative approach to an existing market.

2. Asset managers will drive change.

In 2022, global assets under management by asset managers were valued at $98 trillion.[17] Historical growth has been tied to market increases. Future growth will be tied to innovative strategies and attracting new investment. Since the next generations are a gatekeeper to capital, asset managers are incentivized to adapt and will be drivers of change in digital asset adoption. They have already started.

Franklin Templeton, Apollo, and Hamilton Lane have tokenized private funds, offering a lower minimum investment and opening up their investors base to retail clients. Growing from retail channels is a good bet. Demand for alternative investments opportunities will continue to grow for retail clients, and digital assets will be both requested and the most efficient investment option.

In addition, asset managers are responsible for the flow of trillions of dollars of capital, and a back office expense savings of 1.5 percent is tremendous. More automated systems and blockchain-enabled capabilities will translate into decreased expenses and a stronger bottom line.

Digital assets will help asset managers grow AUM (as discussed in Chapter 5) and decrease expenses. A win-win.

3. Banks will refocus revenue lines.

Banks are the backbone of the financial system as their job is money. Banks are not disappearing upon finance's upgrade, but they will figure out how to work in the new dynamic and technologically advanced ecosystem. Many banks, including Goldman Sachs and Citibank, have already started offering clients tokenization services.

If the ownership structure for money changes to a tech wallet-based world, banks will become custodians (subject to smart regulation) and potentially have a similar structure to what they have today with holding deposits and lending funds. Currencies will be fiat and digital. Banks are clever and capable of adapting.

Most people will not want to be responsible for potential loss, theft, or management of their own finances by self-custody in a wallet. Let's play with numbers and say that 80 percent of people will still keep money within the services of a bank, or have the bank hold their wallets, and the other 20 percent will self-manage or manage wallets elsewhere. Will wallets include investments and look like a brokerage account? Will it be a brokerage account so that it means they have more deposits if you include the securities or possibly commodities for those banking clients? What do the other 20 percent of bank clients actually do? How will fees change for banks?

Investment bank services of M&A, capital raising, and strategic advisory will benefit from technology and efficiency and continue to be a source of revenue. Companies are increasingly choosing to remain private with fewer than 15 percent of companies with revenues over $100 million going public. IPO services may change because the value of becoming public isn't as advantageous in future finance. However, companies will still look for both equity and debt offerings and still need advisors.

Despite the unknowns, banks will preserve in a technologically advanced ecosystem as they will adapt and find opportunities for new services. But don't be a dinosaur. Here is your chance.

4. Retail investors demand a broader investment universe.

Crypto assets have opened up new investment opportunities and met a demand for a less vanilla investment profile. Though the ICO world was ripe with fraud, the idea of offering retail investors the opportunity to partake in a venture investment struck a chord. So did demand for the Rhianna song investment, the Aspen St. Regis, the Kentucky Derby winner, and bitcoin. The job of the Suits is to recognize and use the Hoodie intuition with what is possible now and create a better, regulatory-compliant framework. More opportunities in alternative investments will be available for retail investors, with possibilities for more granular investing and diversification.

Just like the company formerly known as Twitter has become a megaphone for national, political, and business news, many investors follow social media and turn to it for financial advice. The power of online chats, message boards, and social media was shown in the GameStop example. Technology has helped build communities. People are turning to social media more and more for education and recommendations. This trend will continue, and more financial advisors will use it as a medium for advice.

Both the increased utilization in crypto assets and social media highlight changing trends and dynamics. Challengers to the status quo ask, "Are there better ways to do things?"There is a demand for new concepts and new approaches to what we see as the traditional normal, including a world past stocks and bonds. Welcome alternative investments.

The retail investor is shifting the old-school mentality and looking to invest in more than stocks and bonds. The investment markets are expanding from the call for more alternative investments. Thanks to demand and opportunity, the market for alternative assets is expected to grow to $17.2 trillion by 2025 – four times greater than it was in 2010.[18] Historically, access to these investments has been limited and the market has proved illiquid. Digital assets will unlock this market to retail investors with transferability and transparency that was previously lacking. Demand and opportunity.

5. Wealth management and private banking will transform.

Historically, our parents invested in stocks, bonds, and mutual funds of stocks and bonds through a wealth manager. Our parents also invested in a VCR and were incapable of setting the VCR's digital clock. Things evolve. The only constant is change.

With the increase in investment opportunities, wealth managers and private bankers will be more important. Investments with diverse portfolios, wallets, and accounts will need to be consolidated and risk weighted. More investment opportunities means more noise about what to do with money. Managers will bring opportunities to clients as well as financial advice.

Given the rise of the influencer, social media does keep individuals social and encourages conversations, even if they aren't in person. Relationships will not be replaced by technology. Wealth managers will find ways to communicate outside the office and online and optimize portfolios for the changing market dynamics. Wealth management and private banking will tie together the institutional and retail investment opportunities.

Finance is undergoing an upgrade. As Richard Walker, Bain & Company Partner, explained, "The current financial market infrastructure is brittle, high cost, and high risk, but the sunk cost and legacy market structure make it difficult to drive change. What's needed to catalyze the required change is a disruptor, new scale profits pools, or regulatory mandates. Without one of those, it will be status quo with little more than incremental adoption and no structural transformation."[19]

Afterword

"All I'm offering is the truth. Nothing more."

– Morpheus in *The Matrix*

In *The Matrix*, Morpheus offers Neo a choice: a blue pill that leaves his life the same and a red pill that shows him the truth. It's essentially a decision to make between accepting the status quo or opening the mind to possible enlightenment. Though many different groups have adopted the messaging in *The Matrix* to mean various things, when it comes to finance, it's clear: You can choose to ignore the advances in technology or you can learn and leverage it for you, your family, your company, and your industry.

While developing digital assets and its frameworks, the Hoodies are upgrading finance and have made a few mistakes along the way – yes, some of them criminal. But they've also created a groundbreaking technology and laid the foundation to work with the Suits to apply blockchain technology to traditional finance on Wall Street and in corporate America. The more Suits who learn about the capabilities and applicability of the technology developed by Hoodies, the more likely that they'll be a part of the changes that are beginning to revolutionize traditional finance. The rest will be left behind.

The question is: Which will you choose?

Notes

Introduction

1. Friedman, Vanessa. "Mark Zuckerberg's I'm Sorry Suit." *New York Times*, April 10, 2018. https://www.nytimes.com/2018/04/10/fashion/mark-zuckerberg-suit-congress.html.
2. Bellafante, Ginia. "Sam Bankman-Fried Was a Grown up Criminal, Not an Impulsive Man-Child." *New York Times*, November 3, 2023. https://www.nytimes.com/2023/11/03/nyregion/sam-bankman-fried-ftx-trial-cryptocurrency.html.
3. Gura, David. "Criminal Mastermind or Hapless Dude? A Look into Sam Bankman-Fried's Trial so Far." NPR, October 14, 2023. https://www.npr.org/2023/10/14/1205737325/criminal-mastermind-hapless-dude-sam-bankman-fried-trial-ftx.
4. Rodeck, David. "What Is Ethereum? How Does It Work?" *Forbes*, February 16, 2023. https://www.forbes.com/advisor/investing/cryptocurrency/what-is-ethereum-ether/.
5. Dailey, Natasha. "Vitalik Buterin Says He Created Ethereum after His Beloved World of Warcraft Character Was Hobbled by the Developers, Awakening Him to the 'Horrors Centralized Services Can Bring.'" *Business Insider*, 2021. https://markets.businessinsider.com/news/currencies/vitalik-buterin-created-ethereum-following-world-of-warcraft-debacle-2021-10.

Chapter 1: Blockchain Is Not Bitcoin

1. "JPMorgan's Jamie Dimon: Bitcoin is a 'hyped-up fraud.'" YouTube. CNBC, 2023. https://www.youtube.com/watch?v=qdIooHrQeK8.

2. Irrera, Anna. "JPMorgan (JPM) Switches on JPM Coin Payments System in Euros." Bloomberg.com, June 23, 2023. https://www.bloomberg.com/news/articles/2023-06-23/jpmorgan-jpm-switches-on-jpm-coin-payments-system-in-euros.
3. Flitter, Emily. "Banks Tried to Kill Crypto and Failed. Now They're Embracing It (Slowly)." *New York Times*, November 1, 2021. https://www.nytimes.com/2021/11/01/business/banks-crypto-bitcoin.html.
4. "The Future of Wealth Management." JPMorgan, 2023.
5. Frankenfield, Jake. "Cryptocurrency Wallet: What It Is, How It Works, Types, Security." Investopedia, 2023. https://www.investopedia.com/terms/b/bitcoin-wallet.asp.
6. Satoshi Nakamoto, "Bitcoin: A Peer-to-Peer Electronic Cash System." Bitcoin.org, October 2008. https://bitcoin.org/bitcoin.pdf
7. Edwards, John. "Bitcoin's Price History." Investopedia, October 27, 2023. https://www.investopedia.com/articles/forex/121815/bitcoins-price-history.asp.
8. Zoaib Saleem, Shaikh. "The 2008 Global Meltdown and the Birth of Bitcoin." Live Mint, September 13, 2018. https://www.livemint.com/Money/YTYMYUD7dytGK5PGSpdRTN/The-2008-global-meltdown-and-the-birth-of-Bitcoin.html.
9. "Title Insurance Market: Expected to Be the Fastest Growing Industry 2030." LinkedIn, September 4, 2023. https://www.linkedin.com/pulse/title-insurance-market-expected-fastest-growing-industry/.
10. Russo, Camila. "Sale of the Century: The Inside Story of Ethereum's 2014 Premine." CoinDesk, September 14, 2021. https://www.coindesk.com/markets/2020/07/11/sale-of-the-century-the-inside-story-of-ethereums-2014-premine/.
11. "Ethereum (ETH) Price, Charts, and News." Coinbase, 2023. https://www.coinbase.com/price/ethereum.
12. Coinbase, 2023.
13. Peck, Morgen. "The Uncanny Mind That Built Ethereum." Wired, June 13, 2016. https://www.wired.com/2016/06/the-uncanny-mind-that-built-ethereum/.
14. Memoria, Francisco. "Ethereum ICO Participant Resurfaces and Transfers 8,000 $eth after It Appreciated Nearly 600,000%."

CryptoGlobe, May 29, 2023. https://www.cryptoglobe.com/latest/2023/05/ethereum-ico-participant-resurfaces-and-transfers-8000-eth-after-it-appreciated-nearly-600000/.

15. Ariwoola, Abdulrasaq. "Whale Withdraws Eth Worth $15.9m from Binance amid Price Rally." Coin Edition, November 7, 2023. https://coinedition.com/whale-withdraws-eth-worth-15-9m-from-binance-amid-price-rally/.
16. Kharpal, Arjun. "Over 800 Cryptocurrencies Are Now Dead as Bitcoin Is 70 Percent off Its Record High." CNBC, July 2, 2018. https://www.cnbc.com/2018/07/02/over-800-cryptocurrencies-are-now-dead-as-bitcoin-feels-pressure.html.
17. Williams, Sean. "Less than 4% of All Initial Coin Offerings Are a Success." The Motley Fool, June 6, 2018. https://www.fool.com/investing/2018/06/06/less-than-4-of-all-initial-coin-offerings-are-a-su.aspx.
18. "Bitcoin Energy Consumption Index." Digiconomist, February 28, 2023. https://archive.org/web/.
19. Gaur, Nitin. Email message to author, November 10, 2023.
20. "Anonymity vs. Pseudonymity in Crypto." Gemini, May 17, 2021. https://www.gemini.com/cryptopedia/anonymity-vs-pseudonymity-basic-differences.
21. "HSBC, Northern Trust Estimate 5–10% of Assets Will Be Tokenized by 2030." *Ledger Insights*, February 23, 2023. https://www.ledgerinsights.com/hsbc-northern-trust-tokenized-by-2030/.
22. "Kodak Says 'It's Not Playing Grab Ass Anymore' with Digital – in 2007." YouTube, 2012. https://www.youtube.com/watch?v=A1zzehTOKi0.
23. Roose, Kevin. "Kodak's Dubious Cryptocurrency Gamble." *New York Times*, January 30, 2018. https://www.nytimes.com/2018/01/30/technology/kodak-blockchain-bitcoin.html.
24. Daniel, Will. "Bitcoin Has 'Significant Upside' and Could Rise to $38,000, JPMorgan Says." *Fortune*, May 25, 2022. https://fortune.com/2022/05/25/what-is-bitcoin-worth-price-outlook-jpmorgan-significant-upside-jamie-dimon-crypto/.
25. Nelson, Rob. "Nothing Showcases the Value of Bitcoin Like the Larry Fink, Blackrock ETF Pivot." The Street Crypto, October

16, 2023. https://www.thestreet.com/crypto/markets/larry-fink-pivot-blackrock-etf-demonstrate-value-of-bitcoin.

26. Di Salvo, Matthew. "Blackrock CEO Larry Fink: Crypto Will 'Transcend Any One Currency.'" Yahoo! Finance, July 14, 2023. https://finance.yahoo.com/news/blackrock-ceo-larry-fink-crypto-173439344.html.
27. Amoils, Nisa. Email message to author, Nov 10, 2023.

Chapter 2: The House That Crypto Built

1. Moore, Galen. "10 Years after Laszlo Hanyecz Bought Pizza with 10K Bitcoin, He Has No Regrets." CoinDesk, September 14, 2021. https://www.coindesk.com/markets/2020/05/22/10-years-after-laszlo-hanyecz-bought-pizza-with-10k-bitcoin-he-has-no-regrets/.
2. CoinDesk, September 14, 2021.
3. "Cryptocurrency Prices, Charts and Market Capitalizations." CoinMarketCap, 2023. https://coinmarketcap.com/.
4. "Saudi Arabia Datasets." International Monetary Fund, 2023. https://www.imf.org/external/datamapper/profile/SAU.
5. "Saudi Arabia Facts and Figures." OPEC, 2023. https://www.opec.org/opec_web/en/about_us/169.htm.
6. Lee Chaum, David. "Computer Systems Established, Maintained and Trusted by Mutually Suspicious Groups." Nakamoto Institute. Accessed 2023. https://nakamotoinstitute.org/static/docs/computer-systems-by-mutually-suspicious-groups.pdf.
7. "History of Cryptocurrency: The Idea, Journey, and Evolution." Worldcoin, 2023. https://worldcoin.org/articles/history-of-cryptocurrency.
8. Kuhn, Daniel. "'I Jumped in with All 4': Legendary Cryptographer David Chaum on the Future of Web3." CoinDesk, May 11, 2023. https://www.coindesk.com/layer2/2022/06/08/i-jumped-in-with-all-4-legendary-cryptographer-david-chaum-on-the-future-of-web-3/.
9. Daly, Lyle. "How Many Cryptocurrencies Are There?" The Motley Fool, 2023. https://www.fool.com/investing/stock-market/market-sectors/financials/cryptocurrency-stocks/how-many-cryptocurrencies-are-there/.

10. "Cryptocurrency Ownership Data." Triple A, October 22, 2023. https://triple-a.io/crypto-ownership-data/.
11. "Cryptocurrency Prices Today By Market Cap." *Forbes*, 2023. https://www.forbes.com/digital-assets/crypto-prices/?sh=18cdc71f2478.
12. Lee, Jully. "Jeff Bezos Net Worth Breakdown (2023)." Ainutoken, June 28, 2023. https://www.ainutoken.net/net-worth/jeff-bezos/.
13. Ackman, Bill. "Tweet." Twitter, November 20, 2022. https://twitter.com/BillAckman/status/1594456857191628800?s=20&t=209znaO6dy7TGZHbhXyqIw.
14. Royal, James. "Cryptocurrency Statistics 2023." Bankrate, 2023. https://www.bankrate.com/investing/cryptocurrency-statistics/#:~:text=26%20percent%20of%20millennials%20owned,percent%20of%20all%20U.S.%20adults.
15. "New National Survey of 2,000+ American Adults Suggests 20% ..." Coinbase, 2023. https://www.coinbase.com/blog/new-national-survey-of-2-000-american-adults-suggests-20-of-americans-own?homepage_tab=receive-money.
16. "Paxos Survey Finds Users Want to Buy Crypto from Banks." Ledger Insights, March 7, 2023. https://www.ledgerinsights.com/survey-buy-crypto-from-banks-paxos/.
17. Sethi, Ankit. "Bitcoin vs Bitcoin Cash vs Wrapped Bitcoin Explained." Kalkine Media, 2021. https://kalkinemedia.com/ca/stocks/financial/bitcoin-vs-bitcoin-cash-vs-wrapped-bitcoin-explained.
18. Hayes, Adam. "Stellar Cryptocurrency Definition, History & Future." Investopedia, 2023. https://www.investopedia.com/terms/s/stellar-cryptocurrency.asp.
19. Stojan, Jon. "Should You Invest in AAVE Crypto?" *Charlotte Observer*, 2023. https://www.charlotteobserver.com/contributor-content/article274764561.html.
20. "Decentraland Price Today." CoinMarketCap, 2023. https://coinmarketcap.com/currencies/decentraland/.
21. Kumar Sharma, Toshendra. "Security Tokens vs. Utility Tokens : A Concise Guide." Blockchain Council, September 27, 2023. https://www.blockchain-council.org/blockchain/security-tokens-vs-utility-tokens-a-concise-guide/.

22. Georgiev, George. "What Is a Meme Coin? The Biggest Meme Coins You Must Know About." Crypto Potato, September 19, 2023. https://cryptopotato.com/what-is-meme-coin/.
23. Gubadze, Dachi. "What Are Utility Tokens and How Do You Use Them?" Stack Browser, 2023. https://stackbrowser.com/blog/utility-tokens.
24. Browne, Ryan. "The World's Biggest Stablecoin Has Dropped below Its $1 Peg." CNBC, May 13, 2022. https://www.cnbc.com/2022/05/12/tether-usdt-stablecoin-drops-below-1-peg.html.
25. Nicolle, Emily. "Moody's Is Working on Scoring System for Crypto Stablecoins." Bloomberg, January 26, 2023. https://www.bloomberg.com/news/articles/2023-01-26/credit-rater-moody-preps-crypto-stablecoins-scoring-system.
26. Dance, Gabriel J. X. "The Real-World Costs of the Digital Race for Bitcoin." *New York Times*, April 10, 2023. https://www.nytimes.com/2023/04/09/business/bitcoin-mining-electricity-pollution.html.
27. Frankenfield, Jake. "Silk Road." Investopedia, 2021. https://www.investopedia.com/terms/s/silk-road.asp.
28. "Bitcoin: $1bn Seized from Silk Road Account by US Government." BBC News, November 5, 2020. https://www.bbc.com/news/technology-54833130.
29. Best, Raynor de. "COINBASE Users, by Quarter 2018–2022." Statista, October 27, 2023. https://www.statista.com/statistics/803531/number-of-coinbase-users/.
30. "About." Coinbase, 2023. https://www.coinbase.com/about.
31. Tully, Shawn. "Coinbase Seals Its Rank as the 7th Biggest New U.S. Listing of All Time." *Fortune*, April 15, 2021. https://fortune.com/2021/04/14/coinbase-ipo-direct-listing-stock-coin-shares-7th-biggest-all-time-nasdaq/.
32. Ryan, Crypto. "The Rise of Binance: A Brief History." CryptoRyancy, November 29, 2020. https://www.cryptoryancy.com/a-history-of-binance-a-complete-overview-of-everything-to-know/.
33. Almada Lopez, Diego. "Coinbase Lists PayPal USD as Binance Cuts BUSD Support." Crypto Briefing, September 1, 2023. https://cryptobriefing.com/coinbase-lists-paypal-usd-as-binance-cuts-busd-support/.

34. Goldstein, Matthew, Emily Flitter, and David Yaffe-bellany. "S.E.C. Accuses Binance of Mishandling Funds and Lying to Regulators." *New York Times*, June 5, 2023. https://www.nytimes.com/2023/06/05/business/sec-binance-charges.html.
35. Derby, Michael S. "Binance Founder Changpeng Zhao Agrees to Step Down, Plead Guilty." *Wall Street Journal*, November 21, 2023.
36. Gura, David. "The Future of Crypto Hinges on a Fight between the SEC and a Former Burger Flipper." NPR, August 13, 2023. https://www.npr.org/2023/08/13/1188231308/binance-lawsuits-cz-crypto-sec-coinbase-bitcoin.
37. Frankenfield, Jake. "Tzero (T0): Meaning, History, Regulation." Investopedia, 2022. https://www.investopedia.com/terms/t/tzero.asp#:~:text=tZero%20(t0)%20is%20a%20blockchain,same%20technology%20that%20underlies%20Bitcoin.
38. "tZero Homepage." tZERO, 2023. https://www.tzero.com/.
39. Seth, Shobhit. "What Is Kraken? How It Works, How It Stands out, and Issues." Investopedia, 2023. https://www.investopedia.com/tech/what-kraken/.
40. Seth, Shobhit. "Gemini Exchange: Definition, History, Products & Services." Investopedia, 2023. https://www.investopedia.com/tech/gemini-winklevoss-bitcoin-exchange/.
41. "Gemini Homepage." Gemini, 2023. https://www.gemini.com/.
42. Rosenblatt, Joel. "Kraken Ordered to Turn over Its Users' Information to the IRS." Bloomberg, June 30, 2023. https://www.bloomberg.com/news/articles/2023-06-30/kraken-ordered-to-turn-over-its-users-information-to-the-irs#xj4y7vzkg.
43. Jonathan Stempel, "US SEC sues Kraken for Operating Crypto Trading Platform Without Registering," Reuters, November 20, 2023.
44. Temple-Raston, Dina. "Review | Criminals Thought Crypto Was Untraceable. They Were Wrong." *Washington Post*, December 27, 2022. https://www.washingtonpost.com/books/2022/12/29/tracers-crime-cryptocurrency-andy-greenberg/.
45. *Washington Post*, December 27, 2022.
46. "The 2023 Crypto Crime Report." Chainalysis, 2023.
47. "Money Laundering, Proceeds of Crime and the Financing of Terrorism." United Nations: Office on Drugs and Crime, 2023. https://www.unodc.org/unodc/en/money-laundering/index.html.

48. Gapusan, Jeff. "Defi: Who Will Build the Future of Finance?" *Forbes*, April 21, 2021. https://www.forbes.com/sites/jeffgapusan/2021/11/02/defi-who-will-build-the-future-of-finance/?sh=77326df35b8d.

49. Braun, Helene. "Blackrock CEO Larry Fink Says Bitcoin Could 'Revolutionize Finance.'" CoinDesk, July 7, 2023. https://www.coindesk.com/business/2023/07/05/blackrock-ceo-larry-fink-says-bitcoin-could-revolutionize-finance/#:~:text=%E2%80%9CWe%20do%20believe%20that%20if,revolutionize%20finance%2C%E2%80%9D%20he%20said.

50. Fink, Larry. "Annual Chairman's Letter to Investors." BlackRock, 2023. https://www.blackrock.com/corporate/investor-relations/larry-fink-annual-chairmans-letter?utm_source=newsletter&utm_medium=email&utm_campaign=newsletter_axioscryptocurrency&stream=business.

51. Lu, Kevin. "A Dive into Smart Contracts and Defi." CoinMarketCap, August 21, 2021. https://coinmarketcap.com/alexandria/article/a-dive-into-smart-contracts-and-defi.

52. Lopatto, Elizabeth. "The Tech Industry Moved Fast and Broke Its Most Prestigious Bank." The Verge, March 12, 2023. https://www.theverge.com/23635692/silicon-valley-bank-svb-collapse-explainer-startups-venture-capital.

53. Copeland, Tim. "Bitcoin Lending Services Exploded in 2020: Here's Why." Decrypt, December 31, 2020. https://decrypt.co/52271/bitcoin-lending-services-exploded-in-2020-heres-why.

54. Decrypt, December 31, 2020.

55. Decrypt, December 31, 2020.

56. "Crypto's String of Bankruptcies." Reuters, January 20, 2023. https://www.reuters.com/business/finance/cryptos-string-bankruptcies-2023-01-20/.

57. Reuters, January 20, 2023.

58. "Crypto Fear and Greed Index – Bitcoin Momentum Tracker." Coin Tree, 2023. https://www.cointree.com/learn/crypto-fear-and-greed-index/.

59. Kim, Christine. "Here's Why Interest Rates on Cryptocurrencies Could Be a Game-Changer." CoinDesk, May 9, 2023. https://

www.coindesk.com/business/2020/02/22/heres-why-interest-rates-on-cryptocurrencies-could-be-a-game-changer/.

60. Shekhawat, Jaiveer. "Coinbase to Launch New Lending Platform Aimed at Large Institutional Investors." Reuters, September 6, 2023. https://www.reuters.com/business/finance/coinbase-launch-new-lending-platform-aimed-large-institutional-investors-2023-09-05/.
61. Singer, Andrew. "Genesis Capital's Fall Might Transform Crypto Lending – Not Bury It." Cointelegraph, January 28, 2023. https://Cointelegraph.com/news/genesis-capital-s-fall-might-transform-crypto-lending-not-bury-it.
62. "Exercise Caution with Crypto Asset Securities: Investor Alert." SEC, 2023. SEC. https://www.sec.gov/oiea/investor-alerts-and-bulletins/exercise-caution-crypto-asset-securities-investor-alert.
63. Johnson, Katanga. "U.S. SEC Working to Register Crypto Lending Firms – Gensler." Reuters, July 21, 2022. https://www.reuters.com/technology/us-sec-working-register-crypto-lending-firms-gensler-2022-07-21/.
64. "Defi Staking: A Beginner's Guide to Proof-of-Stake (POS) Coins." Cointelegraph. Accessed November 5, 2023. https://Cointelegraph.com/learn/defi-staking-proof-of-stake-pos-coins.
65. Butsch, Chris. "Crypto Staking and Lending: Everything You Should Know." Moneywise, 2023. https://moneywise.com/investing/cryptocurrency/bitcoin-staking-and-lending.
66. Williams, Chris. "Polygon Launches $40m Liquidity Mining Program with AAVE." Crypto Briefing, April 14, 2021. https://cryptobriefing.com/polygon-launches-40m-liquidity-mining-program-with-aave/.
67. Fernau, Owen. "Incentive Programs and Rewards Were Nine-Figure Gushers." The Defiant, December 30, 2021. https://thedefiant.io/defi-incentives-rewards-airdrops.
68. Shumba, Camomile. "UK Crypto Incentives Ban Could Drive Firms Out of Country, Lobbyists Say." CoinDesk, August 10, 2023. https://www.coindesk.com/policy/2023/08/10/uk-crypto-incentives-ban-could-drive-firms-out-of-country-lobbyists-say/.
69. "JP Morgan Rolls Out JPM Coin Blockchain Payments in Euro." Ledger Insights, September 8, 2023. https://www.ledgerinsights.com/jp-morgan-jpm-coin-blockchain-payments-euro/.

70. Castro Margaroli, Isabelle. "Supercharging TASSAT's B2B Blockchain with FedNow." Fintech Nexus, February 6, 2023. https://www.fintechnexus.com/supercharging-tassats-b2b-blockchain-with-fednow/.
71. "FedNow® Service Participants and Service Providers."The Federal Reserve, 2023. https://www.frbservices.org/financial-services/fednow/organizations.

Chapter 3: Crypto as a Proof of Concept for Traditional Finance's Capital Markets

1. Lieber, Ron. "Letter to a Young Crypto Enthusiast (or the Merely Curious)." *New York Times*, August 13, 2023. https://www.nytimes.com/2023/08/13/your-money/cryptocurency-personal-finance-bitcoin.html?smid=nytcore-android-share.
2. Casey, Michael J. "PayPal's Stablecoin Is No Libra. Why the Timing Feels Right." CoinDesk, August 11, 2023. https://www.coindesk.com/consensus-magazine/2023/08/11/paypals-stablecoin-is-no-libra-why-the-timing-feels-right/.
3. Bambysheva, Nina. "PayPal Leads What Could Be a Stablecoin Stampede." *Forbes*, October 4, 2023. https://www.forbes.com/sites/digital-assets/2023/08/09/paypal-leads-what-could-be-a-stablecoin-stampede/?sh=b84da58757e1.
4. Malekan, Omid. "PayPal Revisited." Medium, August 8, 2023. https://omid-malekan.medium.com/paypal-revisited-aef3bd584d6e.
5. Sopov, Vladislav. "PayPal Stablecoin PYUSD FAQ." U. Today, August 18, 2023. https://u.today/guides/paypal-stablecoin-pyusd-faq-guide-on-everything-you-need-to-know.
6. Casey, Michael J. "PayPal's Stablecoin Is No Libra. Why the Timing Feels Right." CoinDesk, August 11, 2023. https://www.coindesk.com/consensus-magazine/2023/08/11/paypals-stablecoin-is-no-libra-why-the-timing-feels-right/.
7. Helms, Kevin. "Bank of America Assesses Significance of Paypal's USD Stablecoin and Fednow System." Bitcoin News, August 15, 2023. https://news.bitcoin.com/bank-of-america-assesses-significance-of-paypals-usd-stablecoin-and-fednow-system/.

8. Waters, Maxine. "Ranking Member Waters' Statement on PayPal's Launch of U.S. Dollar Stablecoin." U.S. House Committee on Financial Services Democrats, August 9, 2023. https://democrats-financialservices.house.gov/news/documentsingle.aspx?DocumentID=410725.
9. Kuhn, Daniel. "PayPal's New Stablecoin and the '2 Wolves' inside Crypto." CoinDesk, August 8, 2023. https://www.coindesk.com/consensus-magazine/2023/08/08/paypals-new-stablecoin-and-the-2-wolves-inside-crypto/.
10. "Bank of America Predicts PayPal's Stablecoin Unlikely to Be Used Widely Anytime Soon." CoinDesk, 2023. https://www.coindesk.com/video/bank-of-america-predicts-paypals-stablecoin-unlikely-to-be-used-widely-anytime-soon/.
11. Adams, Ryan Sean. "Tweet." Twitter, August 7, 2023. https://twitter.com/RyanSAdams/status/1688586470330621953.
12. Kaplan, Talia. "Crypto Markets Are Undergoing a 'flight to Quality,' Says Goldman Sachs Digital Assets Chief." CNBC, February 10, 2023. https://www.cnbc.com/2023/02/10/goldman-sachs-digital-asset-chief-lays-out-blockchain-strategy.html.
13. LaVecchia, Pat. Email message to author, November 11, 2023.
14. "BofA Global Research Launches Coverage of Digital Assets." Bank of America Newsroom, 2021. https://newsroom.bankofamerica.com/content/newsroom/press-releases/2021/10/bofa-global-research-launches-coverage-of-digital-assets.html.
15. Lee, Michael, Antoine Martin, and Benjamin Müller. "What Is Atomic Settlement?" Liberty Street Economics, 2022. https://libertystreeteconomics.newyorkfed.org/2022/11/what-is-atomic-settlement/.
16. Hillery, Michele. "The Road to T+0 and the Future of Settlement." DTCC, 2021. https://www.dtcc.com/dtcc-connection/articles/2021/november/09/the-road-to-t0-and-the-future-of-settlement.
17. "FAQ." Federal Reserve, 2023. https://www.federalreserve.gov/cbdc-faqs.htm.
18. Creer, David, and Alexander Feenie. "Are CBDCs a Ticking Timebomb for Commercial Banks?" OMFIF, April 17, 2023. https://www.omfif.org/2023/04/are-cbdcs-a-ticking-timebomb-for-commercial-banks/.

19. Duggan, Wayne. "Central Bank Digital Currency: What Is a CBDC?" *Forbes*, October 25, 2023. https://www.forbes.com/advisor/investing/central-bank-digital-currency-cbdc/.
20. Jones, Marc. "Study Shows 130 Countries Exploring Central Bank Digital Currencies." Reuters, June 28, 2023. https://www.reuters.com/markets/currencies/study-shows-130-countries-exploring-central-bank-digital-currencies-2023-06-28/#:~:text=Eleven%20countries%2C%20including%20a%20number,commerce%20to%20government%20stimulus%20payments.
21. "What Happens at a Crypto ICO." Bloomberg Originals, YouTube, 2018. https://www.youtube.com/watch?v=T2uJ6cCwqh0.
22. "How to Use Compound Liquidity Pools to Earn Your First Defi Yield – Linen Blog." Linen, 2023. https://linen.app/articles/how-to-use-compound-liquidity-pools-to-earn-your-first-defi-yield/.
23. Shewale, Rohit. "13 Most Expensive NFTs Ever Sold (July '23 Update)." Demand Sage, July 6, 2023. https://www.demandsage.com/most-expensive-nfts/#:~:text=%27The%20Merge%27%20remains%20the%20most,has%20ownership%20of%20the%20thing.
24. Creighton, Jolene. "NFT Timeline: The Beginnings and History of NFTs." NFT Now, 2022. https://nftnow.com/guides/nft-timeline-the-beginnings-and-history-of-nfts/.
25. "What Is the Metaverse?" McKinsey, August 17, 2022. https://www.mckinsey.com/featured-insights/mckinsey-explainers/what-is-the-metaverse.
26. Smith, Craig. "Decentraland: The Ultimate Game Guide: Player Counts and Game Details." Video Game Stats, May 18, 2023. https://videogamesstats.com/decentraland/.
27. Howcroft, Elizabeth. "Virtual Real Estate Plot Sells for Record $2.4 Million." Reuters, November 24, 2021. https://www.reuters.com/markets/currencies/virtual-real-estate-plot-sells-record-24-million-2021-11-23/.
28. "Adidas Metaverse." Adidas, 2023. https://www.adidas.com/metaverse.
29. Energii. "Adidas Metaverse: Everything You Need to Know." NFT Evening, February 23, 2023. https://nftevening.com/adidas-metaverse-everything-you-need-to-know/.

30. Stempel, Jonathan. "U.S. Judge Permits Lawsuit Claiming NBA Top Shot NFTs Are Securities." Reuters, February 22, 2023. https://www.reuters.com/legal/us-judge-permits-lawsuit-claiming-nba-top-shot-nfts-are-securities-2023-02-22/.
31. McDowell, Maghan. "New Gucci NFTs Combine Fashion and Art Using Generative AI."Vogue Business, July 14, 2023. https://www.voguebusiness.com/technology/new-gucci-nfts-combine-fashion-and-art-using-generative-ai.
32. Sato, Mia. "Starbucks Sold 2,000 NFTs in 20 Minutes – Coffee Not Included." The Verge, March 10, 2023. https://www.theverge.com/2023/3/9/23633169/starbucks-nfts-odyssey-siren-collection-rewards-program.
33. Thomas, Lauren. "Walmart Is Quietly Preparing to Enter the Metaverse." CNBC, January 18, 2022. https://www.cnbc.com/2022/01/16/walmart-is-quietly-preparing-to-enter-the-metaverse.html.
34. Hayward, Andrew. "Amazon Prime Is Giving out Free NFTs for This Polygon Game." Decrypt, August 2, 2023. https://decrypt.co/151033/amazon-prime-free-nft-polygon-game-mojo-melee.
35. Citi GPS. "Money, Tokens, and Games: Blockchain's Next Billion Users and Trillions in Value," 2023. https://www.citifirst.com.hk/home/upload/citi_research/rsch_pdf_30143792.pdf.
36. "Bearer Bonds That Almost Floated Away During Katrina, Finally Recovered." YouTube, 2023. https://www.youtube.com/watch?v=i-mD3iYewaY&t=4s.
37. Ruane, Jonathan, and Andrew McAfee. "What a DAO Can – and Can't – Do." *Harvard Business Review*, January 10, 2023. https://hbr.org/2022/05/what-a-dao-can-and-cant-do.
38. Nagarajan, Shalini. "Rihanna Nfts Enable Holders to Earn When This Song Plays." Blockworks, February 10, 2023. https://blockworks.co/news/rihanna-song-nfts-enables-holders-to-earn-when-it-plays.
39. Bain, Katie. "The Chainsmokers Giving Fans a Share of New Album's Royalties as Free NFTs." *Billboard*, May 12, 2022. https://www.billboard.com/business/tech/chainsmokers-free-nfts-royalties-new-album-royal-1235069874/.

40. "Tokenized Royalties: Unlocking the Benefits." CoinFantasy, June 30, 2023. https://www.coinfantasy.io/blog/tokenized-royalties/.
41. Dorman, Jeff. "Amazon Prime Membership Should Have Been a Tokenized Asset." CoinDesk, September 14, 2021. https://www.coindesk.com/markets/2020/07/16/amazon-prime-membership-should-have-been-a-tokenized-asset/.
42. "Amazon Prime Statistics." Statista, 2023. https://www.statista.com/topics/4076/amazon-prime/#topicOverview.
43. Aspen Coin, 2023. https://www.aspencoin.io/.
44. Noonan, Laura. "Bob Diamond Says Digital Currencies to Have 'Very Important Place' in Finance." *Financial Times*, January 10, 2023. https://www.ft.com/content/16089458-3aa9-4f20-82ec-4de47b4b2dd4.

Chapter 4: What FTX, Hubris, and Crypto's Other Mistakes Can Teach Traditional Finance

1. Reuters. "Sam Bankman-Fried's Bid to Dismiss Cryptocurrency Charges Is 'Meritless,' Prosecutors Say." NBC News, May 30, 2023. https://www.nbcnews.com/news/us-news/sam-bankman-frieds-bid-dismiss-cryptocurrency-charges-meritless-prosec-rcna86772.
2. Mayhew, Stewart. "Conflicts of Interest among Market Intermediaries." SEC. Accessed November 9, 2023. https://www.sec.gov/about/offices/oia/oia_market/conflict.pdf.
3. Smith, Timothy. "FTX: An Overview of the Exchange and Its Collapse." Investopedia, 2023. https://www.investopedia.com/ftx-exchange-5200842.
4. Stevenson, Alexandra, and Matthew Goldstein. "FTX's Sister Firm, Alameda Research, Was Central to Collapse." *New York Times*, November 30, 2022. https://www.nytimes.com/2022/11/30/business/dealbook/ftx-almeda-research-sam-bankman-fried.html.
5. Newmyer, Tory. "Sam Bankman-Fried Charmed Washington. Then His Crypto Empire Imploded." *Washington Post*, November 14, 2022. https://www.washingtonpost.com/business/2022/11/12/sam-bankman-fried-ftx-demise/.

6. "Sam Bankman-Fried Donor Detail." OpenSecrets, 2023. https://www.opensecrets.org/outside-spending/donor_detail/2022?id=U0000004705&type=I&super_only=N&name=Bankman-Fried%2C%2BSam.
7. McLeod, Paul. "What Does Congress Do with a Problem Like Sam Bankman-Fried?" *Vanity Fair*, November 18, 2022. https://www.vanityfair.com/news/2022/11/congress-sam-bankman-fried-regulation-crypto-ftx.
8. "Chairwoman Waters Statement on the Arrest of Sam Bankman-Fried." U.S. House Committee on Financial Services Democrats, December 12, 2022. https://democrats-financialservices.house.gov/news/documentsingle.aspx?DocumentID=410026.
9. Edelman, Gilad. "The Crypto Industry Is Getting Too Honest." *Wired*, May 5, 2022. https://www.wired.com/story/ftx-steph-curry-crypto-ad-ponzi-scheme/.
10. Newmyer, Tory. "Sam Bankman-Fried Charmed Washington. Then His Crypto Empire Imploded." *The Washington Post*, November 12, 2022. https://www.washingtonpost.com/business/2022/11/12/sam-bankman-fried-ftx-demise/.
11. "FTX, Tom Brady and Gisele Bündchen Announce Long-Term Partnership." PR Newswire, June 30, 2021. https://www.prnewswire.com/news-releases/ftx-tom-brady--gisele-bundchen-announce-long-term-partnership-301321814.html.
12. Tortorelli, Paige, and Kate Rooney. "Sam Bankman-Fried's Alameda Quietly Used FTX Customer Funds for Trading, Say Sources." CNBC, November 14, 2022. https://www.cnbc.com/2022/11/13/sam-bankman-frieds-alameda-quietly-used-ftx-customer-funds-without-raising-alarm-bells-say-sources.html.
13. Yaffe-Bellany, David. "How Sam Bankman-Fried's Crypto Empire Collapsed." *New York Times*, November 14, 2022. https://www.nytimes.com/2022/11/14/technology/ftx-sam-bankman-fried-crypto-bankruptcy.html.
14. Allaire, Jeremy. "Tweet." Twitter, November 8, 2022. https://twitter.com/jerallaire/status/1590112507632685056.
15. Lipton, Eric, and Ephrat Livni. "Crypto Nomads: Surfing the World for Risk and Profit." *New York Times*, July 23, 2021. https://www.nytimes.com/2021/07/23/us/politics/crypto-billionaires.html.

16. Brooks, Kristopher J. "Sam Bankman-Fried Charged with Fraud and Money Laundering." CBS News, 2022. https://www.cbsnews.com/news/ftx-sam-bankman-fried-indicted-fraud-charges/.
17. "FTX Bankruptcy Filing – John J. Ray III." DocumentCloud, 2022. https://www.documentcloud.org/documents/23310507-ftx-bankruptcy-filing-john-j-ray-iii.
18. "Kevin O'Leary and Hasan Debate FTX, Crypto, and Investments." YouTube. *The Daily Show*, 2023. https://www.youtube.com/watch?v=I30_q6Tjaxk.
19. Singletary, Michelle. "Americans View Crypto Investing as Unreliable. They're Right." *Washington Post*, April 21, 2023. https://www.washingtonpost.com/business/2023/04/21/americans-view-cryptocurrency-unreliable/.
20. "Sam Bankman-Fried Interviewed Live About the Collapse of FTX." YouTube, 2022. https://www.youtube.com/watch?v=IyoGdwVIwWw&t=126s.
21. "Transcript of Sam Bankman-Fried's Interview at the DealBook Summit." *New York Times*, December 1, 2022. https://www.nytimes.com/2022/12/01/business/dealbook/sam-bankman-fried-dealbook-interview-transcript.html.
22. *New York Times*, December 1, 2022.
23. Stieb, Matt. "FTX Wants Back All the Lavish Gifts Sam Bankman-Fried Gave His Parents." Intelligencer, September 19, 2023. https://nymag.com/intelligencer/2023/09/ftx-sues-sam-bankman-frieds-parents-for-millions.html.
24. "Statement Of U.S. Attorney Damian Williams on the Conviction of Samuel Bankman-Fried." *Justice*, November 2, 2023. U.S. Attorney's Office, Southern District of New York. https://www.justice.gov/usao-sdny/pr/statement-us-attorney-damian-williams-conviction-samuel-bankman-fried.
25. Yaffe-Bellany, David, Matthew Goldstein, and J. Edward Moreno. "Sam Bankman-Fried Trial: Fallen Crypto Mogul Convicted in Collapse That Cost Users Billions." *New York Times*, November 3, 2023. https://www.nytimes.com/live/2023/11/02/business/sam-bankman-fried-trial.
26. Bellafante, Ginia. "Sam Bankman-Fried Was a Grown up Criminal, Not an Impulsive Man-Child." *New York Times*, November 3, 2023.

https://www.nytimes.com/2023/11/03/nyregion/sam-bankman-fried-ftx-trial-cryptocurrency.html.

27. Jung, Col. "Earn 20% on USD on Terra's Anchor Protocol-Defi Basics." Medium, June 6, 2023. https://medium.com/coinmonks/forget-banks-earn-20-on-your-usd-in-defi-on-the-terra-blockchain-2b1d2844574#:~:text=Terra's%20USD%20stablecoin%20%E2%80%94%20called%20TerraUSD,just%20be%20your%20dream%20proposition.
28. Barbosa, Vinicius. "Terra Classic (LUNC) Would Trade at This Price If It Hits Its All-Time High Market Cap." Finbold, August 30, 2023. https://finbold.com/terra-classic-lunc-would-trade-at-this-price-if-it-hits-its-all-time-high-market-cap/#:~:text=Terra%20Classic%20%28LUNC%29%20%E2%80%94%20formerly%20Terra%20%28LUNA%29%20%E2%80%94,cap%20of%20%2441%20billion%20on%20the%20same%20date.
29. Davies, Kyle. "Tweet." Twitter, March 29, 2022. https://twitter.com/KyleLDavies/status/1508634652797374469.
30. Kwon, Do. "Tweet." Twitter, April 17, 2022. https://twitter.com/stablekwon/status/1515501798442008577.
31. Sandor, Krisztian, and Ekin Genç. "The Fall of Terra: A Timeline of the Meteoric Rise and Crash of UST and Luna." CoinDesk, December 22, 2022. https://www.coindesk.com/learn/the-fall-of-terra-a-timeline-of-the-meteoric-rise-and-crash-of-ust-and-luna/.
32. "What Really Happened to Luna Crypto?" *Forbes*, 2022. https://www.forbes.com/sites/qai/2022/09/20/what-really-happened-to-luna-crypto/?sh=3cd003f44ff1.
33. Graphenist. "Why Did You Guys Think This Was Going to Work?" Reddit, 2022. https://www.reddit.com/r/terralunacrash/comments/uofcos/why_did_you_guys_think_this_was_going_to_work/.
34. Yaffe-Bellany, David. "Crypto Fugitive Do Kwon Is Charged with Fraud by U.S. Prosecutors." *New York Times*, March 23, 2023. https://www.nytimes.com/2023/03/23/business/do-kwon-arrested-crypto.html#:~:text=Kwon%20over%20his%20management%20of,and%20engage%20in%20market%20manipulation.
35. Kwon, Do. "Tweet." Twitter, May 13, 2022. https://twitter.com/stablekwon/status/1525238416991891457.

36. Nwaokocha, Amaka. "Terra Crash Anniversary: Community Reflects on the Lessons Learned." Cointelegraph, May 11, 2023. https://Cointelegraph.com/news/terra-luna-crash-anniversary-community-reflects-on-the-lessons-learned.
37. Allen, Hilary J. "The Superficial Allure of Crypto." IMF, September 1, 2022. https://www.imf.org/en/Publications/fandd/issues/2022/09/Point-of-View-the-superficial-allure-of-crypto-Hilary-Allen.
38. "The Failure of Long Term Capital Management (LTCM)." Management Study Guide. Accessed November 9, 2023. https://www.managementstudyguide.com/failure-of-long-term-capital-management.htm.
39. Van Boom, Daniel. "Luna Crypto Crash: How UST Broke and What's Next for Terra." CNET, 2022. https://www.cnet.com/personal-finance/crypto/luna-crypto-crash-how-ust-broke-and-whats-next-for-terra/.
40. Ge Huang, Vicky, Caitlin Ostroff, and Corinne Ramey. "Crypto Lender Celsius CEO Alex Mashinsky Arrested, Sued by Regulators." *Wall Street Journal*, July 14, 2023. https://www.wsj.com/articles/crypto-lender-celsius-ceo-alex-mashinsky-arrested-sued-by-regulators-5169ff4d.
41. "What Really Happened to Luna Crypto?" *Forbes*, 2022. https://www.forbes.com/sites/qai/2022/09/20/what-really-happened-to-luna-crypto/?sh=53f33f034ff1.
42. Glover, George. "Bitcoin Is Finally Trading like 'Digital Gold' – But Only Because Nobody Cares about Crypto Anymore." MSN, 2023. https://www.msn.com/en-us/money/markets/bitcoin-is-finally-trading-like-digital-gold-but-only-because-nobody-cares-about-crypto-anymore/ar-AA1eP0GJ?ocid=msedgdhp&pc=ENTPSP&cvid=627bed19dbff45ce8ec8cbdd74428a1a&ei=6.
43. "Afternoon Session – 2018 Meeting." Warren Buffett Archive, June 6, 2018. https://buffett.cnbc.com/video/2018/05/05/afternoon-session--2018-berkshire-hathaway-annual-meeting.html.
44. Colin, Peter. "Facebook's Libra: An Introduction to the next Cryptocurrency." Reuters, 2019. https://www.thomsonreuters.com/en-us/posts/news-and-media/facebooks-libra-cryptocurrency/.
45. Murphy, Hannah, Kiran Stacey, Miles Kruppa, and Dave Lee. "Facebook Libra: The Inside Story of How the Company's

Cryptocurrency Dream Died." *Financial Times*, March 10, 2022. https://www.ft.com/content/a88fb591-72d5-4b6b-bb5d-223adfb893f3.

46. Attlee, David. "Vale Diem: How Facebook's Ambitious Stablecoin Project Came to an End." Cointelegraph, February 2, 2022. https://Cointelegraph.com/news/vale-diem-how-facebook-s-ambitious-stablecoin-project-came-to-an-end.
47. Archie, Ayana. "Dogecoin Price Spikes after Elon Musk Changes Twitter Logo to the Shiba Inu Dog." NPR, April 4, 2023. https://www.npr.org/2023/04/04/1167877216/dogecoin-elon-musk-twitter-logo.
48. Reuters. "Elon Musk Accused of Insider Trading in Dogecoin Lawsuit." *The Guardian*, June 1, 2023. https://www.theguardian.com/technology/2023/jun/01/elon-musk-insider-trading-dogecoin-lawsuit.
49. George, Kevin. "The Largest Cryptocurrency Hacks So Far." Investopedia, 2022. https://www.investopedia.com/news/largest-cryptocurrency-hacks-so-far-year/.
50. Bambysheva, Nina. "Over $3 Billion Stolen in Crypto Heists: Here Are the Eight Biggest." *Forbes*, January 2, 2023. https://www.forbes.com/sites/ninabambysheva/2022/12/28/over-3-billion-stolen-in-crypto-heists-here-are-the-eight-biggest/?sh=192bf20c699f.
51. Maurer, Mark. "More Crypto Exchanges Verify Reserves, but Questions about Assets Remain." *Wall Street Journal*, December 5, 2022. https://www.wsj.com/articles/more-crypto-exchanges-verify-reserves-but-questions-about-assets-remain-11670153687?mod=article_inline.
52. "Wormhole Hack: Lessons from the Wormhole Exploit." Chainalysis, February 3, 2022. https://blog.chainalysis.com/reports/wormhole-hack-february-2022/.
53. Dugan, Kevin T. "Crypto Is Crashing. It Deserves To." Intelligencer, June 13, 2022. https://nymag.com/intelligencer/2022/06/crypto-is-crashing-it-deserves-to.html.
54. Wieczner, Jen. "The Crypto Geniuses Who Vaporized a Trillion Dollars." Intelligencer, August 15, 2022. https://nymag.com/intelligencer/article/three-arrows-capital-kyle-davies-su-zhu-crash.html.
55. Yaffe-Bellany, David. "Their Crypto Company Collapsed. They Went to Bali." *New York Times*, June 9, 2023. https://www.nytimes.com/2023/06/09/technology/three-arrows-cryto-bali.html.

56. NG, Serena. "Crypto Hedge Fund Three Arrows Capital Considers Asset Sales, Bailout." *Wall Street Journal*, June 29, 2022. https://www.wsj.com/articles/battered-crypto-hedge-fund-three-arrows-capital-considers-asset-sales-bailout-11655469932?mod=latest_headlines.
57. Sigalos, MacKenzie. "From $10 Billion to Zero: How a Crypto Hedge Fund Collapsed and Dragged Many Investors Down with It." CNBC, July 12, 2022. https://www.cnbc.com/2022/07/11/how-the-fall-of-three-arrows-or-3ac-dragged-down-crypto-investors.html.
58. Yaffe-Bellany, David. "Their Crypto Company Collapsed. They Went to Bali." *New York Times*, June 9, 2023. https://www.nytimes.com/2023/06/09/technology/three-arrows-cryto-bali.html.
59. C, Hope. "Three Arrows Capital Kyle Davies Will Donate Open Exchange Earnings to Creditors for 'Good Karma.'" Yahoo! Finance, 2023. https://finance.yahoo.com/news/three-arrows-capital-kyle-davies-023602971.html.
60. Singer, Andrew. "Genesis Capital's Fall Might Transform Crypto Lending – Not Bury It." Cointelegraph, January 28, 2023. https://Cointelegraph.com/news/genesis-capital-s-fall-might-transform-crypto-lending-not-bury-it.
61. Segal, David. "Crypto Meltdown, What Crypto Meltdown?" *New York Times*, January 17, 2023. https://www.nytimes.com/2023/01/17/business/crypto-market-meltdown-nft-blockchain.html.

Chapter 5: Institutional Digital Assets: Securities, Only Better

1. "Purpose-Built For Financial Services." Provenance Blockchain Foundation, 2023. https://provenance.io/solutions/.
2. "Provenance's Ou: 'Blockchain is a technology, application for the real world,'" 2023. https://www.radio.finance/episodes/provenance-blockchain-foundations-ou-we-want-our-blockchain-to-be-a-technology-for-true-applications-in-the-real-world.
3. Rothfeld, Merlin. "Will the Digital Asset Boom Be Bigger Than the Internet?" Nasdaq, 2023. https://www.nasdaq.com/articles/will-the-digital-asset-boom-be-bigger-than-the-internet.

4. Kleine, Darren. "JPMorgan Looks to Save Millions with Blockchain-Based Financial Instruments." Blockworks, September 12, 2023. https://blockworks.co/news/jpmorgan-lobban-blockchain-financial-instruments.
5. "What Are Smart Contracts and How Do They Work?" Crypto.com, 2023. https://crypto.com/university/smart-contracts#:~:text=The%20term%20%27smart%20contract%27%20was,parties%20perform%20on%20these%20promises.%E2%80%9D.
6. Amaral, Miguel. "Case 3. Blockchain and Smart Contracts: Regulatory Challenges and Regulatory Approaches." OEDC Library, 2021. https://www.oecd-ilibrary.org/sites/fbf2ebe9-en/index.html?itemId=%2Fcontent%2Fcomponent%2Ffbf2ebe9-en.
7. Gorrivan, Charles. "How Blockchain Is Helping Northern Trust Self-Execute Contracts." American Banker, August 11, 2023. https://www.americanbanker.com/news/how-blockchain-is-helping-northern-trust-self-execute-contracts.
8. "Bank Failures in Brief – 2008." FDIC, 2019. https://www.fdic.gov/bank/historical/bank/bfb2008.html#:~:text=There%20were%2025%20bank%20failures,below%20for%20other%20years%27%20information.
9. O'Brien, Sarah. "Fraud Cost Consumers $8.8 Billion Last Year, Federal Trade Commission Says. That's up 44% from 2021." CNBC, March 1, 2023. https://www.cnbc.com/2023/03/01/ftc-fraud-cost-consumers-8point8-billion-in-2022.html.
10. Indah, Kelly. "How Many Blockchains Are There in 2023? (Statistics)." Increditools, 2023. https://increditools.com/blockchains/.
11. Kumar, Sumit, Rajaram Suresh, Darius Liu, Bernhard Kronfellner, and Aaditya Kaul. "Relevance of On-Chain Asset Tokenization in 'Crypto Winter.'" Boston Consulting Group, 2022.
12. Khan, Roomy. "Asset Tokenization a Trillion Dollar Market Opportunity: JP Morgan, Blackrock, and Goldman Sachs Think So." *Forbes*, July 5, 2023. https://www.forbes.com/sites/roomykhan/2023/06/29/asset-tokenization-a-trillion-dollar-market-opportunity-jp-morgan-blackrock-and-goldman-think-so/amp/.
13. Carroll, Rick. "In $18 Million Deal, Nearly One-Fifth of St. Regis Aspen Sells through Digital Tokens." *Aspen Times*, October 9,

2018. https://www.aspentimes.com/trending/in-18-million-deal-nearly-one-fifth-of-st-regis-aspen-sells-through-digital-tokens/.

14. Leo Rivers, Martin. "The Art of Tokenization: How a Picasso Painted Itself onto the Blockchain." *Forbes*, April 30, 2022. https://www.forbes.com/sites/martinrivers/2022/04/27/the-art-of-tokenization-how-a-picasso-painted-itself-onto-the-blockchain/?sh=7c0e689d7729.
15. Indap, Sujeet. "Apollo Defends Push to Retail Investors amid Blackstone Storm." *Financial Times*, December 13, 2022. https://www.ft.com/content/2084e80d-8bac-4c3a-89d5-0c3eace67e32.
16. "KKR Adds Senior Exec to Expand Focus on Retail Investors and Advisors." The DI Wire, March 24, 2023. https://thediwire.com/kkr-adds-senior-exec-to-expand-focus-on-retail-investors-and-advisors/.
17. Skolnik, Or, Markus Habbel, Brenda Rainey, Alexander De Mol, and Isar Ramaswami. "Why Private Equity Is Targeting Individual Investors." Bain, October 20, 2023. https://www.bain.com/insights/why-private-equity-is-targeting-individual-investors-global-private-equity-report-2023/.
18. Hamlin, Jessica. "The Institutional Share of Global Capital Is Shrinking. What Does This Mean for Managers?" Institutional Investor, March 10, 2022. https://www.institutionalinvestor.com/article/2bstmxkxtc18sjq0b0zr4/portfolio/the-institutional-share-of-global-capital-is-shrinking-what-does-this-mean-for-managers.
19. "Glossary: Money Market Fund." Investor, 2023. https://www.investor.gov/introduction-investing/investing-basics/glossary/money-market-fund.
20. Fujiyama, Yuki. "Trade Finance Guide: A Quick Reference for U.S. Exporters." U.S. Department of Commerce, 2022.
21. Wegner, Carl. "The Real Tipping Point in the Digitalization of Trade Finance." *Forbes*, March 16, 2023. https://www.forbes.com/sites/forbesbusinesscouncil/2023/03/15/the-real-tipping-point-in-the-digitalization-of-trade-finance/?sh=10fde1097561.
22. Knox, James. Email message to author, November 10, 2023
23. Berman, Brian. Email message to author, August 29, 2023.
24. Basar, Shanny. "JP Morgan's Onyx Digital Assets Processes up to $2bn Daily." Markets Media, October 11, 2023. https://www

.marketsmedia.com/jp-morgans-onyx-digital-assets-processes-up-to-2bn-per-day/.

25. Hays, Jeff. "Railroads in Russia." Facts and Details. Accessed November 7, 2023. https://factsanddetails.com/russia/Education_Health_Transportation_Energy/sub9_6d/entry-5155.html#:~:text=around%20%241.7%20billion.-,Railroad%20Gauges%20and%20Russian%20Border%20Crossings,former%20Soviet%20Union%20are%20wider.

Chapter 6: Incremental Wins in Wall Street's Pre-Season

1. Avneri, Itai. "Silvergate, Signature and SVB: What Their Collapse Reveals about the Nature of Banking." INX One Platform, March 15, 2023. https://www.inx.co/learn/inxperts/silvergate-signature-and-svb-what-their-collapse-reveals-about-the-nature-of-banking/.
2. Korn, Jennifer. "SVB Collapse Was Driven by 'the First Twitter-Fueled Bank Run.'" CNN, March 14, 2023. https://www.cnn.com/2023/03/14/tech/viral-bank-run/index.html.
3. 2021. "Deloitte's 2021 Global Blockchain Survey." Deloitte, 2021. https://www2.deloitte.com/us/en/insights/topics/understanding-blockchain-potential/global-blockchain-survey.html.
4. "Digital Assets – Worldwide." Statista, 2023. https://www.statista.com/outlook/dmo/fintech/digital-assets/worldwide#revenue.
5. Smith, Jordan. "Why Big Banks Like JPMorgan and Citi Want to Put Wall Street on a Blockchain." CNBC, July 26, 2023. https://www.cnbc.com/2023/07/26/why-big-banks-like-jpmorgan-want-put-wall-street-on-a-blockchain.html.
6. Bowley, Taylor, and Vanessa Cook. "Beyond Crypto: Tokenization." Bank of America Institute, 2023.
7. Castillo, Michael del. "Distributed Ledger Consortium R3 Closes Record $107 Million Funding Round." CoinDesk, September 11, 2021. https://www.coindesk.com/markets/2017/05/23/distributed-ledger-consortium-r3-closes-record-107-million-funding-round/.
8. Coindesk. "Scanning, Trying and Scaling: Fidelity's Journey in Digital Assets." YouTube, 2022. https://www.youtube.com/watch?v=Xv5fuRHA6r0.

9. Ge Huang, Vicky. "The 'Fidelity Mafia' behind Big Crypto." *Wall Street Journal*, August 27, 2023. https://www.wsj.com/finance/currencies/the-fidelity-mafia-behind-big-crypto-953ad00e?mod=djem10point.
10. Tergesen, Anne. "Labor Department Criticizes Fidelity's Plan to Put Bitcoin on 401(k) Menu." *Wall Street Journal*, May 4, 2022. https://www.wsj.com/articles/labor-department-criticizes-fidelitys-plan-to-put-bitcoin-on-401-k-menu-11651197309?mod=article_inline.
11. Xuan Chua, Jie. "Real-World Assets: State of the Market." Binance, 2023.
12. CryptoPotato. "Tokenized Treasury Market Is Worth over $600 Million: Binance Research." Binance, July 31, 2023. https://www.binance.com/en/feed/post/884381.
13. Morgan, Nicholas. "Defi Startup Ondo Expands Yield-Earning Stablecoin Alternative to Polygon." Decrypt, July 14, 2023. https://decrypt.co/148370/ondo-finance-tokenized-treasuries-stablecoin-alternative-ethereum-polygon.
14. CryptoPotato. "Tokenized Treasury Market Is Worth over $600 Million: Binance Research." Binance, July 31, 2023. https://www.binance.com/en/feed/post/884381.
15. "Laws and Rules." SEC, June 20, 2020. https://www.sec.gov/investment/laws-and-rules.
16. "Interview: Jenny Johnson, President and CEO of Franklin Templeton." TheTruthAboutYourFuture, 2022. https://www.thetayf.com/blogs/this-weeks-stories/exclusive-interview-jenny-johnson-president-and-ceo-of-franklin-templeton.
17. About." WisdomTree, 2023. https://www.wisdomtree.com/about-wisdomtree#:~:text=Relentlessly%20searching%20for%20better%20ways,in%20assets%20under%20management%20globally.
18. Basar, Shanny. "Wisdomtree to Launch Its First Blockchain-Enabled Fund." Markets Media, October 11, 2022. https://www.marketsmedia.com/wisdomtree-to-launch-its-first-blockchain-enabled-fund/.
19. Wisdomtree Announces Nine New Blockchain-Enabled Funds Are Effective with the SEC." Globe News Wire, December 14, 2022. https://www.globenewswire.com/news-release/2022/12/14/2573756/18051/en/WisdomTree-Announces-Nine-New-Blockchain-Enabled-Funds-are-Effective-with-the-SEC.html.

20. Basar, Shanny. "Wisdomtree to Launch Its First Blockchain-Enabled Fund." Markets Media, October 10, 2022. https://www.marketsmedia.com/wisdomtree-to-launch-its-first-blockchain-enabled-fund/.
21. Ricketts, David. "Abrdn Unveils Tokenisation for £16bn Flagship Fund." FN London, June 8, 2023. https://www.fnlondon.com/articles/abrdn-unveils-tokenisation-for-16bn-flagship-fund-20230608.
22. Steves, Rick. "Archax Utilizes Hedera Hashgraph DLT to Tokenize . . . ." Finance Feeds, 2023. https://financefeeds.com/archax-utilizes-hedera-hashgraph-dlt-to-tokenize-interest-in-abrdns-money-market-fund/.
23. "Abrdn Buys Stake in Digital Assets Exchange Archax." Reuters, August 12, 2022. https://www.reuters.com/markets/europe/abrdn-buys-stake-digital-assets-exchange-archax-2022-08-12/.
24. "Ondo Debuts USD Yield (USDY) for Global (Non-US) Individual and Institutional Investors." PR Newswire, August 4, 2023. https://www.prnewswire.com/ru/press-releases/ondo-debuts-usd-yield-usdy-for-global-non-us-individual-and-institutional-investors-301892815.html.
25. "About ArCoin." Arca Labs. Accessed November 8, 2023. https://www.arcalabs.com/about-arcoin.
26. David, Jearld. Email message to author, November 16, 2023.
27. Gottfried, Miriam. "KKR Makes Piece of PE Fund Available on Public Blockchain." *Wall Street Journal*, September 13, 2022. https://www.wsj.com/articles/kkr-makes-piece-of-pe-fund-available-on-public-blockchain-11663014955.
28. Melinek, Jacquelyn. "KKR Dives into Avalanche Blockchain to Tokenize and 'Democratize' Financial Services." TechCrunch, September 13, 2022. https://techcrunch.com/2022/09/13/kkr-dives-into-avalanche-blockchain-to-tokenize-and-democratize-financial-services/.
29. "KKR Closes $4.0 Billion Health Care Strategic Growth Fund II." Business Wire, January 10, 2022. https://www.businesswire.com/news/home/20220110005267/en/KKR-Closes-4.0-Billion-Health-Care-Strategic-Growth-Fund-II.
30. "Partnership with Alta to Expand Access for Investors across Southeast Asia." Hamilton Lane, 2023. https://www.hamiltonlane.com/en-us/news/alta-partnership-tokenize-fund.

31. Betz, Brandy. "Investment Manager Hamilton Lane Opens Tokenized Fund on Polygon Blockchain." CoinDesk, May 9, 2023. https://www.coindesk.com/business/2023/01/31/investment-manager-hamilton-lane-opens-first-tokenized-fund-with-securitize/.
32. "2023 Market Overview: Private Markets." Hamilton Lane, 2023. https://www.hamiltonlane.com/en-us/news/hamilton-lane-2023-market-overview.
33. "Eov Fund Now Available for Investment on Securitize." Hamilton Lane, 2023. https://www.hamiltonlane.com/en-us/news/direct-equity-fund-now-available-on-securitize.
34. "Figure Announces Expansion of Digital Fund Listing Business alongside Leading Asset Managers." PR Newswire, November 22, 2022. https://www.prnewswire.com/news-releases/figure-announces-expansion-of-digital-fund-listing-business-alongside-leading-asset-managers-301684747.html.
35. Lang, Hannah. "Apollo Holds Crypto for Clients as It Expands in Digital Assets." Reuters, October 31, 2022. https://www.reuters.com/technology/apollo-holds-crypto-clients-it-expands-digital-assets-2022-10-31/.
36. Basak, Sonali. "Apollo (APO) to Offer New Private Asset Fund on Blockchain with Figure." Bloomberg, November 22, 2022. https://www.bloomberg.com/news/articles/2022-11-22/apollo-to-offer-new-private-asset-fund-on-blockchain-with-figure.
37. Gkritsi, Eliza. "Apollo Hires JPMorgan's Christine Moy to Lead Digital Assets Strategy." Yahoo! Finance, 2022. https://finance.yahoo.com/news/apollo-hires-jpmorgans-christine-moy-125958253.html.
38. "Figure Announces Expansion of Digital Fund Listing Business alongside Leading Asset Managers." PR Newswire, November 22, 2022. https://www.prnewswire.com/news-releases/figure-announces-expansion-of-digital-fund-listing-business-alongside-leading-asset-managers-301684747.html.
39. https://www.apexgroup.com/technology-platforms/digital-onboarding/.
40. Archibald, Georges. Email message to author, November 10, 2023.
41. "Vanguard Advances Blockchain Technology Pilot to Streamline Asset-Backed Securities Markets." Vanguard, 2020. https://

corporate.vanguard.com/content/corporatesite/us/en/corp/who-we-are/pressroom/Press-Release-Vanguard-Advances-Blockchain-Technology-Pilot-061120.html.

42. Vanguard, 2020.
43. Cromley, Kelly. "Vanguard Group Makes Significant Investments in Bitcoin Mining Companies, Reflecting Growing Interest in Crypto Market." CoinTrust, July 12, 2023. https://www.cointrust.com/market-news/vanguard-group-makes-significant-investments-in-bitcoin-mining-companies-reflecting-growing-interest-in-crypto-market.
44. Strack, Ben. "Vanguard's $600 Million 'Investment' in Bitcoin Miners Isn't What You Think." Blockworks, July 12, 2023. https://blockworks.co/news/vanguard-bitcoin-miners-investment.
45. Berman, Ana. "Chinese State Bank Uses Blockchain to Issue Digital Mortgages Worth $1.3 Billion." Cointelegraph, September 27, 2018. https://Cointelegraph.com/news/chinese-state-bank-uses-blockchain-to-issue-digital-mortgages-worth-13-billion.
46. "Redwood Trust Announces Pricing of the Market's First Non-Agency Residential Mortgage-Backed Securitization Leveraging Blockchain-Based Technology." PR Newswire, September 22, 2021. https://www.prnewswire.com/news-releases/redwood-trust-announces-pricing-of-the-markets-first-non-agency-residential-mortgage-backed-securitization-leveraging-blockchain-based-technology-301383175.html.
47. "Figure Expands Reach of HELOC Products through Four New Partnerships." PR Newswire, July 12, 2023. https://www.prnewswire.com/news-releases/figure-expands-reach-of-heloc-products-through-four-new-partnerships-301875351.html.
48. "Figure Announces First Third-Party Loan Trade on Provenance, Company's Groundbreaking Blockchain Platform." Business Wire, May 13, 2020. https://www.businesswire.com/news/home/20200513005146/en/Figure-Announces-First-Third-party-Loan-Trade-on-Provenance-Company%E2%80%99s-Groundbreaking-Blockchain-Platform.
49. "World Bank Prices First Global Blockchain Bond, Raising A$110 Million." World Bank, September 12, 2018. https://www.worldbank.org/en/news/press-release/2018/08/23/world-bank-prices-first-global-blockchain-bond-raising-a110-million.

50. Nagarajan, Shalini. "World Bank Rolls out First Digital Bond Issuance on Euroclear." Blockworks, October 25, 2023. https://blockworks.co/news/world-bank-digital-bond-euroclear.
51. Blockworks, October 25, 2023.
52. "R3's Corda Powers First Digital Bond Issuance on Euroclear's Digital Financial Market Infrastructure." R3, October 24, 2023. https://r3.com/press-media/r3s-corda-powers-first-digital-bond-issuance-on-euroclears-digital-financial-market-infrastructure/#:~:text=The%20transaction%20represents%20a%20major,of%20the%20bond%20issuance%20process.
53. Noonan, Laura. "BBVA Issues Corporate Loan Using Blockchain." *Financial Times*, April 25, 2018. https://www.ft.com/content/8c5a44e8-4878-11e8-8ae9-4b5ddcca99b3.
54. Khatri, Yogita. "BBVA Puts $150 Million Syndicated Loan on Ethereum Blockchain." CoinDesk, September 13, 2021. https://www.coindesk.com/markets/2018/11/07/bbva-puts-150-million-syndicated-loan-on-ethereum-blockchain/.
55. "BBVA, BME and IDB Issue the First Regulated Bond in Spain Registered with Blockchain." BBVA, July 26, 2022. https://www.bbva.com/en/bbva-bme-and-idb-issue-the-first-regulated-bond-in-spain-registered-with-blockchain/.
56. "Societe Generale Performs the First Financial Transaction Settled with a Central Bank Digital Currency." SG FORGE, October 6, 2020. https://www.sgforge.com/societe-generale-performs-the-first-financial-transaction-settled-with-a-central-bank-digital-currency/.
57. "Societe Generale – Forge Borrows Dai Stablecoin from Decentralised Finance Protocol Maker Dao to Extend Loan." SG FORGE, July 10, 2023. https://www.sgforge.com/refinancing-dai-stablecoin-defi-MakerDAO/.
58. "Socgen Forge Gets French Crypto License." Ledger Insights, July 19, 2023. https://www.ledgerinsights.com/socgen-forge-crypto-license/.
59. "EIB Issues Its First Ever Digital Bond in Pound Sterling." European Investment Bank, February 8, 2023. https://www.eib.org/en/press/all/2023-030-eib-issues-its-first-ever-digital-bond-in-british-pounds.

60. "ABN AMRO Issues Tokenized Corporate Bond on Public Blockchain." Ledger Insights, September 6, 2023. https://www.ledgerinsights.com/abn-amro-tokenized-bond-blockchain/.
61. "Onyx Homepage." J.P. Morgan, 2023. https://www.jpmorgan.com/onyx/index.
62. Khan, Roomy. "Asset Tokenization a Trillion Dollar Market Opportunity: JP Morgan, Blackrock, and Goldman Sachs Think So." *Forbes*, July 5, 2023. https://www.forbes.com/sites/roomykhan/2023/06/29/asset-tokenization-a-trillion-dollar-market-opportunity-jp-morgan-blackrock-and-goldman-think-so/?sh=40e146ac4ff0.
63. Kitonyi, Nicholas. "JPMorgan's Digital Assets Product Onyx Processing Up to $2B Daily." NFTgators, October 5, 2023. https://www.nftgators.com/jpmorgans-digital-assets-product-onyx-processing-up-to-2b-daily/.
64. Allison, Ian. "Tokenization Is 'Killer App' for Tradfi: JPMorgan." CoinDesk, May 9, 2023. https://www.coindesk.com/business/2023/04/27/tokenization-is-the-killer-app-for-tradfi-jpmorgan/.
65. "Broadridge Launches DLT Repo Platform to Execute First Bilateral Repo Trades Using Smart Contracts." *Broadbridge*, 2021. Broadbridge Financial Solutions. https://www.broadridge.com/press-release/2021/broadridge-launches-dlt-repo-platform.
66. "Broadridge's DLT Repo Platform Transacts $1 Trillion a Month. Just Getting Started." Ledger Insights, February 1, 2023. https://www.ledgerinsights.com/broadridges-dlt-repo-dlr-1-trillion/.
67. Liao, Gordon Y., and John Caramichael. "Stablecoins: Growth Potential and Impact on Banking." The Federal Reserve, January 2022. https://www.federalreserve.gov/econres/ifdp/stablecoins-growth-potential-and-impact-on-banking.htm.
68. "Citi Develops New Digital Asset Capabilities for Institutional Clients." Citigroup, September 18, 2023. Citigroup. https://www.citigroup.com/global/news/press-release/2023/citi-develops-new-digital-asset-capabilities-for-institutional-clients.
69. "Societe Generale–Forge Launches 'Coinvertible': The First Institutional STABLECOIN Deployed on a Public Blockchain."

SG FORGE, July 21, 2023. https://www.sgforge.com/societe-generale-forge-launches-coinvertible-the-first-institutional-stablecoin-deployed-on-a-public-blockchain/.

70. "Coinvertible Stablecoin: An Institutional-Grade Stablecoin with Full Transparency." SG FORGE, October 27, 2023. https://www.sgforge.com/product/coinvertible/.
71. "SEC Intends to Narrow Qualified Custodians for Digital Assets." Ledger Insights, February 14, 2023. https://www.ledgerinsights.com/sec-qualified-custodians-digital-assets/.
72. "SEC Spotlights Crypto with New 'Safeguarding Rule' Proposal." Perkins Coie, 2023. https://www.perkinscoie.com/en/news-insights/sec-spotlights-crypto-with-new-safeguarding-rule-proposal.html.
73. "BNY Mellon Launches New Digital Asset Custody Platform." BNY Mellon, 2022. https://www.bnymellon.com/us/en/about-us/newsroom/press-release/bny-mellon-launches-new-digital-asset-custody-platform-130305.html.
74. "Digital Assets: From Fringe to Future." BNY Mellon, 2021. https://www.bnymellon.com/us/en/insights/all-insights/digital-assets-from-fringe-to-future.html.
75. Baer, Justin. "Bitcoin to Come to America's Oldest Bank, BNY Mellon." *Wall Street Journal*, February 17, 2021. https://www.wsj.com/articles/bitcoin-to-come-to-america-s-oldest-bank-bny-mellon-11613044810.
76. Muir, Scott. "SEC Issues SAB 121 on Digital Asset Custodial Obligations." KPMG, 2022. https://frv.kpmg.us/reference-library/2022/sec-issues-guidance-on-digital-asset-custodial-obligations.html.
77. "Digital Assets Account." Fidelity Workplace, 2023. https://www.fidelityworkplace.com/s/digitalassets#:~:text=Fidelity%27s%20proprietary%20Digital%20Assets%20Account,demands%20of%20your%20evolving%20workforce.
78. Watkins, Jon. "Fidelity Digital Assets Granted UK Licence to Offer Custody as Institutional Interest in Crypto Grows." The Trade, December 8, 2021. https://www.thetradenews.com/fidelity-digital-assets-granted-uk-licence-to-offer-custody-as-institutional-interest-in-crypto-grows/.
79. Fenton, Bruce. "Tweet." Twitter, October 19, 2022. https://twitter.com/brucefenton/status/1582806632425062401.

80. Jha, Prashant. "Fidelity: Bitcoin Is a 'Superior Form of Money.'" Cointelegraph, February 1, 2022. https://Cointelegraph.com/news/fidelity-bitcoin-is-a-superior-form-of-money.
81. Kuiper, Chris, and Jack Neureuter. "Bitcoin First: Why Investors Need to Consider Bitcoin Separately from Other Digital Assets." Fidelity, 2022. https://www.fidelitydigitalassets.com/research-and-insights/bitcoin-first.
82. "Digital Assets." State Street, 2023. https://www.statestreet.com/us/en/asset-manager/solutions/digital-assets.
83. "Why Crypto Is Just the Start of the Digital Transformation of Finance." State Street, 2022. https://www.statestreet.com/us/en/asset-owner/insights/why-crypto-is-just-the-start-of-digital-transformation-of-finance.
84. "Northern Trust Creates Digital Assets and Financial Markets Group." Northern Trust, 2022. https://www.northerntrust.com/united-states/pr/2022/northern-trust-creates-digital-assets-financial-markets-group.
85. Castillo, Michael del. "$1.5 Trillion Asset Manager Northern Trust Creates Digital Assets Group to Meet Growing Demand." *Forbes*, June 24, 2022. https://www.forbes.com/sites/michaeldelcastillo/2022/06/23/15-trillion-asset-manager-northern-trust-creates-digital-assets-group-to-meet-growing-demand/?sh=5e2ab6a1774c.
86. *Forbes*, June 24, 2022.
87. "Standard Chartered and Northern Trust Announce Zodia Custody Receives FCA Registration." Northern Trust, 2021. https://www.northerntrust.com/united-states/pr/2021/zodia-custody-receives-fca-registration.
88. Golden, Paul. "Is DLT the Answer to a $2 Trillion FX Settlement Problem?" Euromoney, April 14, 2023. https://www.euromoney.com/article/2baewt9l513y8ln2swwe8/foreign-exchange/is-dlt-the-answer-to-a-2-trillion-fx-settlement-problem.
89. "UBS, NatWest Commit to Intraday DLT Platform Finteum for 2023 Go Live." Ledger Insights, August 8, 2023. https://www.ledgerinsights.com/ubs-natwest-finteum-intraday-dlt-fx-swaps/.
90. Lomax, Jenna. "State Street, Vanguard and Symbiont Complete First Live Trade for FX Forward Contracts through Blockchain." Securities Finance Times, December 7, 2021. https://www.securities

financetimes.com/securitieslendingnews/technologyarticle.php?article_id=225211&navigationaction=technologynews&newssection=technology.

91. "HSBC and Wells Fargo Use Blockchain to Settle Forex Trades." Reuters, December 13, 2021. https://www.reuters.com/markets/currencies/hsbc-wells-fargo-use-blockchain-settle-forex-trades-2021-12-13/.
92. Coghlan, Jesse. "Australia Marks First FX Transaction Using a CBDC as EAUD Pilot Continues." Cointelegraph, May 18, 2023. https://Cointelegraph.com/news/australia-uses-cbdc-in-fx-transaction-pilot-test.
93. "Northern Trust Developing Digital Platform for Institutional Voluntary Carbon Credit Transactions." Northern Trust, 2023. https://www.northerntrust.com/united-states/pr/2023/northern-trust-developing-digital-platform-for-institutional-voluntary-carbon-credit-transactions.
94. Singh, Amitoj. "ANZ Bank Completes Carbon Credits Trading as Part of Australia's CBDC Pilot." CoinDesk, April 6, 2023. https://www.coindesk.com/policy/2023/04/06/anz-bank-completes-carbon-credits-trading-as-part-of-australias-cbdc-pilot/.
95. Lo, Joe. "World Bank Backs Carbon Credit Blockchain Registry to Attract Crypto. . ." Climate Change News, 2022. https://www.climatechangenews.com/2022/08/19/world-bank-launches-carbon-credit-blockchain-registry-to-attract-crypto-investors/.
96. "Blockchain + the Capital Markets: Unlocking a New Era of Speed and Transparency." Goldman Sachs, 2021. https://www.goldmansachs.com/intelligence/pages/blockchain-and-the-capital-markets.html.
97. "Digital Assets: Beauty Is Not in the Eye of the Beholder." Goldman Sachs, June 22, 2021. https://www.goldmansachs.com/what-we-do/consumer-and-wealth-management/private-wealth-management/intellectual-capital-f/beauty-is-not-in-the-eye-of-the-beholder/.
98. Biekert, Mary. "Morgan Stanley Backs Blockchain with Investment in Securitize." Bloomberg, 2021. https://www.bloomberg.com/news/articles/2021-06-21/morgan-stanley-backs-blockchain-with-investment-in-securitize#xj4y7vzkg.
99. Bloomberg, 2021.

100. Citi Survey Finds Significant Jump in Institutional Adoption of DLT, Crypto." Ledger Insights, August 23, 2023. https://www.ledgerinsights.com/citi-survey-dlt-crypto-institutional-adoption/.

Chapter 7: How Tomorrow's Investors Will Expect Change

1. bawse1. "How'd You Guys Manage to Win So Big It Made These Old Guys Drown in Their Tears?" Reddit, 2021. https://www.reddit.com/r/wallstreetbets/comments/l3z0n8/howd_you_guys_manage_to_win_so_big_it_made_these/.
2. Podkul, Cezary. "The Regrets of Lewis Ranieri." *Wall Street Journal*, September 7, 2018. https://www.wsj.com/articles/the-regrets-of-lewis-ranieri-1536240610.
3. "Distribution of Household Wealth in the U.S. since 1989." Federal Reserve, 2023. https://www.federalreserve.gov/releases/z1/dataviz/dfa/distribute/table/#quarter:119;series:Assets;demographic:generation;population:all;units:levels.
4. Hayes, Adam. "Boomer Effect (Baby Boomer Factor): What It Is, How It Works, FAQ." Investopedia, 2022. https://www.investopedia.com/terms/b/boomer-effect-baby-boomer-factor.asp.
5. Joseph Smith, Talmon, and Karl Russell. "The Greatest Wealth Transfer in History Is Here, with Familiar (Rich) Winners." *New York Times*, May 14, 2023. https://www.nytimes.com/2023/05/14/business/economy/wealth-generations.html.
6. Joseph Smith, Talmon, and Karl Russell. "The Greatest Wealth Transfer in History Is Here, with Familiar (Rich) Winners." *New York Times*, May 14, 2023. https://www.nytimes.com/2023/05/14/business/economy/wealth-generations.html.
7. "U.S. Population by Generation 2022." Statista, August 29, 2022. https://www.statista.com/statistics/797321/us-population-by-generation/
8. "Mobile Fact Sheet." Pew Research Center, April 7, 2021. https://www.pewresearch.org/internet/fact-sheet/mobile/.
9. Taylor, Petroc. "Smartphone Penetration in the US (Share of Population) 2010–2021." Statista, January 18, 2021. https://www.statista.com/statistics/201183/forecast-of-smartphone-penetration-in-the-us/.

10. Silverman, Dwight. "Your Smartphone Is Light Years Ahead of NASA Computers That Guided Apollo Moon Landings," 2019. https://www.houstonchronicle.com/local/space/mission-moon/article/Your-smartphone-is-light-years-ahead-of-NASA-13757565.php.
11. McSpadden, Kevin. "Science: You Now Have a Shorter Attention Span than a Goldfish." *Time*, May 14, 2015. https://time.com/3858309/attention-spans-goldfish/.
12. "Millennial Home Buying Statistics – 2021 Guide." New Silver, May 14, 2021. https://newsilver.com/the-lender/millennial-home-buying-statistics/.
13. Tergesen, Anne. "Millennials on Better Track for Retirement than Boomers and Gen X." *Wall Street Journal*, October 26, 2023. https://www.wsj.com/personal-finance/retirement/millennials-on-better-track-for-retirement-than-boomers-and-gen-x-1aebf00.
14. Koop, Avery. "Ranked: The World's 25 Richest Millennial Billionaires." Visual Capitalist, July 2, 2021. https://www.visualcapitalist.com/worlds-25-richest-millennial-billionaires/.
15. "Millennial Life: How Young Adulthood Today Compares with Prior Generations." Pew Research Center's Social and Demographic Trends Project, February 14, 2019. https://www.pewresearch.org/social-trends/2019/02/14/millennial-life-how-young-adulthood-today-compares-with-prior-generations-2/.
16. Pew Research Center's Social and Demographic Trends Project, February 14, 2019.
17. Bump, Pamela. "5 Things Gen Z Will Spend Money On and Why Marketers Need to Care." HubSpot, December 5, 2022. https://blog.hubspot.com/marketing/what-gen-z-spends-money-on#:~:text=According%20to%20a%202021%20Consumer,%2C%20home%20goods%2C%20and%20furniture.
18. Francis, Tracy, and Fernanda Hoefel. "'True Gen': Generation Z and Its Implications for Companies." McKinsey & Company, November 12, 2018. http://www.mckinsey.com/industries/consumer-packaged-goods/our-insights/true-gen-generation-z-and-its-implications-for-companies.
19. Wenner Moyer, Melinda. "Kids as Young as 8 Are Using Social Media More than Ever, Study Finds." *New York Times*, March 24, 2022. https://www.nytimes.com/2022/03/24/well/family/child-social-media-use.html.

20. Coe, Erica, Andrew Doy, Kana Enomoto, and Cheryl Healy. "Gen Z Mental Health: The Impact of Tech and Social Media." McKinsey and Company, April 28, 2023. https://www.mckinsey.com/mhi/our-insights/gen-z-mental-health-the-impact-of-tech-and-social-media.
21. Buller, Abi, and Savannah Scott. "Stat: Generation Z Are at the Forefront of Black Lives Matter." ISN Global, 2020. https://www.lsnglobal.com/youth/article/25685/stat-generation-z-are-at-the-forefront-of-black-lives-matter.
22. Francis, Tracy, and Fernanda Hoefel. "'True Gen': Generation Z and Its Implications for Companies." McKinsey & Company, November 12, 2018. https://www.mckinsey.com/industries/consumer-packaged-goods/our-insights/true-gen-generation-z-and-its-implications-for-companies.
23. Gough, Christina. "Top Esports Players by Earnings 2023." Statista, September 12, 2023. https://www.statista.com/statistics/518010/leading-esports-players-worldwide-by-earnings/.
24. Schwartz, Casey. "Jean Twenge Is Ready to Make You Defend Your Generation Again." *Washington Post*, April 20, 2023. https://www.washingtonpost.com/books/2023/04/20/generations-jean-twenge-boomers-gen-z-millennials/.
25. "Helping Those Who Care about Young People, Care Better." Springtide Research Institute, April 6, 2023. https://www.springtideresearch.org/post/generation-alpha/more-insights-on-generation-alpha.
26. Pinsker, Joe. "Oh No, They've Come up with Another Generation Label." *The Atlantic*, February 21, 2020. https://www.theatlantic.com/family/archive/2020/02/generation-after-gen-z-named-alpha/606862/.
27. Nuttall, Caitlin. "5 Key Characteristics and Data of US Generation Alpha." GWI, 2022. https://blog.gwi.com/marketing/us-gen-alpha-characteristics/.
28. Fry, Richard. "Millennials Are the Largest Generation in the U.S. Labor Force." Pew Research Center, April 11, 2018. https://www.pewresearch.org/short-reads/2018/04/11/millennials-largest-generation-us-labor-force/.
29. Chugh, Abhinav. "What Is the 'Great Resignation?' an Expert Explains." World Economic Forum, 2021. https://www.weforum.org/agenda/2021/11/what-is-the-great-resignation-and-what-can-we-learn-from-it/.

30. "How Long Do Millennials Really Stay at a Job?" Zippia, 2022. https://www.zippia.com/answers/how-long-do-millennials-stay-at-a-job/.
31. Fisher, Catherine. "Ready for Anything: Jobs Come and Go, But Your Career Is Here to Stay." LinkedIn, January 18, 2023. https://www.linkedin.com/pulse/ready-anything-jobs-come-go-your-career-here-stay-catherine-fisher/.
32. Pendell, Ryan, and Sara Vander Helm. "Generation Disconnected: Data on Gen Z in the Workplace." Gallup, 2022. https://www.gallup.com/workplace/404693/generation-disconnected-data-gen-workplace.aspx.
33. "3 in 4 Managers Find It Difficult to Work with Genz." Resume Builder, May 15, 2023. https://www.resumebuilder.com/3-in-4-managers-find-it-difficult-to-work-with-genz/.
34. Smith, Morgan. "Gen Z and Millennials Are Leading 'the Big Quit' in 2023-Why Nearly 70% Plan to Leave Their Jobs." CNBC, January 18, 2023. https://www.cnbc.com/2023/01/18/70percent-of-gen-z-and-millennials-are-considering-leaving-their-jobs-soon.html.
35. "The History of Banks." Worldbank. Accessed November 8, 2023. https://www.worldbank.org.ro/about-banks-history.
36. Tkachenko, Tim. "This Is Where Gen Z Goes for Financial Advice." World Economic Forum, 2022. https://www.weforum.org/agenda/2022/08/finfluencer-gen-z-financial-advice/.
37. World Economic Forum, 2022.
38. "Gen Z Investors: A Look at the Attitudes and Behaviors of the Youngest Investors." FINRA, July 11, 2023. https://www.finra.org/media-center/gen-z-investor-attitudes.
39. "Robinhood Markets, Inc. Reports May 2023 Operating Data." Robinhood, June 12, 2023. https://investors.robinhood.com/news/news-details/2023/Robinhood-Markets-Inc.-Reports-May-2023-Operating-Data/default.aspx.
40. "Gen Z and Investing: Social Media, Crypto, FOMO, and Family." FINRA, 2023. https://rpc.cfainstitute.org/en/research/reports/2023/gen-z-investing.
41. Duggan, Wayne. "8 Stocks That Generation Z Loves." *U.S. News*, 2019. https://money.usnews.com/investing/stock-market-news/slide shows/stocks-that-generation-z-loves.

42. Csernyik, Rob. "Future Returns: Millennials and Sustainable Investing." *Barron's*, November 23, 2021. https://www.barrons.com/articles/future-returns-millennials-and-sustainable-investing-01637695579.

Chapter 8: The Building Blocks of Securities

1. "Set Value: 40511 Lego Minions Kung Fu Training." BrickEconomy, 2023. https://www.brickeconomy.com/set/40511-1/lego-minions-kung-fu-training.
2. "Toys Prove to Be Better Investment than Gold, Art, and Financial Securities." HSE University, 2021. https://www.hse.ru/en/news/research/536477053.html.
3. Dobrynskaya, Victoria, and Julia Kishilova. "LEGO: The Toy of Smart Investors." Science Direct, 2022. https://www.sciencedirect.com/science/article/pii/S0275531921001604?via%3Dihub.
4. "Lego Investing Is Booming. Here's How It Works." *Wall Street Journal*, 2022. https://www.wsj.com/video/series/in-depth-features/lego-investing-is-booming-heres-how-it-works/5F2B44FE-2789-46E2-B280-9CA089EAB458.
5. SEC v. W.J. Howey Co., 328 U.S. 293 (1946).
6. Boiron, Marc. "Sufficient Decentralization: A Playbook for Web3 Builders and Lawyers." Variant, 2022.
7. "Futures and Commodities." FINRA, 2023. https://www.finra.org/investors/investing/investment-products/futures-and-commodities.
8. FINRA, 2023.
9. "Gold Prices – 100 Year Historical Chart." MacroTrends, 2023. https://www.macrotrends.net/1333/historical-gold-prices-100-year-chart.
10. "Loan." Legal Information Institute, 2021. https://www.law.cornell.edu/wex/loan#:~:text=A%20loan%20is%20a%20form,to%20lend%20money%20to%20another.

Chapter 9: Here Come the Regulators

1. "SEC Charges Coinbase for Operating as an Unregistered Securities Exchange, Broker, and Clearing Agency." SEC, 2023. https://www.sec.gov/news/press-release/2023-102.

2. "Custody of Digital Asset Securities by Special Purpose Broker-Dealers." SEC, 2021.
3. "Official Compilation of Codes, Rules and Regulations of the State of New York Title 23. Financial Services Chapter I. Regulations of the Superintendent of Financial Services Part 200. Virtual Currencies." Westlaw. Accessed November 9, 2023.
4. "Stablecoin Policy Issues for the 118th Congress." Congressional Research Service, 2023.
5. "Order Instituting Cease-and-Desist Proceedings Pursuant to Section 8a of the Securities Act of 1933, Making Findings, and Imposing a Cease-and-Desist Order." SEC, 2008.
6. Ehrlich, Steven. "Congressman French Hill Sees Urgency in Congress to Pass Crypto Legislation." *Forbes*, October 4, 2023. https://www.forbes.com/sites/digital-assets/2023/08/23/congressman-french-hill-sees-urgency-in-congress-to-pass-crypto-legislation/?sh=1cd4d13f3a69.

Chapter 10: Don't Be Afraid of Change

1. Sorrel, Charlie. "Briton Invented iPod, DRM and on-Line Music in 1979." *Wired*, September 9, 2008. https://www.wired.com/2008/09/briton-invented/.
2. "The Strange Story of the MP3 Player." YouTube, 2018. https://www.youtube.com/watch?v=pSJi5YuK3gQ.
3. Richter, Felix. "Farewell iPod: The Rise and Fall of an Icon." Statista, May 11, 2022. https://www.statista.com/chart/10469/apple-ipod-sales/.
4. Wouters, Sam. "Top Banks Investing in Crypto & Blockchain Companies." Blockdata, 2022. https://www.blockdata.tech/blog/general/banks-investing-blockchain-companies.
5. Wouters, Sam. "Top Banks Investing in Crypto & Blockchain Companies." Blockdata, 2022. https://www.blockdata.tech/blog/general/banks-investing-blockchain-companies.
6. "Crypto/Digital Assets: 2022 Banking Industry Survey." KPMG, 2022. https://kpmg.com/us/en/articles/2022/crypto-digital-assets.html.
7. McCracken, Harry. "How the Bloomberg Terminal Made History – and Stays Ever Relevant." Fast Company, 2015. https://www.fastcompany.com/3051883/the-bloomberg-terminal.

8. "Beginner's Guide to the Bloomberg Terminal." Investopedia, 2023. https://www.investopedia.com/articles/professionaleducation/11/bloomberg-terminal.asp.
9. Kenton, Will. "What Is a Bloomberg Terminal? Functions, Costs, and Alternatives." Investopedia, 2022. https://www.investopedia.com/terms/b/bloomberg_terminal.asp.
10. "Here's What the 5 Biggest Innovations in the History of Lending Technology Have in Common." Coviance. Accessed November 9, 2023. https://www.coviance.com/resource-library/heres-what-the-5-biggest-innovations-in-the-history-of-lending-technology-have-in-common.
11. Zetter, Kim. "Sept. 2, 1969: First U.S. ATM Starts Doling out Dollars." *Wired*, September 2, 2010. https://www.wired.com/2010/09/0902first-us-atm/.
12. Bennett, Karen, and Matthew Goldberg. "Survey: ATM Fees Hit Record High While Overdraft and NSF Fees Fell Sharply." Bankrate, 2023. https://www.bankrate.com/banking/checking/checking-account-survey/#atm-fees.
13. Faverio, Michelle. "More Americans Are Joining the 'Cashless' Economy." Pew Research Center, October 5, 2022. https://www.pewresearch.org/short-reads/2022/10/05/more-americans-are-joining-the-cashless-economy/.
14. Pew Research Center, October 5, 2022.
15. O'Connell, Brian. "History of PayPal: Timeline and Facts." The Street, 2020. https://www.thestreet.com/technology/history-of-paypal-15062744.
16. Freakley, Simon. "2023 AlixPartners Disruption Index: Growth Leaders." AlixPartners, 2023. https://disruption.alixpartners.com/?utm_source=bing&utm_medium=ppc&utm_campaign=paid-search&utm_term=disruption_insights.
17. McQuillan, Susan. "Why Do Humans Resist Change?" *Psychology Today*, 2019. https://www.psychologytoday.com/us/blog/cravings/201910/why-do-humans-resist-change.
18. Hill, Diana. "Why You Resist Change and What to Do about It." *Psychology Today*, 2022. https://www.psychologytoday.com/us/blog/from-striving-to-thriving/202210/why-you-resist-change-and-what-to-do-about-it.

19. Kanter, Rosabeth Moss. "Ten Reasons People Resist Change." *Harvard Business Review*, September 26, 2018. https://hbr.org/2012/09/ten-reasons-people-resist-chang.
20. "How Fast Is Technology Accelerating?" *The Atlantic*, 2015. https://www.theatlantic.com/sponsored/prudential-great-expectations/how-fast-is-technology-accelerating/360/.
21. "What Is Tokenization?" McKinsey & Company, October 6, 2023. https://www.mckinsey.com/featured-insights/mckinsey-explainers/what-is-tokenization.
22. Erni, Stephan, Richard Walker, Clara Albuquerque, Thomas Olsen, Samit Soni, and Sen Ganesh. "WEB3 Experiments Start to Take Hold in Banking." Bain, 2022. https://www.bain.com/insights/web3-experiments-start-to-take-hold-in-banking/.
23. Cocheo, Steve. "Explainer: What Is Web 3.0? (And Why Should Banks Care?)."The Financial Brand, April 7, 2022. https://thefinancialbrand.com/news/digital-banking/explainer-what-is-web-3-0-and-why-should-banks-care-131680/.
24. Prohaska, Michelle. "Council Post: Ready or Not, Web 3.0 Is Coming. Bold Banks Can Seize the Opportunity." *Forbes*, March 4, 2022. https://www.forbes.com/sites/forbesfinancecouncil/2022/03/03/ready-or-not-web-30-is-coming-bold-banks-can-seize-the-opportunity/?sh=367b745961cc.
25. Solomon, David. "Blockchain Is Much More than Crypto." *Wall Street Journal*, December 6, 2022. https://www.wsj.com/articles/blockchain-is-much-more-than-crypto-david-solomon-goldman-sachs-smart-contracts-11670345993.
26. Rogers, Taylor Nicole. "Mobile Deposits Surpass in Person Transactions at Bank of America."The Street, 2018. https://www.thestreet.com/technology/mobile-deposits-surpass-in-person-transactions-at-bank-of-america-14652141.
27. "2024 Banking and Capital Markets Outlook." Deloitte, October 25, 2023. https://www2.deloitte.com/us/en/insights/industry/financial-services/financial-services-industry-outlooks/banking-industry-outlook.html.
28. Deloitte, October 25, 2023.
29. Allison, Ian. "Banking Giants Abuzz about Tokenization of Real-World Assets as Defi Craves Collateral." CoinDesk, October 4, 2023.

https://www.coindesk.com/business/2023/09/28/banking-giants-abuzz-about-tokenization-of-real-world-assets-as-defi-craves-collateral/.

30. Das, Samburaj. "Blockchain Explored by 90% of Major North American and European Banks, Survey Finds." CCN, March 4, 2021. https://www.ccn.com/blockchain-explored-90-major-north-american-european-banks-survey-finds/.
31. Lurie, Mark. "Stablecoins Promote Dollar-Dominance and U.S. Interests." *Forbes*, October 17, 2023. https://www.forbes.com/sites/digital-assets/2023/10/13/stablecoins-promote-dollar-dominance-and-us-interests/?sh=3e94e06858d3.
32. "Central Bank Digital Currency Tracker." Atlantic Council, July 14, 2023. https://www.atlanticcouncil.org/cbdctracker/.
33. Conti, Robyn. "What Is an NFT? Non-Fungible Tokens Explained." *Forbes*, March 17, 2023. https://www.forbes.com/advisor/investing/cryptocurrency/nft-non-fungible-token/.

Chapter 11: Finance's Imminent Upgrade

1. Mookerjee, Ajay S. "What If Central Banks Issued Digital Currency?" *Harvard Business Review*, October 15, 2021. https://hbr.org/2021/10/what-if-central-banks-issued-digital-currency.
2. Somensatto, Jason. "The U.S. Risks Its Position as a Stablecoin Leader." Nasdaq, 2023. https://www.nasdaq.com/articles/the-u.s.-risks-its-position-as-a-stablecoin-leader.
3. "S&P Global Ratings Launches Stablecoin Stability Assessment." S&P Global, December 12, 2023. https://press.spglobal.com/2023-12-12-S-P-Global-Ratings-Launches-Stablecoin-Stability-Assessment.
4. Lang, Hannah. "US Fed Clarifies Process for Banks to Transact in Stablecoins." Reuters, August 8, 2023. https://www.reuters.com/technology/us-fed-clarifies-process-banks-transact-stablecoins-2023-08-08/#:~:text=Aug%208%20(Reuters)%20%2D%20State,a%20new%20supervisory%20letter%20Tuesday.
5. Jones, Marc. "Study Shows 130 Countries Exploring Central Bank Digital Currencies." Reuters, June 28, 2023. https://www.reuters.com/markets/currencies/study-shows-130-countries-exploring-central-bank-digital-currencies-2023-06-28/.

6. Wee, Rae. "China's Digital Yuan Transactions Seeing Strong Momentum, Says Cbank Gov Yi." Reuters, July 19, 2023. https://www.reuters.com/markets/asia/chinas-digital-yuan-transactions-seeing-strong-momentum-says-cbank-gov-yi-2023-07-19/#:~:text=SINGAPORE%2C%20July%2019%20(Reuters),as%20of%20August%20last%20year.
7. Reuters, July 19, 2023.
8. Carapella, Francesca, Grace Chuan, Jacob Gerszten, Chelsea Hunter, and Nathan Swem. "Tokenization: Overview and Financial Stability Implications." The Fed - Tokenization: Overview and Financial Stability Implications, August 9, 2023. https://www.federalreserve.gov/econres/feds/tokenization-overview-and-financial-stability-implications.htm.
9. Clark, Julia, Anna Metz, and Claire Casher. "850 Million People Globally Don't Have ID – Why This Matters and What We Can Do About It." World Bank Blogs, February 6, 2023. https://blogs.worldbank.org/digital-development/850-million-people-globally-dont-have-id-why-matters-and-what-we-can-do-about.
10. "Maker Governance 101." MakerDAO, 2023. https://MakerDAO.com/en/governance/.
11. "ASSA 2022 Virtual Annual Meeting." American Economic Association, 2022. https://www.aeaweb.org/conference/2022/preliminary.
12. Guttmann, A. "Estimated Revenue Generated by Bloomberg LP Worldwide from 2015 to 2022." Statista, June 2, 2023. https://www.statista.com/statistics/1387634/bloomberg-lp-revenue/.
13. O'Meara, Patrick. Email message to author, November 11, 2023.
14. "Summary: Circle." Crunchbase, 2023. https://www.crunchbase.com/organization/circle-2.
15. "About Fireblocks." Fireblocks, October 18, 2023. https://www.fireblocks.com/about.
16. "Fireblocks: Company Overview & News." *Forbes*, 2023. https://www.forbes.com/companies/fireblocks/?sh=19886df016b4.
17. McIntyre, Chris, et al. "The Tide Has Turned." BCG Global, May 15, 2023. https://www.bcg.com/publications/2023/the-tide-has-changed-for-asset-managers.

18. Wang, Michael. "Alts for All: The Growth of Alternative Investments, Explained." Nasdaq, 2022. https://www.nasdaq.com/articles/alts-for-all%3A-the-growth-of-alternative-investments-explained.
19. Walker, Richard. Email message to author, November 10, 2023.

Index